T0146696

# A Silk Purse
## from a
# Sow's Ear?

# A Silk Purse from a Sow's Ear?

STEPHANIE HARRINGTON

# A SILK PURSE FROM A SOW'S EAR?

iUniverse books may be ordered through booksellers or by contacting:

iUniverse
1663 Liberty Drive
Bloomington, IN 47403
www.iuniverse.com
1-800-Authors (1-800-288-4677)

ISBN: 978-1-5320-0226-7 (sc)
ISBN: 978-1-5320-0247-2 (e)

Library of Congress Control Number: 2016912704

Print information available on the last page.

iUniverse rev. date: 08/27/2016

*Grant me the serenity to accept the things I cannot change,*
*the courage to change the things I can,*
*and the wisdom to know the difference.*

When Georgina Jackson, age sixty-five—divorced several times, retired, and happily and contently living the single life for the past eighteen years—looked back over her life, she began mulling over its major events. The main thought in her mind was, *Could I have done that better?* But realizing one can't change the past, she concluded the best she could do was accept that maybe she couldn't have done better and should be at peace with that.

She knew that she had had no influence over certain events in her life. They had taken her down an almost predetermined path that shaped her actions. She knew she could have thought, *Well, if it hadn't been for …*, but she knew that would achieve nothing.

But that didn't stop her from considering the ebb and flow of her life. Crows flying in an out of the snowcapped pine trees allowed her to ponder these events.

And so it began.

# CHAPTER 1

# *I Was Only Two ...*

"**O**KAY, IT'S YOUR TURN, SUZIE. You have to say what's your first memory, the very first. No hiding stuff now."

"I reckon I can go back to when I was five. I remember a birthday party, I think."

"Oh, c'mon. I can do better than that. I remember camping when I couldn't have been more than three and a half!"

This is a game played by students all over the world in every college whether in a dorm or a bar or with the family sitting around the fire at Christmas. Memories of our childhood don't seem very important when we're young; we just take for granted that as we get older, the memories will make us what we are, and we assume that the more positive and happy the memories are, the more vital they will be to developing a sound and secure adulthood. But what happens if your memories aren't positive?

Georgina's memories appear to go back to when she could have been no more than about eighteen months old. What was so indelibly imprinted on her mind then? What made her different from most other people who can cast their minds back only so far as age five, four, or at best three?

Her life appears to be a catalogue of odd and unusual events from the beginning, as you will learn as her story unfolds. It begins early in 1952 on a beautiful, sunny day, and for some reason, she's sitting under the utilitarian wooden kitchen table on a rough, brown blanket. The outside kitchen door's open, and she can see down the steep concrete steps that lead to the small backyard enclosed by a high whitewashed wall.

Someone is doing something on the table, and occasional flurries of fine white flour fall to the floor in front of her. She hears the thump, thump of the wooden rolling pin as it irons out pastry. She listens to a quiet, unfamiliar jazz tune and someone occasionally asking, "You okay under there, poppet?"

We can only assume it's her mother, but poppet learned at an early age not to take anything for granted, so it could have been anyone.

Evocative smells of cinnamon and hot sugar come from the freshly baked cakes and the bread been baking in the old, prewar stove. Wartime rationing had all but finished, but some items were still difficult to come by—chocolate, spices, and sugar for a good bake-up, so when they were available, everyone made the most of it.

Most days seemed to be the same or at least very similar, and at that early age, only the very specific memories were worthy of Georgina's recall.

One thing that appeared to be lacking, however, was any memory of her father back then. As it was the end of the war, menfolk had to take work were they could find it, and it would seem that Daddy was away. Maybe at sea?

Days rolled into weeks and months. The next memory she can recall was possibly six months later, around her second birthday. She can remember vividly waking up and becoming very excited because when she had gone to bed the night before, it was with the words "Now go to sleep quickly, darling, and let's see what might be waiting for you in the morning" ringing in her ears. So come the following morning, she clambered out of her cot bed and ran into the kitchen, not knowing what to expect but knowing it was something special.

"Mumma? Mumma? It's my birfday!" she whooped.

"Yes, my little darling! And see what's here for you."

She spied a shiny, brand-new tricycle apparently bought by her absent father. It was decorated with a pink bow wrapped around the frame and the seat, and once she'd attacked it and torn it all off, she saw a bright red and blue seat and handlebars.

"Let's go down to the yard and have a play on it, shall we?" her mum asked with a laugh. Georgina in one arm, trike in the other, she headed down the steps.

It very quickly became her favorite toy, and she enjoyed riding it after learning the basics of how to stay on it and pedal. She would spend hour after hour playing in the yard just scooting round and round.

Ian, her brother, was about two and a bit years her elder. He was at preschool during the day, but when he came home, he would constantly demand that she let him ride it. "Come on, it's my turn now" was almost the first thing he would say as he came in the door.

We all know what big brothers are like, and after all, she was only two for heaven's sake! She didn't have much of a say in the matter. He would ride her pride and joy fast around the yard, yelling like a banshee and sporting a look of total devilment in his big, brown eyes. Of course, one day, the inevitable happened.

He'd been charging around the yard for some time when suddenly there came a resounding crash. She rushed to the top of the steps and was mortified to see Ian standing over her lovely tricycle, which was just a mangled heap of metal, having been ridden at force into the yard wall. He had a huge grin on his face. All he could say while laughing was "Oops!"

Oh how she cried! Through her tears she wailed, "Mumma, Ian broke my bike!"

Memories are of course very selective, and there are always gaps that can't be filled in. There is therefore a period of a few months during which life must have carried on as normal until the next thing Georgina is able to recall vividly—her daddy calling her to him.

"Now then, little maid, let's get dressed up because we're going to see some nice people for the afternoon." Pleased to be in his company, she felt very special. This could have been because she seemed to have

3

had no recollection of her mummy or her brother, Ian, having been around for some time.

She came to understand later that this was when her mum and dad had separated and Ian had gone away with her mum. She was too little to work any of this out for herself, and no one was telling her anything, but hey! She was still only a baby.

So her memory of this particular day was that Daddy helped her dress like a little princess with pretty blue ribbons in her hair to match the new dress and shiny black shoes and new white ankle socks with pink bows.

"My, don't you look so pretty, little maid," said Daddy with a big smile.

They walked to the bus stop on the busy road that led to the city. They boarded the number 24, a big, red, double-decker bus. The ride seemed endless (it would have been maybe thirty minutes), but they eventually climbed off the bus and started walking up the road past an elegantly manicured park with a new, shiny-black, wrought-iron fence. She stared with excitement and longing at the swings and roundabouts inside but carried on past all the big houses. Her father was chatting to her intermittently while holding her hand tightly and showing her the children playing and laughing. "Maybe if we have time, toots, we can play on the swings on the way back." He laughed as she looked longingly at the toys. It was a beautiful, tree-lined road with an abundance of pretty pink and white flowers on them.

Occasionally, the lightest of winds would blow and a shower of the petals would cascade on Georgina. She thought it was truly magical. "It's pretty, Daddy, it's really pretty."

"Yes, isn't it just," her father said with a wistful look. "Nearly there."

They came upon a three-story house surrounded by an amazing garden. A maze of flowers welcomed them as they opened the gate and walked up the path to the huge, red front door. Her father banged the brass knocker; she heard it echo throughout the house. "Rat-tat, rat-tat, rat-tat." Soon, the door swung open and revealed a pleasant-looking woman with a huge smile. She was wearing a pink pinny, and it looked as if she'd been cooking as there was white dust in her hair.

"Why hello there. You must be Stephen, and this must be Georgina. My, what a beautiful dress you've got on, my dear."

Her father shook hands with the woman, who took Georgina's hand. "Come on in then and let's see what's upstairs, shall we?"

They were taken upstairs and shown into a large, warm, cozy room with a fire burning in the grate. There were pictures on every wall and many squishy-looking chairs. Apparently, the folks they were visiting lived on the top floor and the attic, and the woman's mother used the ground floor as her home.

They were made exceptionally welcome; cups of tea and chocolate biscuits were passed round.

"Go on, m'dear, have another one," said a cheerful gentleman with a beaming smile. "There's plenty more where they came from."

The roaring fire burned in the grate, and the enormous chairs were on either side of the fireplace. A large sofa was against the wall. Her dad sat in one of the chairs while she sat happily at his feet.

The nice couple sat on the sofa looking the epitome of a kind, middle-class couple who wanted to help this nice chap and his pretty, freckle-faced girl.

After the tea and several delicious chocolate biscuits (Oh such a luxury!) and much grown-up chatter, it was decided that because her dad had to go away to America for a couple of months to secure a job and a home for them, she would stay with the nice man and woman. They promised to take care of her as if she were their own.

"She'll be as happy as can be here with us. It'll be an absolute joy to have her."

They apparently had no children, so there it was. It was all arranged. Little did she and they know that their meeting would alter the course of everyone's lives forever and not necessarily for the better.

# CHAPTER 2

## A Court Appearance

So it was that she became part of her new family. She was dressed in the prettiest of dresses, and her hair was cut in a very fetching bob, popular even then for little ones. It was a pleasant time, though she was still not sure where her mum and dad were, but because the couple made her so welcome, she didn't let it bother her too much.

On the occasions when it did bother her and she got upset, she was told, "Don't you worry, dear. It'll be alright soon. Don't you cry now. Let's see what we can find in the sweetie box."

The old woman downstairs was to be called Granny, and she was a great source of sweeties (though still rationed) and creamy cakes whose smell emanated throughout the house daily. "Are you there, dearie?" she'd call up the big staircase. "Come and see what Granny's got for you today."

Georgina would hurtle down the wide stairway, hanging onto the wooden banister, and launch herself into the kitchen where she'd be greeted with fairy cakes or gingerbread men. If she was very lucky, she'd be allowed to help decorate the little cakes with colored icing and little silver balls she would sprinkle over the top. Granny just laughed about those that made it to the floor; she'd get out the dustpan and brush and sweep them up.

One day, the woman came into her bedroom and said, "Today's a very special day, sweetie pie, and we've all got to look our best." After her bath, she was dressed in a dainty yellow floral dress with matching hair ribbons and a new pair of socks like she's never seen before with white lace around the top. The whole thing was finished off with brand-new white shoes. She looked and felt like a princess again.

Great attention was paid to everyone's appearance that day, and even Granny had on her best hat with a big feather in it.

"Are we all ready?" asked the gentleman. "My, don't we all look grand!"

The three left the house, walked to the road, and boarded the number 17. After a long ride and lots of chatting and laughing, they stepped off the bus and walked toward an enormous, tall, elegant building with what seemed to be endless steps leading up to huge, wooden doors. For some time—hours it seemed—they sat in a grandiose, dark-paneled room.

A man with funny hair (We now know this to have been a wig) made all the people sit in a box by his side, and they talked to him, but about what she had no idea.

There seemed to be an air of familiarity about some of the people he talked to, as Georgina recognized some of the people who had visited the house, but after a while, she lost interest in the proceedings. She heard her name mentioned several times, but it was all grown-up talk. She resorted to coloring and playing hangman with Granny.

After what seemed to be an age, the man with the funny hair banged the big desk with a wooden mallet, making Georgina and Granny jump out of their skin.

Everyone stood, and she was rushed out of the building with the man and woman who had taken over the role of her mummy and daddy recently each holding a little hand. It must have been a comical sight because they were walking so quickly that her feet didn't touch the ground. She had no idea what was going on, but she vividly remembers looking over her shoulder and seeing all the other people who had been in the room emerging from the building. One looked very familiar, but she was told, "Don't look at that man. He's very bad."

We now know that was the day the family named Frazer took her father to court, stating that he had deserted her and that they thought the best option for all concerned was for them to adopt her.

The rules of adoption were thankfully changed in 1956, when apparently, the suitable ages of potential adoptive parents were reduced and more-stringent rules as to the suitability of potential parents were adopted.

Unfortunately for Georgina, in 1953, a childless couple ages sixty and fifty-one were able to say whatever they wanted, make whatever accusations, and not have to prove any of it, or so it would appear. The events of the next years were the reason this should never have been allowed and why the rules had to be reviewed and updated.

# CHAPTER 3

Getting to Know Her "Family"

T HAT DAY AND SO MANY more passed by, and life went back to normal, with Georgina unwittingly playing the role of the little girl who had been rescued. Days, months, and years went by, and all memories of her father were pushed to the back of her mind. No one ever mentioned him, and she was encouraged to lead the life they had mapped out for her. She looked forward to hairdresser's appointments on Friday for Mummy, who would cut up a Mars Bar before leaving and give Georgina a slice and a promise of another if she was a good girl.

It was a lonely life. There weren't many callers, though various "uncles" and "aunties" were occasionally introduced. While the mum's family came from the same county, his family were Scottish and were spread around from Surrey to Buckinghamshire right up to Argyllshire on the western highlands of Scotland.

Occasionally, they visited the woman's sister, Vera, and her husband, Jim, but it was never a joyous event; it seemed more of a duty than a pleasure. They were always very nice to her, but she was aware there weren't many shows of emotion between the grown-ups.

The visits were so infrequent that at Christmas time, Auntie Vera and Uncle Jim brought her two presents. "Here you are then, dear. One's for your birthday and the other one for Christmas. But you can open them both now, I expect. Isn't that fun?"

She obviously enjoyed the two gifts, but it never crossed her mind to question why she didn't see her aunt and uncle on her birthday.

Another sister, Phyllis, was married to John; they had three children. Philip was the eldest, but she had memories of only the girls, Marion and Marguerite. They were older than Georgina; Marion was about fourteen and Marguerite was twelve when Georgina was about four. They didn't visit the Frazers at all, but there was one day she would recall, a day when she was wearing a very pretty cream dress she'd never seen before, and after lunch she and her mum got on a bus.

After a short time, they got off and walked for maybe five minutes until they arrived at Auntie Phil's house. The front door was knocked quite heavily. From behind the door came hoots of laughter and the sounds of children running around. A surprised Auntie Phil opened the door. She looked at her sister and Georgina. "Oh … er … Hello. This *is* a surprise." Georgina realized it was Marguerite's birthday party. She was sent to join the other children though they were considerably older than she was. They played games such as pass the parcel and pin the tail on the donkey.

"Who are you?" asked one of the little boys.

"Oh she's a cousin or something," Marion replied.

It would appear that the two sisters (Auntie Phil and her mum) must have been in the other part of the house, but Georgina could remember thinking even at that time that they hadn't actually been invited. This was her mum letting her sister know she expected them to be included whether they were wanted or not. This was the first time she felt uncomfortable and not really wanted by their host.

And then there was the wedding. Georgina knew it was to be a very special occasion because everyone was dressed in their best and taken by coach to a church in another part of the country. Afterward, everyone went to the village hall for food, singing, and dancing. But again, Georgina felt a total outsider, not included in Marion's wedding and festivities as the other guests had been. She was also aware that the

Frazers didn't seem to join in with the festivities as much as everyone else did. Even at the tender age of six or seven, she was developing an inferiority complex.

And then of course there had been all the preparation for the first day of school. This meant repeated shopping trips for new clothes that had to be just so. Apparently, everyone had to wear the same, so Georgina was kitted out with bottle-green gym slips and white blouses and a very smart green blazer with a special badge on the pocket. Then there was a gabardine coat and two hats—one for summer, a straw boater with a green and gold band around it, and the other was felt with the same band. There was also a PE kit as well which was the same green but consisted of a skirt, knickers, and black shoes. Georgina didn't understand what was going on; all she was told was that it was vital she looked the best she could because everyone else would.

The big day arrived. She was meticulously dressed in her uniform. She and her mum walked up the road to the infants' school on the corner of their road and another; it took only about ten minutes to get there. Georgina noticed all the other children passing them were wearing the same as her.

"Come along. Stop dawdling. You don't want to be late on your first day, do you?" It wasn't so much a question as an instruction, but she was getting used to that sort of talk. It seemed everything had to be done one way only.

As they approached gates, Georgina was fearful. She had no idea what to expect and wondered if it would be like a party.

With her birthday falling in August, it meant she was one of the youngest in her class, but she was by far the tallest. Many of the children also seemed to know each other prior to starting school, having played with each other at their homes and in the park. Georgina had not been encouraged to make friends; no one had ever been invited to their house. On the rare occasion she received an invite to someone else's house, she was told she wasn't able to go. From that first day at school, she was ostracized by her classmates, and even at that age, she believed it was all about how different she was.

Somewhere at this time, Granny must have passed away, but it didn't affect Georgina emotionally because she had had very little to do with her once she had started school. The old woman had spent more and more time in her part of the house, and the baking seemed to have stopped as well.

# CHAPTER 4

## Acceptance Isn't Automatic

I T WASN'T LONG AFTER SHE started school that they moved. We can only assume this was because with the old woman gone, they were free to do so. They moved to a bungalow a distance away but in the same town, Southampton. This meant Georgina changed schools, so there were more uniform-buying trips, this time for a navy and gold outfit.

Of course there was more space—a big garden with lawns, flowerbeds, and a greenhouse. But she wasn't allowed anywhere but the drive and the patio lest she damage the grass and plants. And woe betide her if she went anywhere near the greenhouse.

The Barretts lived across the road from them; the family included two boys maybe two or three years older than Georgina who attended her school. They were kind enough to occasionally invite her over for tea and to play with them. However, the invitations soon stopped after they were consistently and curtly declined by Mrs. Frazer, who said Georgina wasn't interested in being their friend. Georgina was told she was not to go because they were only being polite. "They don't really want you there, so you wouldn't like it."

After one fractious dinner, the conversation drifted to an area Georgina had never been party to before, the fact that she must appreciate they had been good and kind enough to adopt her.

"We could have had any boy or girl, but we chose you. You should be very grateful because if we hadn't taken you, heaven only knows where you'd have ended up. In some children's home more than likely."

Georgina was confused by this revelation but had a feeling it wouldn't be a particularly good idea to continue that line of conversation. She pushed it to the back of her mind, not realizing those words would go deeper than she could imagine.

School wasn't pleasant. A clique of girls, some her age and others older, took great pleasure in taunting her because of her height, which made her appear gangly. "Hey, skinny, you been stretched or summat?" She was jibbed because she had very old parents. She desperately wanted acceptance and therefore looked for something that would make her stand out and be different from anyone else. With this in mind, she told them the big secret—that she had been adopted, thinking that made her special. But my, did that backfire. How wrong could she have been? This information was digested and resulted in merciless taunting because now the jibes were that "Your parents didn't want you then" and "The old folk were the only ones who would take you." She realized what a huge mistake she'd made. It was one of many she was to make over the years as she tried to gain acceptance.

Another mistake she made was trying to buy friendship. She worked out a way of stealing small amounts of money from her mum's purse (about two shillings old money, just over ten pence nowadays), which was a lot then when you could buy a jamboree bag full of sweets for three pence and eight black-jacks for a penny from the sweet shop just outside the school gates. Armed with her loot, she would hotfoot it to the playground armed with all the goodies and thinking she could entice others to like her if she had a continual supply of sweets.

The kids took them of course, but when they ran out, she had two options. Either steal more money or go back to being humiliated. So steal it was. However, she wasn't very good at it because she was soon caught. When asked why she had done it, she was daft enough to tell the Frazers the reason, and this led to more scorn, a good hiding, and being locked in her bedroom as soon as she returned from school each day for about two weeks.

This was not, however, before Mrs. Frazer frog-marched her to the school and took her to the headmaster. You might think this was an opportunity for the Frazers to speak up for her and try to stop the bullying and name-calling they were obviously aware of, but you'd be wrong. They informed the head she had come from bad stock, was close to a delinquent, and should be watched at all times.

After that, school got worse. Somehow, the gang had learned about the visit and ridiculed her even more.

Even after that miserable attempt to become popular, she developed yet another "wheeze" she thought would help her popularity issues and make her some money. She acquired a load of school notebooks from the stationary cupboard and tore apart some old wallpaper sample books that became covers for special notebooks she sold on the playground. She then had some pocket money she could spend in the tuck shop, which put her on a par with her classmates for a change.

Around this time, her mum was apparently taken ill. She remained at home, but the doctor attended the house regularly. Dad stayed at home, very concerned about her. Georgina was to keep away and stay as quiet as possible; she resorted again to staying in her bedroom.

This seemed to go on for several weeks, and while she was never very happy, Georgina still thought of her mum as most little girls do and was worried. After perhaps six weeks of doctor visits, it was apparent she was recovering, so Georgina would go into her mum's room and talk about school and such. She had a captive audience as her mum just lay there. Sometimes, Georgina was allowed to take the tea tray in and would sit and chat until the food was gone.

Two or so weeks later, it was her mum's birthday. Georgina and her dad went to a little shop a few roads away, and she chose a box of chocolates for a birthday present. It was a box of Milk Tray; he was confident it was her mum's favorite. Georgina wrapped the present and skipped into the bedroom singing, "Happy Birthday."

With a bored sigh, her mum unwrapped the gift. Georgina hoped it would be a happy evening with at least some kind words or at least a smile. She heard, "Oh thanks … but I'd have sooner had Black Magic."

Georgina looked at her dad, devastated. *I'm so sorry*, he mouthed at her, but she ran from the room in tears.

"Why did you let her buy those?" her mum asked her dad in a bitter voice. "You should know better."

"Okay, I got it wrong, but did you have to say so in front of her? You know how she only wants to please you."

"Not much chance of that, is there?" she said resignedly.

Georgina lay on her bed asking herself, *Can I do nothing right? Obviously not.*

When she was about eight, the school music teacher, Mrs. Titford, a kindly, plump, matronly woman with a soft voice and gentle smile, took her under her wing. She had seen something in Georgina and encouraged her to join the school choir. Georgina blossomed with the attention and got better and better; she looked forward to her weekly music lessons. Her first solo performance was at an interschool competition at which she sang "Jerusalem" and "Blow the Wind Southerly." Rapturous applause from the several hundred mums and dads in the audience made up for the fact that hers weren't there. Reveling in the praise, she began to feel worthy at last. She had finally found something she could excel at.

Anything to do with music, she was there, and when Mrs. Titford suggested she try some of the school instruments stored in the music room, she couldn't believe her ears. There were all types of instruments—woodwinds, brass, string, and percussion. She had seen these being played by the orchestra but had had no idea the school had such a cornucopia of instruments. She was in heaven.

Having no idea how to play any of them, she picked up one by one and tried to do what she'd seen others do. One afternoon after music class, Mrs. Titford showed her how they were played.

"Come on, dear. Let's see if any of these suit you."

Mrs. Titford, already very high in Georgina's estimation, went even further because she could play to some degree the saxophone, clarinet, trumpet, and trombone. While she was not in any way proficient with string instruments, she introduced Georgina to the violin.

That was for Georgina an epiphany. She considered holding the violin the same as holding a jewel. So delicate, so smooth, but capable of such wondrous sounds even by just plucking the strings. That was her introduction to the world of the orchestra. Did Mrs. Titford know then what she was unleashing in this tall, lanky misfit?

Georgina ran home that day with a newfound joy in her heart. She wanted to believe that nothing could dampen her spirits. She burst into the kitchen. "Mum, it was brilliant! They have all sorts of instruments … I can learn to play any of them … And it doesn't cost anything." She added that in case her mum threw up they couldn't afford it. She expected to hear, "Why do you think you'd be any good at it? That silly teacher has no right to go getting your hopes up."

But that time, her desire was met by a different response. Her mum's initial comments trailed off to total disinterest; while she expressed no enthusiasm, she expressed no resistance. "Do whatever you want. Just don't expect us to come to any of your silly music shows" was all she heard. She couldn't have asked for more. It meant she could get on with what was becoming the most important thing in her life. She could hide from her classmates' ribbing and her parents' put-downs in music.

Her elation at her mum's response was heightened just weeks later when her dad returned from his work on Southampton docks with a violin. He had apparently chatted to a pal he worked with about Georgina's latest craze; his friend's daughter had gone through the same phase but had dropped it. His friend was more than happy to get rid of that dust collector.

Georgina became absorbed in the choir and orchestra; that gave her the lust for life she'd lacked and a creditable role in the school. She had a valuable part to play, and people relied on her for her contributions.

By that time, she was about nine, and her parents were glad they could abdicate an amount of responsibility for her to school choir practice and orchestra rehearsals.

She entered several interschool competitions and musical shows and regularly sang solos and took leading parts in productions. She passed her progressive violin exams and reached grade six after just over a year, but neither Frazer attended recitals even when she was invited to play for the Southampton Youth Orchestra.

It was usual for Georgina to catch the ten past seven bus home from school, getting home around twenty to eight. But one day, close to a big recital, rehearsals had been very intense and there was so much fine tuning to be done. She missed the usual bus and had to wait for the next one, which wasn't until a quarter to eight. This meant it didn't get her to her stop until quarter past eight. She was in fear of what would be said when she got in, but she wasn't prepared for the reception she received at the bus stop. Her very aggressive mum was flailing her arms and shouting, "You dirty, street-walking, little prostitute!" Her mum's blow to her head knocked her sideways.

Remember that Georgina was very tall for her age; she didn't look nine—more like twelve or thirteen. The fact that she was carrying a violin case wouldn't have made anywhere near as much of an impression on those aboard the bus as did the wild woman attacking Georgina and screaming.

Sobbing hysterically, Georgina ran frantically up the hill to the house. She ran to her room, threw herself on her bed, and tried to hide her crying in her pillow. She had done nothing wrong but had as usual not been given the opportunity to defend herself.

Nothing else was said that night, but she was so upset at being shouted at and hit in public that she wasn't able to clear her mind let alone sleep. She threw up a few times, something that had started a couple of years earlier whenever there was a confrontation. Restless, tossing and turning, she heard her parents retiring.

Their room was next to hers; she could hear her mum through the wall. "What have we done to deserve this? We made a huge mistake taking her on. How on earth will we put up with this for the next eight or ten years?"

She lay in the darkness, thinking, *I just want this to end. How can I get away?* But of course she had nowhere to go—no friends, her mum's family didn't want to know, and her dad's family was in other parts of the country and were too … good. She was stumped. Her only option was to pretend it had never happened and accept it would more than likely happen again.

However, what she couldn't accept was the injustice of it all. She was never asked to explain why she had been late and never given the opportunity to explain herself. It was as if it hadn't happened.

But there was one thing shouted from her parents' bedroom door that night. Under no circumstances would she to play at the upcoming recital. All those months of practice, all the anticipation wasted. Georgina needed to talk to the only person she knew had any interest at all in her well-being.

Mrs. Titford tried to get the Frazers to change their mind but to no avail. She wrote to them, invited them to come to the school, and finally turned up at the house.

"She has such potential, Mr. and Mrs. Frazer, I'll personally guarantee she's home on time."

But the answer was still an emphatic no.

One of the worst feelings Georgina suffered at that time wasn't just the embarrassment of having to face the members of the orchestra, who for the first time treated her as an equal, or even letting down Mrs. Titford, who was the only person so far in Georgina's life who had any faith or pride in her. The worst feeling was new to her; she felt she had let everyone down. She's never been an integral part of anything before; no one had ever relied on her before she joined the orchestra. She was as important as any of the other fifty-one members. She enjoyed feeling she belonged and had responsibilities, a new experience for her. The feeling she had failed ate away at her.

# CHAPTER 5

# Getting to Know His Family

OVER THE PREVIOUS FOUR OR five years, they had taken regular train trips to see his family in Surrey, Buckinghamshire, and Scotland. They were a different kettle of fish. Her dad was one of four brothers and a sister. One of the brothers, Donald, and his wife, Flora, lived in Surrey in what seemed to Georgina a huge, rambling, old house with servants' quarters downstairs. She was allowed to entertain herself (Keep out of our way!), so she would seek out wee Mary, the Scottish housekeeper who always had a friendly and welcoming smile. As soon as Georgina appeared at the kitchen door, she would put an arm around her and say, "Come on, hinney, let's away."

She was a tiny, frail-looking woman whose hair was always the same—pinned back in a bun and covered with a net. Her kitchen and rooms were downstairs. The kitchen had a huge wooden table in the center on which she would prepare wonderful dishes for the family.

Georgina was also told by kindly Auntie Flora that she could go wherever she liked in the house, and that meant she naturally gravitated to the music room, where there was what seemed to her to be a huge, black, shiny grand piano. She had never seen one like it except on stage where the orchestra was performing.

There was also a big, old-fashioned wind-up gramophone with an image of a dog sitting by the funnel, something she'd never seen before. There were hundreds of black, shiny, seventy-eight rpm records all meticulously wrapped in the sleeves with wonderful pictures of the musicians and scenes of musical treats. Wee Mary would wind up the machine, and she and Georgina would start dancing to the records. "Why, hinney, this is one of my very favorite records. Let's dance!"

They listened to Frank Sinatra, Mario Lanza, Joan Sutherland, and many orchestral works, some of which she recognized from concerts. They would dance to Strauss waltzes, pretending to be at one of the wonderful balls Mary had spoken about. She had so many stories of grand parties and beautiful women in elegant dresses and men wearing long, black coats.

The ringing of a bell would interrupt the magic. Ten bells on springs were all labeled with the room they were connected to. Mary would look to see which one had been rung and scurry up to the room to take an order for tea.

She and Georgina would lay up trays with the finest china cups and saucers so thin you could see through them. They would place the little cakes wee Mary had made that day on a three-tiered china cake plate with a silver handle on top. Another would have scones on, and there were the little glass dishes with jam and clotted cream. Once all this was ready, Mary would load all into what looked like a box in the wall, pull down a shutter, and press a button; the tea would trundle its way up to the hallway on the second floor outside the drawing room. She would run up the stairs and retrieve the trays one at a time, and tea would be served.

Georgina was sent to wash her hands and face because Mary might just have let her lick the spoon with the cream on before it was sent on its journey upward.

And of course there were instruction that Georgina had to go immediately upstairs as well and join the grown-ups.

Uncle Donald was considerably older than her dad but was a great bear of a man with a twinkle in his eye and a wonderful, soft, Scottish lilt. They always went out of their way to make Georgina feel she was a member of the family, and they always asked her about school and music. She would ache to tell them about her last concert or a new piece she'd learned for the violin, but she was never allowed to engage in too much of the conversation, and she got used to the odd put-down form you know whom. There were even occasions when Uncle Donald would say to the Frazers, "Let her speak. Go on then, Georgina." This gave her a wonderful feeling of satisfaction, knowing that they must have felt a bit put down for a change.

After tea, the bell pull by the side of the fire was tugged, and Mary would bustle in again and clear away the cups and saucers and the remains of the cakes. Usually at that point, Uncle Donald would look at Georgina with a smile and say, "Away now, my dear, if you'd like to. And enjoy the music room downstairs. You don't want to be sitting here listening to us old folk now, do you?"

"Thank you, Uncle Donald. May I play the piano?"

Before her parents could admonish her for being rude, Uncle Donald would reply with a smile, "Of course you may. Have fun."

Almost with a feeling of smugness, Georgina would run down the large flight of stairs that twisted through the middle of the house and into the music room. Of course she had no idea how to play, but she would sit on the music stool with a piece of music she had taken from the seat and find the notes she could from the music. She had learned to read music for her violin, but piano music was very confusing to her then.

Another game she would play was to think of a song, maybe a hymn she'd learned at school or a piece she'd sung at a concert and try to find the notes on the piano. It would have been described as a racket by the Frazers, but the music room was far enough away from everyone else, so it didn't matter.

Sometimes, wee Mary would come up with a glass of juice and some shortbread she'd made, and she (who could play well) would pick a simple Scottish song and teach Georgina the words. If it wasn't "The Skye Boat Song," it could be "Marie's Wedding" or "There Was a Soldier, a Scottish Soldier."

These visits, while unusual because Georgina was generally excluded from the adults, Uncle Donald and Auntie Flora seemed to understand this was mutually beneficial. The parents were able to forget about Georgina for a while, and she was able to lose herself in a world completely different from hers, and she enjoyed that. She was treated like a cherished child, something that didn't happen at home.

Another trip would be to Great Missenden in Buckinghamshire, where another brother, Uncle John, and his wife, Auntie Ethel, lived. Theirs was a huge house with a terraced garden, and statues of lions were on either side of the steps from the first lawn down to the second.

The gardens were always immaculate no matter what time of year. In the summer, the borders were full of brilliantly colored flowers and looked like a rainbow to Georgina. Then there was the rose garden. Oh, the scent that came from them! Georgina had never experienced anything like it. She sniffed every one. It seemed to her that the more beautiful the color of any one rose, the less it smelled. She was overcome by the smell of a plain white rose.

Here too, Georgina was allowed to run anywhere she pleased, including across the lawn, of course being careful to miss the metal croquet hoops. Down she went onto the next lawn, where there was a pond with goldfish of all sizes and colors. Some were bigger than her hand, and others had markings like zebras.

Then it was down to the orchard, a magical place. Depending on the time of year, she could find apples, pears, red and yellow plums, and cherries waiting to be picked, and rows of raspberries, gooseberries, and red and black currants growing on sticks. Elsewhere were luscious strawberries growing on beds of straw. Georgina couldn't understand why there was so much fruit in one garden, too much for Auntie Ethel and Uncle John.

One day, Georgina plucked up courage to ask Aunt Ethel, "When do you have time to eat them all, Auntie? There's lots on the ground now. What happens to them?"

Aunt Ethel took her hand. "Come with me, poppet." Georgina was led into a walk-in cupboard off the kitchen. Shelves up to the ceiling on three walls were straining under the weight of dozens of jars. "There you are, poppet. That's what happens to it all. When we have dinner tonight, we'll have rhubarb crumble. You like that if I remember rightly. So there's the rhubarb."

Georgina looked as her aunt pointed to one of the shelves. All the jars were neatly labeled and dated. There were apples, plums, gooseberries, raspberries, strawberries, and rhubarb on one wall. On another were smaller jars of pickles and chutneys of every variety. The last wall was full of jams and jellies and marmalade, and she remembered that when she had been there the previous time, there had been three or four jars on the breakfast table. She'd been allowed by Uncle John (much to the disgust of her mum and dad) to have a little from of each one of the jars, and oh, did they taste good!

She remembered that dessert was usually a fruit pie or a crumble, and that when dinner was served, there were always several dishes of chutneys and such on the table to have with the cheese.

"Don't you have too much, Auntie?" asked Georgina.

"Well no, poppet, because if by the time next year's fruit is ready to be preserved, I take those that are left to the old folks' home up the road."

An endless supply coming from the garden, and none of it went to waste.

When visiting them, they caught the train from Southampton Central Station to Waterloo and were usually met by one of Uncle John's and Auntie Ethel's sons. It was either John, who "worked in the city," whatever that meant, or Dowling, who was a doctor, a skin specialist. He was always her favorite; she had always had a crush on him.

There would then be a thirty-minute journey on a smaller train. Georgina was always amazed at this journey because they had to go downstairs at Waterloo and get on an underground train that had many windows, but all she could see was blackness rushing past. But daylight would occasionally appear in bursts, and the darkness would end totally above ground. It was a complete mystery. On this journey, the normal niceties where exchanged: "How are you keeping? Terrible weather isn't it," and so on.

On one occasion, when Georgina was maybe ten, cousin Dowling had met them at the train. He towered over them all, but he always had a big, gentle smile. He asked how she was doing at school and if she had any idea of what she wanted to be.

She was speechless; she never thought anyone would be interested in that. So eyeing her parents from under her hair, she mumbled something like, "I'd love to be a singer," which sent her mum and dad into fits of laughter and ended in her dad saying, "There's always a black sheep of the family. You can't make a silk purse from a sow's ear, can you?"

She wasn't sure what all that meant, but she knew by the tone of voice it was another put-down.

Dowling looked surprised, as if not sure he'd heard right. "It's great to have something to aim for, isn't it," he said in a kind voice and patted Georgina's hand. "Have you sung in many concerts? And is your school supportive?"

Before she had chance to answer, her mum quickly injected, "She's not going to get any support from us taking into consideration the way she behaves. And what sort of career is singing anyway?"

Georgina could only imagine the comment had been prompted by the missed-bus incident, but nothing more was said. Dowling must have realized there was more to this issue than what had been said and wisely left it alone. But Georgina felt she had been given a friend in the form of her cousin that day.

On that visit, there was general merriment in the evening, as John, the other son, and Edith, the daughter, the headmistress of a private girls' school in Oxford, turned up with their respective partners and joined them for dinner.

It was a grand affair. Uncle John and Auntie Ethel sat at either end of a huge dining table. The food was brought in by the housekeeper, Mrs. Albright, a friendly woman who always appeared in a spotless, white apron over her clothes with a large pocket in the front.

The meal seemed to go on forever. Or so thought Georgina, who was seated between Edith and John's fiancée, Susanna. If only she could have sat next to Dowling. She knew he would have talked to her, but it was not to be. Edith made small talk with her about school and how she thought that the eleven-plus exam was the most important event of a pupil's life because it decided whether he or she went to a grammar school or not. Georgina was about to take her exam in a few months; the conversation did nothing to put her at ease, but Edith was oblivious to Georgina's discomfort and held forth to anyone listening how it was each child's responsibility to pass the exam.

After what seemed hours, everyone rose, and Georgina was what only could be described as dismissed. It was just after 9:00 p.m., so she climbed two flights of stairs to her bedroom that to her seemed to be up in the roof. She got undressed, clambered into bed, and lay in the dark worrying about the eleven-plus exam.

Much later that night, or so it seemed, Georgina was awakened by much noise coming from downstairs. She had no idea of the time. She tiptoed to the door and peered into the semi-darkness. "It's all right, I can get him … Watch the chair … Keep his head up." Too frightened to leave her room and fearing reprisal if she dared investigate further, she crept back into bed and hugged her knees, listening. She saw colored lights outside blinking on and off and shining across the garden. She heard voices she didn't recognize in the house.

She heard an engine start and saw the blue lights of an ambulance drive off. The noises in the house seemed to have subsided, so she cautiously peeked out her bedroom door, but there were still lights on all over the house. She returned to bed mystified and unable to sleep. She was startled at a knock on her door. "Yes? Who is it?"

"It's Dowling. May I come in?"

"Oh … um … yes, I suppose so." No one had ever asked permission to come into her room before; she was taken aback at this apparent consideration for her privacy.

"Listen, pet," said Dowling in his gentle voice, "I'm sorry if you were woken up, but it's nothing to worry about, really, it's not. Your dad was taken ill, and we've had to get an ambulance and take him to hospital. He'll be okay, but he'll have to be there for a little while I think."

"What's wrong with him?" asked Georgina, who was worried.

"We're not too sure, but it's something to do with his tummy possibly. Look, everyone's gone back to bed now. Do you think you can get back to sleep?"

"I'll try," said Georgina as she slid under the covers. Dowling tucked the covers in and around her and gave her a gentle kiss on the forehead.

"Try to sleep, pet. I'll see you in the morning. Night night."

Georgina woke late the next morning. She washed and dressed and went down to the breakfast room. No one seemed to noticed her as she slipped into her place and poured some cereal into her bowl. The conversation was animated; everyone was offering opinions on various aspects of the previous night's events.

No one included her in the conversation, but she learned she and her mum were going back to Southampton by train the following day without her dad.

This confused her, because while the Frazers weren't very demonstrative to each other, she thought she would want to stay near her husband.

Anyway, it was decided that John would drive them to Waterloo the next day. It appeared to be all settled. Still, no one spoke about the events of the previous night to Georgina, so she wandered about and ended up on the seat outside the kitchen window, watching the birds swoop around the garden, where there were several nesting boxes and birdbaths.

Mr. and Mrs. Albright were always friendly to Georgina, and that day, seeing her sitting alone outside the window, called out, "Would you like some cocoa, love? I've got some jam tarts just out of the oven."

"Ooh yes, please!"

While it wasn't in the same league as wee Mary's, Mr. and Mrs. Albright's kindness was very welcome that day. Theirs was a situation different from wee Mary's. They didn't live in the house, so once their work was done, they left for the day. Mr. Albright helped Uncle John with the garden and with the general upkeep of the rambling house while Mrs. Albright helped Auntie Ethel with the housekeeping and entertaining.

Georgina was left to her own devices that day as Uncle John and Dowling drove her mum to the hospital to see her dad after breakfast. She kept a low profile as she enjoyed the hot chocolate and to a certain degree the peace and quiet.

Around twelve-thirty, Auntie Ethel came down to the bottom garden and brought Georgina a scrumptious lunch of fresh, warm bread, juicy tomatoes, and homemade pickles followed by fruit tart and ice cream, which they ate on the big, old bench that had been carved out of a tree. They ate in silence, just looking out into the orchard, watching the birds popping in and out of the feeder boxes.

"Now don't you worry about your dad, poppet. He'll been fine in a few days and be back at home with you before you know it."

Georgina didn't know how she felt. Not sad, not worried; she wasn't sure what the feeling was. At one point, she felt angry that their plans had been upset and life wouldn't be back to normal for a while. She wasn't looking forward to spending time alone with her mum. The train journey was going to be awful, she knew, and then when they got home, well, anything could happen.

In a way, she had a fondness for the old man certainly more than she did for her mum. He sometimes had a kindly word or even a look of sympathy when the ranting started. A world without him, only her mum, would be awful—not a situation she wanted to think about. She spend the rest of the afternoon wandering around the garden, talking to herself, pretending she was having a conversation with Dowling, her new special friend.

The evening slipped by without event after a subdued evening meal with just Aunt Ethel, Uncle John, her mum, and her. Georgina was more than happy to go to her bedroom and read. Books were great. She could hide in them and pretend to be someone else, someone who had an exciting life.

Her favorite books at that time were Enid Blyton's *The Famous Five*; the lead character was George, short for Georgina, so she could easily pretend to be her. The five were always getting up to some wonderful adventures, along with Timmy the dog, and as an added benefit, George was in charge; she was someone Georgina could only dream about being.

The following day, they had a subdued drive to Waterloo Station with John. After the farewells and see you again soons, let us know what's happening, and so on, they caught the train to Southampton, bringing with them some of Auntie Ethel's jams and chutneys. Well, there was that to look forward to at least.

Her dad came home about two weeks later minus his gall bladder, whatever that was, and things gradually got back to normal. As normal as they ever could be anyway.

The youngest of the four Frazer brothers was Uncle Martin, who lived just outside Glasgow with his wife, Fiona, but there weren't many visits there; thought she was young, Georgina sensed there was an undercurrent that bordered on dislike. Whenever they met, they were very frosty to her mum almost to the point of rudeness. However, she was thick-skinned and seemed oblivious to that. While she had no way of knowing what had transpired previously, Georgina realized Uncle Martin and Auntie Fiona would never be there for her as the other two uncles were.

Then finally, there was Uncle Bob and Auntie Mary (Yes, another one). Mary was her dad's only sister. They lived in the beautiful fishing town of Tarbert, on the banks of Loch Fyne in Argyllshire on the western coast of Scotland.

Most years, the three of them went there on holiday around Easter time, and this was a huge adventure for Georgina. It took her out of the normal way of life and gave her so much to look forward to. The journey meant a train ride to London and a sleeper train to Glasgow. While the Frazers slept, she would peer out the blind from the top bunk and imagine all types of people, towns, and villages dashing past in the night. The clickety-click, clickety-click was comforting in a weird way.

In the early morning, the train would pull into its destination, Glasgow central. The guard would come along maybe half an hour later and rat-tat on the door, saying, "Breakfast is now being served in the restaurant car." This would result in a quick wash and dress for them in the tiny bathroom and a short walk past maybe twenty doors just like theirs to the restaurant car. They could smell the bacon at about the sixteenth door, and by the time they reached their destination, their tummies were rumbling.

Breakfast would consist of cereal, toast, and then bacon and egg, sausage, black pudding, mushrooms, and baked beans. It was heaven for Georgina; cooked breakfasts simply weren't on the menu at home.

After breakfast, they alighted the train and took a taxi to the port of Gourock. At about 9:00 a.m., there would be a lot of activity on the dockside, from small ferryboats that took travelers and commuters up the river to Glasgow to small boats carrying sand and ballast to the islands along the various lochs.

A short walk to the end of the dock got them to where the McBaine ferry was tethered. It took them Tarbert, about two hours away. They boarded by way of a rickety, steep, wooden ramp, showed their tickets, and sat in the saloon, a Spartan, enclosed area at the bow. The wind and rain would often come from nowhere as the old boat lumbered up and around the bends of the loch.

Other travelers would chat to each other in a variety of accents, many of which Georgina couldn't understand, and would take their places in the chairs, ideally by the windows. Her dad sauntered off after a while and returned with a tray of hot coffee and a soft drink for Georgina.

After some time, a low, dull rumbling rose from the bottom of the boat and there was shouts of "Okay, cast off aft" and "Let go the ropes." The next part of the adventure began. After getting a nod from her dad and of course a disapproving frown from her mum, Georgina ran out to the deck to watch the departure. She enjoyed that. For some reason, she was allowed to roam around the boat. She would explore all the nooks and crannies and the various decks, and look into the distance, waiting to catch sight of the first of five stops before Tarbert. Some of the stops, such as Dunoon, were insignificant; it was a simple wharf with a dilapidated shed at the end. Rarely did anyone get off or on there; the boat would tie up long enough to load any mail and parcels.

The most memorable stop along the way was for Georgina was Rothsay; there was always—no matter the weather or the time—a welcoming pipe band. The announcement came over the public address: "We will be arriving in Rothsay in approximately ten minutes." Georgina rushed to the rail and spotted the twenty or so men and boys dressed in kilts and white socks with daggers stuffed into them playing bagpipes and drums. They would play while travelers disembarked and embarked and the post and parcels were loaded. The steamer cast of again, and still they played. Georgina stayed on the rails listening to the fading strains of the music as the boat navigated the bends in the river past the Kyles of Bute and into Loch Fyne. That meant they were about twenty-five minutes before they would reach Tarbert, and Georgina knew to go back to the lounge.

True to form, her mum glowered at her. "Where on earth have you been? We've been worried sick!" Georgina looked at her and then at her dad. She'd had her drink and then asked if she could wander. No one had told her to be back at a specific time. She looked pleadingly at her dad, hoping he would stand up for her, but there was no way he would take her side against her mum.

"Okay, I'm sorry, but you didn't tell me when to come back," she retorted with a scowl. They sat in silence until the announcement came that arrival at Tarbert was in ten minutes. "Can I go and see, please? I'll be by the gangway thing."

"Oh for goodness sake go!" said her mum.

Before her mum could change her mind, Georgina picked up her hold-all and legged it out of the lounge to the gangway and climbed on the rail. She watched the dock get larger and larger. There was no band, but Uncle Bob and Auntie Mary would always be there to meet them. The whole boat journey had taken about two and a half hours. Georgina jumped from the rail and ran to the saloon, shouting, "We're here!"

"I can see the dock, Come on, let's go. All right. Just calm down," said her dad with an amused smile. They got all the bags together, disembarked, and walked down the gangplank onto the quay. They say the happy faces of Uncle Bob and Auntie Mary, whose arms were outstretched. Georgina ran into their waiting arms. "Well hello there, little one! It's so good to see you again. Where's Mummy and Daddy?" Auntie would ask.

"They're just coming down now—there—see?" yelled Georgina. She disentangled herself from Auntie and launching herself at Uncle Bob.

"So you're back again then," he said with a laugh as he picked her up and snuggled her neck. "It's good to have you back. My, you've grown!"

They had no children and seemed to relish making a fuss of Georgina, who did not complain.

After "Oh so good to see you" and "How was the journey?" and "Did you manage to sleep?" and the bags were distributed, they began the ten-minute stroll up the hill to the house, which stood in the shadow of the hill overlooking the water. Georgina watched the steamer disappear around the point on its way to Lochgilphead, its last point of call before returning to Gourock.

Unlike her brothers, Auntie Mary didn't have a grand home. It was a two-story, turn-of-the-century house built in the typical Scottish style of the fragmented islands that made up the Western Highlands. It was stone and granite and so had an air of loneliness about it standing all on its own, a big grey statue that blended into the surrounding rocks.

A large front garden offered an abundance of raspberry, gooseberry, and blackcurrant bushes. They turned off the road and up the long, sloping drive to the back of the house. In the courtyard to the side of the house was Uncle Bob's smoking shed, which separated the small courtyard from a hill. There was a low wall with an ancient, rickety wooden gate. Georgina smiled. That gate was her way into her special, private world where she could go rambling off up to the top of the hill, climbing over the outcrops of rock and across the gorse and heather to her outlook post.

They headed up to the rooms allocated for them; Georgina's was always the same little one that made her feel at home. It was exactly as she remembered it from the previous year even down to the three little bears on the pillows. Though it was small, it looked out over the water. She could see the loch twisting away from the town heading north toward the towns, villages, and hamlets hiding from view.

Baking smells permeated the house. After she put her things into drawers and wardrobes, she ran downstairs to the huge kitchen with the great big range oven. There would be a pot of tea and a plate of freshly baked scones and Scottish pancakes along with a dish of jam and another of cream. Oh she did so enjoy it there!

For reasons she didn't really understand, she was allowed plenty of freedom there. It was almost as if the Frazers felt able to abdicate all responsibility for her. They had very little to do with her, and some days, apart from mealtimes, she wouldn't see them. They would sit and talk and sometimes wander down into town, but Georgina was not required to go with them the majority of times. She got into the habit of telling Auntie Mary were she was going, usually up the hill or down to the beach, promising to be good and coming in when called.

She spent most of her time alone going through the gate at the back of the house and up what seemed a huge mountain to her, across the wild purple heather and the spikey yellow gorse. She took care to avoid the sheep that grazed up there. She would arrive at a large, flat rock, at the edge of the cliff. It was her spot. She loved it there.

Auntie Mary, who knew just how much she loved the hill, always left an old patchwork quilt on the chair in her room she would take with her to her lookout spot. She would lie on the quilt and look over the water. Around one every afternoon, she would see the steamer pull in and tie up at the quay. She would watch the travelers disembark and walk up the road to the town. She would occasionally see the taxi drive past the house on its way to the quay to wait for its fare to arrive.

The rest of the time up there, Georgina would fantasize about mysterious women arriving on the steamer and being taken by taxi up to the manse, a big, old, rambling house that had an air of mystery about it. It stood all alone on the other side of the water. It was apparently where the rector once lived, but of course it was at that time haunted by a girl who was so sad her brother had drowned in the loch that she had taken her own life so she could be with him. Well, that was one story she'd made up. There were several others; it all depended on what the person had looked like as he or she boarded the taxi any one day.

Not long before that, Uncle Bob had been the captain of a fishing trawler there that fished in the North Sea past the Hebrides. He had retired several years earlier but was still held in high esteem by the other boat crews. It was because of this that Auntie Mary would knock gently on Georgina's door early every morning and whisper, "Are you ready, lovey? Let's go down to the dock."

They would walk down the hill carrying a basket to the fish dock. If they got there as the boats came in (which they always did, of course), they would be called over to one and presented with half a dozen fresh herring. They would walk home, and Auntie would gut and clean the fish and grill them for breakfast.

The sounds of the fish sizzling and the smell stayed with Georgina forever. And the taste? There was nothing like it.

They would usually stay for around two weeks, it being the Easter holidays. It was a different world for Georgina—no bullying at school and no nagging from her mum and dad.

The only downsides were of course that she wasn't able to take her violin and she missed the choir. But when weighing it up, it was worth it.

# CHAPTER 6

The First of Many Exams

IT WAS AROUND APRIL 1961. Georgina was aware that the dreaded eleven-plus exam was looming at the end of May. The school did some preparation work. The teacher would call out questions, and the pupils would write the answers. They also replicated the exam conditions—the pupils sat at single desks and received papers from the adjudicator. The students would turn their papers over and complete the test in the given time.

Georgina was usually about third or fourth in her class of thirty-seven kids and was able to answer most of the question correctly. This bode well … you would think. Unfortunately, that wasn't the case. When she took the mock exam, she froze! She turned the paper over when told, looked at the questions, and couldn't think of a single answer. At the end of the hour, she'd completed fewer than half the questions, and she was sure half of those were wrong.

Her teacher, Mr. Chapman, collected the papers for marking, and at the end of the day, she was summoned to his office. "Georgina Frazer! What on earth is happening here?" he asked angrily. "You know the answers to these questions. I've got your answers we did last week, and you got ninety-one percent. What happened?"

"I'm s … sorry, sir," stuttered Georgina. "It's just that when I looked at the questions on the paper, it was if I couldn't understand them."

"Okay," said Mr. Chapman, unconvinced. "Let's see if you *do* know the answers."

He asked Georgina about twelve of the questions on the paper, and she answered them all correctly of course. "Well Georgina, I don't understand. You know the answers to all of those. That would have gotten you eight-seven percent. I'll have to speak to the headmaster about this. Off you go."

Georgina wasn't sure what that meant. Was she going to have to sit the mock exam again, or did they think she was playing around? Whatever the outcome of the meeting between Mr. Chapman and Mr. Guillimont, the head, she didn't want it to get back to the Frazers. Her life wouldn't be worth living.

The exam was hanging over her head like black cloud. She couldn't sleep, she was being sick again, her habit when she was under pressure, and she couldn't concentrate on anything, even her one solace, music. She even tried to speak to her one ally, Mrs. Titford, but even encouraging words from her didn't help.

"You're blowing this up out of all proportion you know," she had said, but Georgina knew she wasn't and that it was going to be an unmitigated disaster. At last, the Frazers would have proof that she was no good, a waste of space, and all the other things they'd been calling her for years.

Georgina walked the twenty-five minutes to school the day of the eleven-plus exam with a heavy heart. She loitered at the gate until the bell sounded, not wanting to get involved in any conversations with the other students. She headed into class, hung up her jacket and satchel, and took her seat. After an assembly, the pupils would learn in which classroom they would take the exam. The three classes sitting the exam were mixed up; it wasn't all the same friends in one room. Not that that mattered to Georgina; no one would help her.

Assembly over, she went to room D. She saw one friendly face; Russell was a boy from the C stream but was a superb clarinetist. He smiled, gave her a thumbs-up, and carried on with a friend.

The teacher who was adjudicating was Miss Symes, whom Georgina didn't know well as she took the first and second years. She appeared at the door of the classroom and called for attention. "Right now, fifth year. You know the drill. Take a place at any of the desks, leaving any bags, pencil cases, or books at the front on my desk. I shall distribute the papers, and you will leave them facedown until I tell you to turn them over, understood?"

"Yes miss," came the low grumble from the class.

It mattered not to Georgina where she sat. She didn't need to see the board, and there were no friends for moral support, so she took her place halfway down the second row. Unfortunately, next to her in the third row was Stella Nunn, one of the nastiest bullies. Stella whispered, "You've got no chance, Frazer. You may as well leave now."

That was all Georgina needed.

Miss Symes distributed the exams. Silence had fallen over the classroom. Everyone was anticipating what the questions would be. *Did I do enough studying? Did I study the right things?*

When the noisy classroom clock reached ten o'clock, Miss Symes broke the silence. "Okay class, you have two hours. If you finish early, you're to bring your paper to me quietly and leave the room. Turn over your papers and begin. Good luck!"

Georgina's nightmare had arrived. She turned the paper over and stared at the questions. *I'll do all the easy ones and then go back to the others.*

The eleven plus covered seven subjects; six were on the paper in front of her, and the seventh, to be held later that afternoon, was a practical music exam, the only one she had any confidence in.

She started with the math section, her next favorite, and moved through the English, history (ugh), geography, science, and the RE sections.

After about an hour and a half, the first student rose, delivered her paper to Miss Symes, and left. Over the next twenty minutes, most others left, leaving Georgina and five others.

At the appointed time, Miss Symes tapped her desk. "Okay, children, pencils down finished or not."

*No surprises then*, thought Georgina. It was as she had expected. Terrible!

At lunch, the fifth-year pupils were huddled in groups comparing their successes, but Georgina kept her distance, not wishing to get involved in any jibing that might come her way. "Hey George, how'd ya get on?" came a friendly voice.

It was Russell and a couple of his friends. "It was bloody awful, wasn't it?"

"No worse than I expected," said Georgina in a solemn voice. "I think there was only about twenty that I know for sure I got right. The rest just muddled up into a fog. I hate exams. It was like the mocks."

"Ah well, it's all over. All we've got to do now is wait until end of term to be told our future. Not that it'll be any surprise to me! Secondary modern here I come! Are you coming to practice tonight?"

"Yup, you bet. See you there," said Georgina as she walked to the food hall, her head stooped. She kept her eyes on the floor so as not to catch anyone's eye.

An unusual irony in all this was her mum's attitude to the exam and Georgina's lack of ability. This came to light when back in January, all parents received a letter from the headmaster asking them to choose what school they'd like their children to attend in September at the start of the senior school term.

There had been talk about that between her mum and dad (not of course with Georgina), and it had been along the lines of, "Well, Marion went to Convent High, and Marguerite went to St Anne's. They were good schools." They were talking about Auntie Phil's girls. But those were the two top grammar schools in Southampton! Did she really think Georgina was good enough to get into either?

No, she didn't; it was pure snobbery and one-upsmanship. She couldn't bear to think of her child not being as good as Phil's three. But of course she had consistently refused to take into consideration Georgina's exam phobia.

Mr. Chapman had sent a letter to them after the mock exam incident that voiced his concerns and asked them to come and talk to him, but they hadn't bothered.

So May drifted into June and then July, and the end of term arrived. Georgina was resigned to failing. The saving grace was that several of the orchestra felt the same. So she placated herself with the notion of being able to concentrate more on music.

School was due to break up for the summer holidays on July 21. Three days before, each pupil went up at the morning assembly to receive a sealed envelope with the results of the exam.

Encouraged by each other, one by one, they opened their envelopes. Russell said to Georgina, "Let's synchronize, shall we?" in a despondent tone. "Okay, on three. One … two … three." They drew out their sheets of paper and looked at each other. "What you expected?" asked Russell. "Mine is." He turned the paper so she could see the large capital letters in the right-hand column of the paper: Overall Fail. She looked down at hers and saw what she'd sort of expected but didn't really want to see: Overall Fail.

"Shit," Russell said. "I was close on math, English, and history. What was the pass mark?"

"Seventy-four percent, I think," said Georgina. "I wasn't even close! The highest I got was fifty-nine percent. Except music of course."

"I'll catch up with you later," said Russell, who headed toward his pals.

There was a vibrant buzz in the hall as the other pupils compared their marks with each other. Georgina slipped into a reverie all her own with only one positive note—she had achieved 94 percent overall in her theory and practical music exam. But she knew that result wouldn't do her much good when she got home that evening. She just wished she could crawl into a hole and die.

She somehow got through the day in spite of her sadness. She steered clear of the other students. They were all too busy with their cliques to bother with her; she felt grateful for small mercies. But even music class didn't raise her spirits as it did normally.

# CHAPTER 7

## First Love: Music

T HE NEW TERM STARTED THE first week in September, and Georgina was for the first time glad to get back to school. Resigned to the secondary modern part of the senior school, she determined to make the best of it; she had no option.

Dressed in her new school uniform, she joined the rest of the "no goods," as her mum had described them. Getting Georgina kitted out for the uniform had been apparently so embarrassing for her that she had taken to bed with a mysterious illness apparently brought on by "traumatic disappointment," her self-diagnosis.

Georgina went on her own to the school outfitters with the list of items she needed. Not the full list of course; some items had been deemed "a waste of money" such as the official shoes and gym wear. "We can get that anywhere and cheaper too."

Joining her "no good" peer group, Georgina settled into the routine of her first year at senior school. Because of her previous placing in class, she had been put into the top stream, there being A, B, and C. She kept her head down, did the homework, put in case work on time, and was a model student. Let's face it—she didn't have the distractions many other kids had. There was no TV at home, she didn't play out, didn't have friends coming around, and she took part in very little sports. The only things she was any good at was cross-country, rounders, and netball.

Unbeknown to Georgina, it had become obvious to the faculty in the first two terms that she had more to offer than her exam results had led them to believe. After Easter and after a consultation between Mr. Chapman and Mr. Guillimont from the junior school and surprisingly enough (though under sufferance) the Frazers, it was decided Georgina should be moved up to the grammar school.

That did nothing to appease the Frazers; they (she predominantly) were still not content with the situation. "She could have gone to St Anne's, you know," said her mum one day when she had unexpectedly bumped into Phil in town.

With a wry smile on her face, Phil posed the question, "Really? Is that right? Then why don't you take her out of Bitterne Park and put her into St Anne's?"

Phil hadn't the time or the inclination to get into the conversation with her sister and was pleased to hear, "Oh, I really can't be bothered now, and anyway, it would mean wasting more money on the new uniform."

Georgina had to settle again into the new school after the Easter holidays, and she immediately felt the pressure again of the bullies, but it was a subtle form of bullying, at least at first. It was almost as if the other students knew she'd been bumped up from the secondary modern stream and didn't want to give her the credit. That resulted in her still feeling on the periphery of her peers. They would spend their breaks talking about programs they'd seen on TV, pop singers they'd heard, and singles they'd bought, but of course none of that was part of Georgina's life because the Frazers stuck rigidly to the view that a TV would allow sin and debauchery into the house. It wasn't that they were particularly devout, but they wanted nothing to do with anything that would bring the outside world into the home.

They did, however, have a radio, and Georgina enjoyed sitting next to it on a Sunday afternoon. She attended church in the morning, and then they would all sit down to Sunday lunch, so the afternoon was a bit of free time.

The programs she enjoyed most would include such nonsense as "Educating Archie" and "The Navy Lark." She enjoyed the inane humor and silliness. She had to sit right next to it, however, so the volume was low enough not to disturb anyone whether it be her mum, who would read the paper from cover to cover, or her dad, who would fall asleep until teatime.

She continued to be heavily involved in the orchestra and the choir. While Mr. Rice, the new music teacher, was not as demonstrative in his praise as Mrs. Titford had been, he obviously recognized the same thing she had. Georgina knew she had talent, and she was determined to get as much out of her music lessons as possible. She took every opportunity to appear in any school and interschool concerts. That resulted in something unexpected—she began to receive approval from some of her peers though maybe a bit begrudgingly.

Nonetheless, other students knew the right buttons to push. She did her best to stay away from them, but that wasn't always possible, for instance, when it came to rounders, netball, and cross-country. The running was okay because she was usually in front, alone, and losing any pent-up aggression. But the teamwork required in netball and rounders often resulted in her being physically knocked to the ground or pushed off base. But life went on, and she accepted that it wasn't the biggest part of her life, so she just put up with it.

It was about that time the Frazers decided to move again, and Georgina was to accompany them while they looked for a suitable home. There was no discussion that involved her, nor was she asked for an opinion, but she didn't expect to be involved. After all, what did she know?

One weekend about three months later, she was told to box all her things because the move was to take place the following Monday. "Where are we going?" she asked. "When was all this decided? No one told me!"

Her dad responded, "I'm sorry, love, I thought you knew. We're moving to the house in Bitterne, the one with the large garden and the cellar. You remember, don't you? You came with us. There was that kitten there."

She vaguely remembered it was one of the last they'd seen. It was about half an hour's walk to school.

"So you'll come back to the new house on Monday, okay? You remember how to get there, don't you?" asked her dad.

"You better give me the address," said Georgina.

That was all that was said.

She dutifully stayed in that weekend and packed up her stuff. It meant she had to miss a rehearsal, but there was no way she would have been allowed to go anyway. Packing took her longer than she thought it would. She hadn't realized how much paperwork, music, and books she'd collected over the years. She enjoyed reminiscing about some of the rubbish she'd written and the schoolbooks she'd saved.

She headed off to school on Monday like any other day and went through the day without any thought of the move. After school, she went to the music room and enjoyed the hour-long lesson as always. They were rehearsing for a recital that was to take place in three weeks, so it was intense, just the way Georgina liked it.

She left and without thinking started walking to her former home. It wasn't until she got there that she realized, *Of course! They'd moved.* She was shocked. She sat on the curb and cried. It was as if she'd been deserted. Her imagination went into overdrive. All types of scenarios flew around her mind, including that they'd purposefully gone, hoping she wouldn't find them, that she was going to be on her own from then on. She fell into a state of self-pity, but she was in a strange way resigned; it seemed to be the ultimate act of disapproval and isolation.

She really should have expected nothing more. After all, she was worthless, a burden, unpopular, a disappointment, and all the other belittling adjectives she's heard over the years. Ironically, she shut out the fact she had been told and had been given the address, but she hadn't taken enough notice and had basically forgotten.

"Are you okay, Georgina?" A voice penetrated the haze of her tears. "Can I do anything?" It was rosy-faced, plump Mrs. Piggott from down the road. She had two boys—Andrew, two years younger than Georgina, and Matthew, in the year above. They too had often tried to offer friendship in the early days but had given up when their invitations to tea or to a birthday party had always met with the same response as the Barretts': "No thanks. Georgina doesn't want to come!"

"Oh Mrs. Piggott, I don't know what to do. We moved today, and I've forgotten where the new house is. I feel so stupid."

"Don't you worry, dear. Come on in and have a drink. We'll sort it all out," said the kind woman who had every reason to ignore Georgina and her problems.

But she didn't, and after some time, several cups of tea, and delicious cheese on toast, her husband drove Georgina home. The Frazers had left the address with the old woman who lived in the bungalow next door in case there was any post or the new owner needed any help. Just as well, really!

## CHAPTER 8

# A Talent Recognized

Life went back to as normal as it ever was. Georgina was doing exceptionally well at school and of course was excelling in music. Her music teacher, Mr. Rice, was a tall, middle-aged man with a mass of unkempt grey hair and a wild beard. He was almost bohemian in appearance as if nothing mattered but his music.

This of course boded well for Georgina; he worked very closely with her. He too could see something he was confident he could work with and develop. When Georgina was in her second year of senior school, he mysteriously sent a letter to the Frazers asking them to come to school the following Monday after rehearsal.

"What on earth is all this about, Georgina. What have you been doing now?" moaned her mum. "Doesn't he think we've got better things to do?"

"I really don't know, Mum. He just told me he was going to write to you, and when I asked him why, he said, 'You'll just have to wait and see.' You will come, won't you, Mum? He made it sound important."

"Oh I suppose so, but don't think we're paying out any more money if that's what he's after."

The following Monday, Georgina somehow got through the day, but she was frustrated at not knowing why it was all so secret. She knew she hadn't done anything wrong, so it could only be something like he was considering putting her forward for the county orchestra and was anticipating problems with rehearsal times and weekends away.

*Yes,* she thought. *That has to be it! Gosh, does he really think I'm that good? Or could it be the school choir exchange in November?* She's listened excitedly when Mr. Rice had made an announcement about that, but she had of course quickly put it in the back of her mind. She didn't for one moment think the Frazers would let her go.

She finished the school day and made her way up to the music room ready for whatever was to come. Rehearsals started and finished with Mr. Rice paying her no more or less attention than normal or giving her a clue as to what was to come. When all the instruments were away and there was no one in the room except for Georgina and Mr. Rice, there was a soft knock on the door.

"Enter," said Mr. Rice. The door opened to reveal Terry Speight, a sixth-form prefect, and the Frazers. *So they've come!* Georgina wondered how long it had taken them to decide to come. She was used to them ignoring open days and teacher-parent evenings; she had come to expect their indifference to anything relating to her.

Mr. Rice approached them and extended his hand. "Mr. and Mrs. Frazer, thank you for taking the time to come in this afternoon. I hope it hasn't caused you too much inconvenience." He nodded to the prefect. "That will be all, Speight. Close the door, will you?"

"This isn't going to take too long, is it? We've several other things we need to be doing," mumbled Mrs. Frazer.

*So they haven't allowed too much time for me then,* thought Georgina, smiling to herself. She hadn't expected anything else. She was still in shock that they'd bothered to come at all.

"Okay," started Mr. Rice once everyone had sat. "Georgina knows nothing about the reason I've asked you to come in, so I'll get to it and put her out of her misery. You must have had quite a day, eh, Georgina?"

"Yes sir, just a bit," She chuckled nervously.

He smiled again, running his hand through his disheveled hair. He spoke with a very soft Welsh accent. He had the knack of putting people at their ease.

"Well now, as you will know, Mr. and Mrs. Frazer, Georgina is a bright star in our orchestra as well as the choir. Do you enjoy her playing and singing at home?"

*Oh this is going to be good! Go on! Be truthful! How are you going to get out of that one then?*

But it was blatantly obvious they weren't going to admit to making her practice her violin in her bedroom with the door shut and that they'd told her they didn't want her singing in the house at all.

"Well to be honest, we can't tell whether it's good or bad, really," said her dad. "And she tends to stay in her bedroom a lot."

*Well, that got them out of that one.* But Georgina knew not to say anything. However, she had a sneaky feeling Mr. Rice was well aware of the truth.

"That's such a shame, but I'm here to tell you she has a great talent. And it would be a real shame to let it go to waste, don't you agree?"

They just looked at each other, but Georgina could see with a certain amount of pleasure that they were a bit uncomfortable.

Mr. Rice continued. "You may not be aware, but there are every year a limited number of opportunities for talented youngsters to go to South of England Music College in Bournemouth on scholarships, and I would like your permission to put Georgina forward for one of these places."

Georgina was stunned. While she knew of the college because the school had played a concert there once, she had no idea how one became a student there. She had assumed it was for the kids of rich parents.

"It's a residential school, much like a boarding school," continued the teacher, leaning forward in his chair and folding his hands together as if in prayer. He was talking directly to the Frazers. "Georgina would be one of four scholarship students this year if she was to be accepted. There would be no cost whatsoever to you other than the uniform. What do you think of that?"

He leaned back in his chair and looked at Georgina with the hint of a smile. "Well, before you comment, Mr. and Mrs. Frazer, let's hear from the star, shall we? What do *you* think about it, Georgina?"

She felt the flush in her cheeks. "But sir, I had no idea … I thought you wanted me to go to Germany on the exchange … I don't think I'm that good … What if I'm not good enough? I don't think …" She was struggling to keep the tears back but not doing very well.

"What about you, Mr. and Mrs. Frazer? Are you prepared to hear more about this wonderful opportunity your daughter has at her fingertips?"

And so it was that the unkempt, bohemian, long-haired Mr. Rice convinced the Frazers (who would have totally disapproved of him at a single glance) to let Georgina take the scholarship exam for entry into music college in the Easter term of 1962.

He was exceptionally astute; he played on the fact they didn't really care. He had already noticed the looks between the two of them and had read into them that maybe this could be played to Georgina's advantage. He explain at length about the accommodation, the catering, the holidays, the curriculum, and the opportunities. It was a win-win situation, and they bought it.

The Frazers would be rid of Georgina for a huge part of the time while saving face with the family. They would be able to say, "It's an opportunity we couldn't miss" and "She's worked so hard, and with our support, she'll have a wonderful opportunity."

And Georgina would finally be able to mix with students who loved the same things she did, and she would be away from the Frazers. She couldn't believe her luck!

Mr. Rice said the program had a very comprehensive curriculum of academic work undertaken from 8:30 in the morning until 1:00. After lunch, music classes went to 4:30. Saturday morning was available for extra tuition, and very strict standards were imposed. The aim of the college was to bring students to O and A levels as soon as possible, and a pass rate of 85 percent or above of A and B grades was the expected standard.

Georgina saw this immediately as a potential stumbling block. If they put such store in the academic side, how would she get on with her exam phobia? But Mr. Rice had thought of everything, it seemed.

"There is of course a far smaller ratio of students to tutors, and this I believe will help Georgina with her exams. I see no reason at all why she can't get the required marks, so you needn't worry about that either." He said that last sentence with such a flourish that Georgina could have kissed him. The Frazers had nowhere to go.

He continued. "Once these exams had been taken and level seven and eight grades been reached in the chosen instrument, a university degree course is the next stage. This could therefore mean students could stay at the college until age twenty-two. At that time, they would leave with a degree in their chosen field along with introductions to orchestra or operatic facilities leading to a full music career."

As soon as Mr. Rice had gained their consent for Georgina to sit the exam, they left. She hung back, wanting to ask Mr. Rice if he really believed she had a chance, but there was a sharp call from the hall outside the room: "Georgina! Get your things. We've spent far too much time here." With one last look at her teacher, she left the room, but not before Mr. Rice gently touched her arm, smiled, and with a knowing look said quietly, "I'll speak with you tomorrow after assembly, okay?"

The three walked home, Georgina trailing behind in a euphoric haze. She heard them muttering and knew they would be putting down this fabulous opportunity with their normal negativity, but she didn't care. She was sure they considered this the answer to their prayers. While taking credit for her achievement, they could absent themselves from the day-to-day responsibility of having a daughter, something they'd been trying to achieve for years.

That night, she lay awake wondering what her life would be like if she became a professional singer or a member of one of the large orchestras. She imagined herself playing first violin dressed in a long, black evening dress and standing to shake the hand of the conductor at the end of a recital; she'd seen that happen at orchestra recitals and at the ballet. She imagined receiving a standing ovation after having sung one of the beautiful Italian arias she'd heard on a record Mr. Rice had played. She thought of the countries she could visit. Her mind raced with such reveries until she fell into a fitful sleep.

She awoke with a start. She realized she had to talk with Mr. Rice about the entrance exam. She quickly showered and dressed, and without even looking at the breakfast table, she charged out of the house and ran to school. So many thoughts were milling around in her head, and one kept niggling at her. *Suppose I don't pass the exam? After all this excitement, suppose I discover I'm not good enough?* How the Frazers would gloat. She would be at their mercy yet again. *Stop it, Georgina. You can do this! You really can.*

She made it through the gates just as the assembly bell stopped ringing. That gave her less than five minutes to squeeze on the end of the bench, breathe, and stand as the faculty paraded in. The assembly seemed to take twice as long as normal that day. She hurried up the stairs to the music room desperate to hear more about the exam. *You can do this!*

A smiling Mr. Rice entered the room. He patted her shoulder. "Get any sleep then?"

She felt he was on her side. "Not a lot, sir."

He launched into the details and explained how the process worked. The next step involved his contacting the college and arrange a date for her to take the oral and written exams. After about half an hour, he said, "You mustn't let this distract you from your lessons. You do understand that, don't you?"

"Yes sir. I'll do my best."

"Right then. Back to classes now. I'll let you know when I hear something."

"Thank you sir, thank you … You just don't know …"

"I think I do, Georgina. I really think I do. Now go!"

About three weeks later, Georgina and Mr. Rice set out for Bournemouth in his old Morris Minor, the split-windscreen model from about 1952. As it chugged and rattled its way around the corners, Georgina wasn't convinced they'd make it. They were on the A27 near Ower, and Mr. Rice was humming, oblivious to the engine's noises.

She touched his arm. "Is it meant to make this much noise?"

"Take it easy, girl. This old lady's never let me down yet."

She stared out of the window, not really watching as the houses became fewer and fewer. They entered the New Forest. It was quiet on the road, so they made good time. The car continued to creak and groan, but as predicted, it kept running, and soon, they were on the outskirts of Bournemouth.

They arrived at the college in Landsdown with about fifteen minutes to spare. It was a huge, rambling, old house with creepers all over the brickwork. There appeared to be three floors and an attic with three rows of nine windows on each floor. Georgina wondered what it would have been like to have been in the family that had lived there originally. She imagined it was maybe two hundred years old. She tried to picture women in bustled dresses and maids running up and down the stairs. She remembered getting a book from the school library where the three generations of aristocrats lived in an old mansion house, with young maids running around below stairs. It was that sort of house. She determined to explore its history. That's if she got in. *Oh dear.* Back to the moment. And the self-doubt.

"Are you feeling okay?" asked Mr. Rice, putting him arm gently around her shoulder and smiling. "You're going to be fine. You know that, don't you?"

They entered the stone-floored hallway as the old grandfather clock chimed forty-five minutes past the hour. A young male tutor in a black gown descended the staircase with a huge grin. "Hi! You must be Georgina. We've been looking forward to seeing you. And Mr. Rice, I assume?"

After such a pleasant welcome, Georgina felt at ease in the beautifully oak-paneled room they were led into.

"We've got a bit of time. Would you like some tea?" asked another of the staff.

"That would be lovely," said Mr. Rice.

"Georgina?"

"Yes please. That would be nice."

After a while, they were ushered into a huge, high-ceilinged room, and after having the process explained to her, Georgina was ushered into an anteroom where she sat the theory exam. She was then brought back into the main room, where she sang her heart out with a rendition of "Jerusalem" and "The Skye Boat Song" to three male and two female judges.

All that was left was her violin solo, and as she completed the last bars of "The Trumpet Voluntary," she heaved a sigh of relief. The had taken two and a half hours, and she was drained.

Everyone was very friendly, and as they made their way down the stairs, several students passed heading up to the dormitories. Each smiled, and a couple said, "Hi."

*What a difference!* Georgina thought. *I could be happy here.*

She would hear within two weeks. The drive back to Southampton was in almost total silence. Mr. Rice hummed quietly. He dropped her off at her house. He gave her a huge smile and a gentle squeeze on her arm. "You did fine, dear. I'm sure you did enough."

The Frazers didn't question her about the trip or the audition, so Georgina had no way of releasing her pent-up excitement. And so she was unsurprisingly getting herself in quite a state after the first week. She couldn't concentrate and found herself staring mindlessly out the window during her lessons.

On the Wednesday of the second week, she went into assembly as normal, and after prayers and the hymn, the headmaster as usual went through announcements: Miss Jones's class was to double up with Mr. Williams's class as she was not in today … Today is the last day for volunteers for the chess match in Birmingham … and so on. They were usually boring. The students would be shuffling from one foot to another waiting to hear the words, "Okay, dismissed. File out."

But that morning was different.

"I have a very pleasant announcement to make," droned Mr. Parsonage, the head. He had one of those voices that was stuck on one note. "As you all know, we're very keen here to encourage you to achieve the best you can, and I have pleasure of telling you that one of our pupils has done just that."

*Oh get on with it*, thought Georgina, looking forward to the domestic science class due to start at 9:30.

The head was still talking. "… and so I'd like to ask Georgina Frazer to come to the stage."

Georgina froze. Everyone was looking at her, and she could hear mumbles all around. She moved from her place in the middle of the line, passing six or seven classmates in a daze, and walked to the front of the hall. She felt as if she were walking in slow motion. She could feel her heart beating. She mounted the steps to the stage, where all the teachers were sitting in a row.

"As some of you know, Georgina is a very valuable member of our choir and orchestra. It is with regret that I tell you we will no longer have the privilege of her company. Mr. Rice encouraged Georgina to sit an entrance exam for the SEMC in Bournemouth, and we heard yesterday she passed with flying colors and will be leaving us at the end of term."

Georgina stood there open-mouthed. She looked at Mr. Parsonage, turned to Mr. Rice, and burst into tears. She couldn't process what she'd just heard. *I'm dreaming!* She looked into the sea of faces and couldn't make out anyone through her tears.

"Well done, Georgina." The clapping started. "We will watch your progress with pride." Mr. Parsonage moved forward on the stage, as did Mr. Rice, and she suddenly realized what this meant.

"Thank you sir." She turned to Mr. Rice. "Thank you so very much." She was crying tears of joy in anticipation of what was to come.

"Just so you know, dear, you achieved eighty-eight percent on the written academic exam and a magnificent ninety-two percent on the music practical exercise."

She didn't care. She'd gotten in. That was all that mattered.

And so Georgina was kitted out in her third uniform in twelve months and started on her dream adventure of studying music with like-minded students.

She packed and moved out of the Frazers' house just after Easter of 1962 with only the holidays to put up with. She felt free. She was sure the Frazers felt so too. It was a new start for everyone, and it should have been a recipe for success and a wonderful future. But every silver lining has a cloud. Georgina was going to find out her beautiful silver lining could hide several clouds.

# CHAPTER 9

## *New Opportunities*

THE SOUTH OF ENGLAND MUSIC College was everything Georgina had hoped for, and she was more than happy to let it absorb her completely. She was living and breathing music, and she couldn't have been happier. Apart from having to go back to the Frazers for the holidays, she felt her life was at last looking up.

Because of the student/teacher ratio being so low, sometimes down to eight students to a class, she was able to successfully come to grips with most of the academic subjects and even began to understand logarithms.

Her end-of-year exams put her in the top of most of her streams to the extent that she and a few of the other students were able to sit their O and A levels a year early. That was one of the great prides of the college, one that made it stand out even before "centers of excellences" had been thought up.

Georgina found herself in the midst of a group of about nine students who hung out together regularly. She'd never encountered the camaraderie before; up until then, she had been the outsider, the odd one out. She was invited to Durham, Plymouth, Coventry, Sussex, and places she'd never heard of where her friends came from.

She became good friends with quite a few other students; they were a very mixed bag who came from all over the country and from all walks of life. One of her best friends was a tiny girl named Sarah who was studying the clarinet and oboe. She came from East Sussex and was a year older than Georgina. They would laugh at the same things, and the two developed a strong friendship though they made an unlikely couple; Sarah was about four foot nine while Georgina stood an impressive if not gangly five foot nine.

Sarah's family ran a hotel near Lewis, and she invited Georgina to stay with them over some holiday periods. When this happened, Georgina would write to the Frazers about the invitation, and they always quickly wrote back telling her to do as she wished.

Sarah's brother Shaun would drive down to Bournemouth at the end of term to pick up the girls, and the journey to Sussex would be constant chatter not least of all from Shaun, who was at Bristol University studying dentistry. He would regale them with tales of drunken parties, girls he fancied, and what he and the four other guys he shared a house with got up to. The girls were sworn to secrecy; they promised not to utter a word of his antics to the parents.

This lifestyle was of course heaven for Georgina, and to her surprise, the Frazers didn't seem to care. They'd become increasingly used to the fact that they were almost free of their responsibility of her, and when she would write and ask if she could stay with Sarah in Lewis, or Dianna in Eastbourne, or Jennifer in Plymouth, they were always more than happy for her to do so. She even became relaxed enough to talk to her friends about the weirdness of the Frazers' way of life.

That explained to her friends why reciprocal visits were never going to happen. While she had initially expected to be ridiculed or judged for this, she wasn't. That was the start of her realizing her family situation wasn't her fault.

On visits to her friends, she sometimes found it confusing and even difficult mixing in with what were of course normal families. She'd had no experience of the interaction or the dynamics that took place in such environments. She would sometimes retire to bed in her friends' houses feeling sad that this was an aspect of family life she'd missed out on and would never experience for herself. It struck her more than once that she'd lost the opportunity to be a child and enjoy sweet memories of that.

She would listen to the families asking, "Do you remember …?" and the hoots of laughter that would follow—what a grandma had said, the look on a daddy's face, and so on. Photos were so much a part of the family life past and present, but she had none.

Actually, she did have a photo. She remembered once seeing a sheet of what would now be called thumbnail shots, about fifty small photos no more than an inch square on a sheet of photographic paper. They were all of her head and shoulders only and of course black and white taken when she was about three, around the time of her adoption. She had been allowed to choose one, which was cut from the page. She'd kept it not knowing it was her only pictorial link to her childhood.

Her day-to-day life continued along the very pleasant path of study, music, friendship, and acceptance. She began putting behind the bullying and other bad memories.

But one day came a phone call that brought her joy and peace to an end. Her dad had been taken seriously ill again and would be in the hospital for several weeks. He had been working part-time until then but wouldn't be able to resume that. He was nearly seventy-five, but he had always been dictated to by Mrs. Frazer and enjoyed being away from her even for a few hours of work, his "quiet" time.

Her mum demanded that Georgina return home immediately. "I don't care what your plans are. You need to stop this silliness and come home. You'll have to get a job!"

"But I have exams coming up soon," she said between sobs.

Her mum seemed to enjoy the conversation. "Dad can't work anymore, so it's about time you started to pay your way. I'll expect you home by the end of the week. I mean it now! No trying to get out of it. You can tell the head whatever you like."

In a terrible state, Georgina went to the bursar. The faculty spoke with Mrs. Frazer and beseeched her to take into consideration the life Georgina would have if she stayed and took her degree. But as Georgina expected, they were unable to sway her. Georgina was to give up all she'd worked for and return home.

In early March of 1967, at age sixteen, she packed her belonging and tearfully said good-bye to all her friends, promising to keep in touch, to call and write, and even visit them. She reluctantly made the journey home on the train and discovered that her dad was weaker and had aged terribly. He had lost his stature; he shuffled around the house and garden with bowed head. He wouldn't stand up to his wife; he didn't have the stamina. Georgina lost what little respect she'd had for him.

What good were O and A levels if you had no thought of a career other than music? She had previously decided that as she had an aptitude for figures, she would do her degree in economics as well as music. She had felt it would give her some security; if she didn't make the top grade in music, she would be able to support herself while enjoying playing and singing.

But all her plans had been cut short. She would have to have a complete rethink as soon as she had mourned the loss of her new life and readjusted to her old life. The bitterness she felt toward the Frazers was phenomenal and growing daily.

She very soon found out that there were very few jobs available to a sixteen-and-a-half-year-old who had supposedly dropped out of college. Even though she'd taken her O and A levels a year early, she hadn't received the A level results yet. She'd gotten nine O level passes and had taken six A levels, and she wasn't about to expand on the reasons for this to any prospective employer. That would simply expand the circle of people who knew of her misery, which in turn would put her at an immediate disadvantage (or so she thought).

She got a job as an assistant at an herbalist's in Southampton. It wasn't anything of a career, but it brought in money. She went to work every day and became more and more convinced this state of affairs couldn't go on. She thought about it and formulated a plan. The startings of one anyway.

She went home one evening from work and announced to them very calmly that she was leaving home. She couldn't have prepared herself for the response she received.

"You stupid child! Do you really think it's that easy? After all we've done for you, you selfish little beast! Let me tell you some facts, shall I? First, you're under seventeen, so if you attempt to leave, we'll tell the court about your wayward behavior and make you a ward of the court!"

Georgina was taken aback. Her mum's reaction was the opposite to what she thought would happen. She expected to have her things packed for her before she'd finished her announcement. Instead, she was making her stay. It certainly couldn't have been for the money. Georgina was made to give up 50 percent of her earnings to the family pot, but she didn't see how that was more valuable than the freedom they'd have if she were no longer there. Then it struck her. Because the old man wasn't able to help much anymore, her mum needed a gofer. And it appeared they expected Georgina to continue to play that role.

She went into her bedroom, trying to make sense of what she had just experienced and rethink her plans. She had for some time been able to confide in Mrs. Wetherby, one of the woman she worked with at the pharmacy. After the initial disbelief that any parent could treat a child adopted or not that way, she had generously offered Georgina a room in her family home should she ever need it. Her son and daughter had left home, and she and her husband were finding life rather quiet for the first time in twenty years. Georgina would have to tell her she wouldn't be able to come after all, at least not then. It was March; she had to stay at least until she turned seventeen in August.

She didn't question the validity of the Frazers' comment about her age, but how had they known? They must have been expecting some sort of reaction from Georgina to have gone to the lengths of finding it out.

*If I have to stay here until August, it'll damned well be on my terms!*

She walked purposefully down the stairs and entered the lounge, where they were sitting on the sofa, he reading his paper and she doing her knitting. A stranger walking into the house at that time would never have known of the previous hour; it would appear a normal evening.

"Okay," announced Georgina, "you leave me no option. I'll stay until my birthday, but rest assured, I'll be out of here that day! And as it's you who are saying I must stay, I'll give you only twenty-five percent of my pay. If you don't like it, let me go!"

They looked at each other. Her dad started to speak. "But what about—"

"That's enough!" said her mum, throwing him a vicious look "Let her stew in her own juice. You'll get nothing from here, young lady! No food, dinners, or anything. You won't get the better of me. You should know that by now."

"But—" said her dad.

"That's the end of it!" she shouted.

Georgina wasn't sure who'd won that battle. As always, the battle-axe had thrown a huge monkey wrench into the works. She just hoped she could manage on the money. She would go to work tomorrow and see if Mrs. Wetherby would let her still move in but in August.

After giving notice of her intent to leave the day after her seventeenth birthday, she and Mrs. Frazer didn't utter a word; they used her dad as a communication vessel. It was an exceptionally uncomfortable period, not a situation anyone would volunteer to be in, but on the eighth of August, Georgina left the house for good.

# CHAPTER 10

## *Independence at Last*

THE SEVENTH OF AUGUST, THE day of freedom, was sunny. There was no thought in Georgina's mind of *Oh goody, it's my birthday,* only of escape from a miserable chapter in her life and a new beginning. There was of course an element of concern: *Oh my God! Can I manage on my own?* But there was no going back.

Mr. and Mrs. Wetherby had come up trumps and assured her she was more than welcome to move in with them, so at least that part of the transition was in place. Also, having been at boarding college for five years was going to help. *It shouldn't be too daunting.* Anything was better than the last four months, and she knew that once she'd made the move, life would get back to a different routine and one she'd control.

Georgina had asked Audrey, one of the girls at work who had a car, if she would mind helping her with her things. Audrey had agreed, suggesting they make a day of it and maybe fit in some fun as well.

She didn't have a lot of baggage. She had packed her clothes in great anticipation of the day. All Georgina had to do was a final check through the drawers and wardrobes. Taking a last look at what had been her purgatory for the last few months, she made her way downstairs for the last time.

Audrey had said she would be at the house around ten-thirty. It was ten past ten. She went to the cupboard under the stairs for her violin, put it with the rest of her things by the door, and entered the lounge. The Frazers were at the table, and as she walked in, she saw her mum holding something wrapped in tissue paper.

"So then, you're going now, are you?" asked her mum in a flat voice.

"Yes. Don't pretend you're surprised or sad. You've had enough notice! I'm sure we're pleased this has finally ended. I just have one question, but I don't suppose even you know the answer."

Her mum halted and looked at the item in her hand. "I've got one thing to say to you too, but go on, what's the question?"

Georgina took a deep breath. "What did you expect when you adopted me? That I'd always be three? Didn't you at any time consider would happen as I got older? Why didn't you just let me go back to wherever I was meant to go?"

Her mum threw her head back and laughed. With a sneer, she said, "You're joking of course! *He* didn't want you and never did! All he wanted you to have was this! He had nothing else to give you." She thrust whatever she was holding at Georgina. "This is all your bloody father left you, a stupid cross." She sat and sipped her tea as if nothing untoward had occurred.

Georgina looked at a silver crucifix about two inches long on a silver chain nestled in a thin, white hankie. "When did he give me that?" she whispered.

"When you first came to us. It was obvious even then that he wasn't going to come back. Get used to it. He didn't want you either!"

Georgina stared at the cross. Tears welled up in her eyes. "I don't believe you. I'll find him. He'll tell me the truth."

"You won't get anywhere, you stupid girl! He's got a new life now and a new family. He won't want you messing it up again."

Georgina was dumbstruck. She walked out of the room in a daze. *Have they been in touch with my father all this time? Why hadn't he contacted her? How much did he know? I have to get out of here!*

Someone knocked. It was Audrey.

"Thank God you're here! Get me out of here!" Georgina screamed as she flung open the door.

"Hey girl, you look awful. Was it that bad?" asked her friend, never having seen Georgina shed a tear.

"Worse! You'd never believe it."

Audrey picked up some boxes and made her way to the car. Georgina picked up her last case and the violin.

"Where the hell do you think you're going with that?" came the scream from the lounge doorway. "That stays here."

"But why? What are you going to do with it? Stop being stupid. It's mine. You know it is. Dad got it for me years ago."

"That may be so, but it stays just where it is. If you take it, I'll call the police and tell them you've stolen it."

Georgina couldn't believe her ears. Neither could Audrey, who had returned to the doorway. "Leave it, girl," she said, throwing a disgusted look at the Frazers. "You can get another one."

"Yes, but not like that one," sobbed Georgina. "It always sounds so much better than the others."

And then something suddenly dawned on her. Some time ago, Mrs. Titford had admired its sound and had asked to look at it. She had spotted the maker's label in it and had shown it to Georgina. "That's why yours sounds so nice," she'd said. It had meant nothing to Georgina until just then. It wasn't a common violin. She remembered the label read "Nicolas Amati 1877."

But she desperately needed to get away from the house; she had no choice but to leave her beloved violin. She should have been use to such irrational actions on the part of her mum, who was wicked and selfish. The Frazer woman knew the violin was very valuable to Georgina not for the label but because it was her love.

They drove off. Georgina thought she should be feeling something other than anger at losing her violin, but she felt cold and empty. She had lost all she had known of family. She wondered if she would ever see the Frazers again. Though she didn't want to, she felt she wasn't allowed to think that by some strange rule and thought she wouldn't be able just to just discard them after fourteen years. She was relieved that part of her life had concluded, but she still felt empty.

Around lunchtime, they reached Mrs. Wetherbys' house, which was in a pleasant, leafy cul-de-sac with about fourteen other houses all similar in appearance and beautifully kept. Their owners obviously took great pride in them. There was no one in when she knocked, but she'd been expecting that as both the Wetherbys worked. They had already given Georgina a key.

She and Audrey took her stuff upstairs to the room Mrs. Wetherby had said would be hers. Her bedroom was a lovely room with pale-blue wallpaper and matching curtains and bedspread. Fresh flowers were in a crystal vase on the dressing table. A big picture window looked out on the immaculate back garden with beds of colorful flowers. She saw tubs and hanging baskets in abundance and a little wooden summer house on a raised area at the bottom of the garden. It was obviously someone's beautiful labor of love.

Her room had a double bed, a large wardrobe, two chests of drawers, and a big, squishy chair. The room was twice the size of her former room. She took in her new surroundings. She spotted a music stand in the corner. A tear formed in her eye. Mrs. Wetherby had already said she was more than happy for Georgina to practice in her room, and a piano was in the study. She had said she would be more than willing to help Georgina with rehearsals. *There won't be much of that*, Georgina thought sadly, certainly not until she could afford another violin. That added to her emptiness and sadness. She wanted to climb into bed and hide under the covers until it all went away.

Audrey could see Georgina was becoming maudlin, so with a cheery smile, she ushered her out of the room, downstairs, and out of the house, insisting on lunch at a café near Mayflower Park she knew of that served wonderful pasta.

Georgina realized she hadn't celebrated her birthday, so she agreed to go. The café did offer wonderful pasta served by a flattering waiter who was very dishy. They consumed two bottles of Leibfraumilch; Audrey was eighteen and Georgina looked it!

After eating and drinking far too much, they left the café and headed to the car. Georgina had consumed much more wine than Audrey had, but the latter was a bit squiffy. "You can't drive us home. You're pissed," slurred Georgina. "How on earth are we going to get back?"

The thought hadn't occurred to Audrey. She lived about eight miles from the café, and Georgina's new home was about four miles the other way. "Oh shit!" said Audrey. "I'll call my brother Johno. He can pick us up."

Thankfully, he did just that. He turned up about thirty minutes later in his beaten-up Vauxhall Victor. He laughed as he helped the two girls into the back. "Can't use the front seat. It's knackered."

"This is really good of you—hic—" Georgina giggled. "I hope you weren't doing anything."

He looked at her in the rear mirror and laughed again. "Just washing the car."

Georgina thought that was terribly funny as the car had more rust and holes than anything else; she thought any washing would make more of the car drop off.

He took Georgina home, though she had a hard time thinking of it as home, and she almost fell out of the car and onto the curb. She turned to thank Audrey for her help and saw she was fast asleep on the backseat.

"Well that's no surprise," said Johno. "She's always does that. She'll be fine in the morning. Nice to have met you."

"Thanks for the lift, Johno. See you again maybe?"

"Sure thing," he yelled as he rattled off into the distance.

She looked up at the house feeling sad that she didn't really have a home. She knew that would change, but she had no idea when.

She let herself in. Luckily, no one was home as it was only about four. She made her way upstairs and flopped onto her bed. That made her feel sick. She made her way to the bathroom, and after throwing up most of her lunch, she returned to her room and fell asleep.

The next thing she knew, Mrs. Wetherby was peering around the door and encouraging her to get undressed and into bed properly. "Can I get you anything, dear? Some tea? Toast?"

"What time is it?" whispered Georgina, not sure where she was.

"It's about nine-thirty, dear, and you've been asleep since I came in about five. You obviously celebrated your birthday with gusto."

"Oh Mrs. Wetherby, I'm so sorry. Audrey helped me move out, and then we went for lunch, and then, well we had some wine, and … Oooh! My head hurts."

Mr. and Mrs. Wetherby continued to do their best to make her feel welcome and comfortable and were really sweet to her, offering to chat if she wanted to but also respecting her need of occasional solitude.

The head of the Southampton Youth Orchestra (with whom Georgina had keep in touch while she was in college) was more than happy to loan her a reasonable violin until she was able to buy one, so she was able to practice at least.

Her life began to get back to a routine of traveling to work with Mrs. Wetherby, getting back into the choir scene in Southampton, and ice-skating at a rink about a mile away. It was very new to her but not to Audrey and her brother, and she started to make some friends among the regulars there. She was uncomfortable with her newfound freedom and independence, but she soon got used to it. She was still livid with the Frazers for the loss of her education options and knew that feeling would last for years, but she also knew life had to go on.

She wanted to start things afresh, so a few weeks later, she took a couple of days off work and took the train to SEMC. She had phoned before she went to let them know she was coming, and faculty and the students welcomed her with hugs and kisses. They wanted updates on what she'd been doing with herself.

She spent a while chatting to the students she'd had so much in common with for so long; she caught up with all the gossip—who was doing what, who'd gotten a role in this or that opera, who was playing in which orchestra. After a while of that, she set off for the dean's office.

One of the main reasons for this visit apart from catching up with her friends had been for her to find out what her educational options were. She didn't imagine for a minute she'd be able to go back there, and within thirty minutes of talking to the dean, that was made abundantly clear not because they didn't want her but because places were at a premium and hers had been taken within two weeks of her leaving.

However, the chat with Mr. Hodgson gave her a better picture of what she wanted to do versus what she'd be able to do and how she could go about achieving it. Apparently, all was not lost.

He suggested that with her O and A results (she'd passed all six), she'd be able to get back into mainstream university, and while music was her first love, she wasn't naive enough to think she could rely on that solely. It was suggested that she apply to Southampton University to take economics, something she'd been planning to do previously anyway.

Mr. Hodgson told her he knew the head of music there very well; he was sure that with a letter from him, she would be able to participate on the sidelines of music and develop at her own pace. He advised her on how to apply for a grant, as she had no means of support, and he gave her the necessary paperwork.

That seemed to her to be her best option. At the beginning of the January term, she enrolled in the European economics class and immediately started catching up with the other students, who were a term ahead of her.

Mr. and Mrs. Wetherby were of course more than happy for her to continue to stay with them; they even refused to charge her rent. They had become used to her being in the house and enjoyed her company. But after a while, it became apparent that wasn't the best option; she was becoming involved in many campus activities and spending more and more time with other students. When the opportunity arose, she moved into a house share in Portswood, only about a fifteen-minute walk to campus.

She slipped easily back into the student routine and the learning mode. She kept her job at the herbalist on Saturdays for a while, which helped with her finances, and she took a few shifts at a pub near campus. But when the holidays came, she realized she had to get something with more hours. She was lucky enough to get a few hours at a Marks & Spencer store.

At the end of most days, the store would sell off the food that had that day's "sell by" date for pennies. The others in her house were more than happy with these morsels, which beat the pie and chips or pizza they were used to. She was also able to get good lunches on workdays again for pennies.

She took an active part in all the usual student activities such as debating the politics of the day, drinking, parties, and more drinking. While not overly politically minded, she did have an acute awareness of what was and wasn't fair.

England's imminent move to the Common Market and eventually the European Union in a few years' time played a vital part of her economics studies. An issue that made her and other students see red was the apartheid in South Africa. With fairness in mind and the feeling they ought to do something, about thirty of them piled into a couple of VW campers and some cars very early one Saturday morning in June and drove the sixty or so miles to London.

The argument then was that the South African government wasn't doing enough to solve the problem and it was being exacerbated by the likes of companies such as Barclays banks and Safeway supermarkets that still insisted on segregating their business locations and therefore the employees and customers.

After meeting up at the McDonalds near Trafalgar Square at about nine that morning, some went to the bank headquarters and to South Africa house, both nearby, and others to the Safeway head office just off Cromwell Road.

Georgina joined the larger group and took her place with banners (and a few rotten eggs and tomatoes they had been saving for the last few weeks in the warmth of several of the houses) on the steps outside SA House. They attracted a crowd with their chanting and rowdiness; everything was very good-humored.

"Black and white, both all right!" was the motto of the day. Some sixty or seventy more young folk joined in the demonstrating over the hours. While this added to their voice, it also attracted the attention of the police, who "respectfully suggested" the group disband. As it was apparent that wouldn't happen, they called for reinforcements, and within thirty minutes, forty police officers (a bit of overkill) along with several Black Marias were hell-bent on dispersing the more than a hundred demonstrators.

Georgina and her pals sat on the steps and chanted, "Stop apartheid now!" They were still chanting as they were manhandled into the black wagons and taken to a police station, where they were charged en masse with disturbing the peace. They were locked up for the night.

They were released the following morning on their own recognizance and made their way back to Southampton having not actually achieved much but with adrenaline still pumping. They felt if nothing else virtuous.

Unfortunately, the faculty wasn't at all pleased with them. They had to attend the dean's office one by one and listen to a lecture on adult responsibilities, bringing the university into disrepute, and what their parents would have to say about their activities. The last part didn't bother Georgina.

That was the last infraction of the rules she was actually caught at. While of course she joined in the student lifestyle, the rest of her days at university passed uneventfully, and she was perceived as a (near) perfect student.

# CHAPTER 11

## "This Man Could Be Your Father"

ANOTHER SIGNIFICANT EPISODE IN HER life unfolded during her penultimate year at university. It all started on a normal, frosty morning in February when she got out of bed to get the mail that had been dropped noisily through the mail slot.

The amount of junk mail the three living there received daily was amazing; proper mail was quite an event. She picked up the pile of post and made her way to the kitchen. She put the mail on the table, filled the kettle, retrieved cups, and returned to the mail. She was hoping to be asked to compete in the initial round of BBC's Young Musician of the Year. She rummaging through the post and came across a letter addressed to her franked not by the BBC but by the Salvation Army. The red ink on the front of the letter where the stamp should be read "Bureau of Missing Persons."

Intrigued, she returned to her bedroom, flopped onto the bed, and tore open the envelope. After the preamble, she read that the Salvation Army had been asked to locate her on behalf of someone who thought he might be her father!

She reread the letter repeatedly as she wandered the house. She sat on her bed again with legs curled under. She was confused. Dazed. Stunned. Her heart raced. She found it hard to breathe. She stood, and luckily, Janey, one of her housemates, noticed Georgina's white face and caught her as she swayed precariously. "For God's sake, George, what is it? You look as if you've seen a ghost." She helped her back onto the bed. "Christ, girl, tell me. What is it?"

'Oh my God! I don't believe it, not after all this time."

'What? Tell me before I bloody throttle you!"

Georgina regained her composure, gave an abridged version of what had happened back in the early fifties, and brought her up to date with the letter.

'What are you going to do?" Janey asked. 'Do you really want to find out who this guy is after all this time? You've managed okay without him so far, haven't you?"

Janey, from Southsea, had grown up with the traditional security of a mum and dad, two younger sisters, and an older brother. She could in no way imagine what life had been like for her friend. She thought Georgina's reaction was weird.

Georgina's head was spinning as if she were watching a movie at the wrong speed. *Do I want to find out who he is? Do I ever! This guy has come looking for me!*

This proved the Frazers yet again had lied to her.

"You can't rush into this," said Janey trying to be wise but not understanding what this could mean to Georgina. "Why does he want to know you now? It could be trouble, you know. You don't know him."

Georgina knew Janey was possibly right, but she knew she was unable to explain to anyone how she felt after having learned someone was trying to locate her. After all the years of rejection, that was huge.

"Did you make the coffee?" asked Janey.

"No I … I … only got as far as the kettle."

Her friend made her way down to the kitchen and came back a few minutes later with a cup for each of them and some toast.

"Look, do what you like, but for God's sake be careful! You're just too trusting. I have to get to class. Will you be okay?"

After assuring Janey she would think carefully about it, she waited until the house was empty before calling the Salvation Army. "Er …

I received a letter from you. My name's Georgina Frazer. What do I have to do?"

A soft-spoken woman said, "Now slow down, my dear, and let's go back to the beginning. So you've had a letter from us, have you?"

After establishing who Georgina was, the woman cross-referenced the information and found the file with the details of the request. She told Georgina someone had written to them a few months earlier, just before Christmas.

She wasn't able to give her a name or the whereabouts of the enquirer, but she informed her that if Georgina wanted him to contact her directly, the Salvation Army would write him with the news it had received a positive response from her and that she was happy to receive a direct communiqué from him. "Now are you absolutely sure, dear? Have you someone you can talk this over with? It's a huge step, you know. Are you sure you've had enough time to give this plenty of thought? You've only just received the letter, haven't you?"

"Yes!" She couldn't control her impatience. *What's with these people? First Janey and now her. They have no idea what this means to someone like me.*

The letter had come at an extremely important part of her university life; it added to the pressure of her busy schedule. As part of her final course work, she'd been offered an internship with the Deutsch Bundesbank in a small town in Germany. But after convincing the woman she was fully aware of the consequences, she learned that the next step was for the Salvation Army to contact the gentleman concerned and that Georgina should expect to hear from him soon. She was warned that at times, those who initiate such searches panic and don't take the enquiry to the next stage. She tried to prepare herself for that as well as everything else.

But just as she was about to leave for Germany for the exchange, she saw three letters on the table for her when she got in from classes. Of course, she didn't recognize the exceptionally neat handwriting on one. At times, she had received letters from the students at SEMC, so she didn't give too much importance to that specific letter. She dropped her books on the table, put the kettle on, and took her mail up to her room and threw it on the bed. She changed, went back to the kitchen, made tea, and sorted out her books. Sipping her tea, she wandered back to her room.

One letter, from Mrs. Wetherby, was as gracious as the others Georgina had received from her—what was going on at the pharmacy, her daughter's graduation, her son's new girlfriend, and so forth. It was sweet of her to keep in touch; she was always inviting Georgina to visit. Georgina felt guilty about not having gone, but it was as if she'd not only turned over a new page but had also started a new book. Her life was so different then, but she decided to ring the Wetherbys and see them one weekend.

She turned to the other two letters and recognized the handwriting on one as being that of Sarah's from the college. *I'll leave that till later.* She turned her attention to the third, which had been precisely written with a fountain pen. *Almost calligraphy.*

"Hey George! You coming to the pub?" Janey yelled from the bottom of the stairs. "You did promise Billy after all. It's his twenty-first. Come on, we're going now if you want a lift." Several of her friends had been discussing it over lunch, and she had agreed to go, so she put the letter on the bed, picked up her bag, and bounced happily down the stairs and out the door.

Later that evening, after declining to go on to the Concorde, an after-hours drinking club they frequented most weekends with the others, she returned to the house and decided to do some work on the essay she'd started a few days earlier that needed finishing before she left for Germany.

She went into the kitchen to put the kettle on again and ran upstairs to retrieve her books. She saw the letter again. She'd forgotten about it. She grabbed it and her study book and descended to the lounge, stopping only to make her drink. She took a sip of tea and slit open the letter—two meticulously handwritten pages with the lines, "I know there's nothing I can ever do to make things better, but I hope you will give me the chance to at least explain a little. May I come and see you?"

Her father! He explained a little about his new life; he was remarried with four children from the marriage. She read and reread the letter until she practically knew it by heart. There was an address in Devon and a telephone number.

"You can call me any time you wish."

She looked at her watch; it was 10:15 p.m. *There's anytime, and then there's ten-fifteen. He wouldn't appreciate a call this late.* Containing herself the best she could, she put the letter back into the envelope and turned to the essay she'd intended to finish. She realized she wouldn't do it justice that night. Giving up on studying, she went upstairs and got ready for bed. Slipping under the cool, crisp sheets and pulling the covers around her chin, she put the envelope under her pillow. *Tomorrow morning. I'll make the call tomorrow morning.*

After an understandably disturbed night and after having read the letter again at about 3:00 a.m., she got up and showered at seven. She read the letter again and could think of no reason it wouldn't work. It was he who had come looking for her, and she wasn't asking him for anything.

She managed to occupy herself until about ten that morning. She couldn't wait any longer. No one else was in the house. She went down to the hall and lifted the phone off the hook. She took it into the kitchen, sat at the table, and dialed the number. She had been practicing all morning what she was going to say, but nothing made any sense. And then a smooth voice. "Hello, Jackson speaking."

"Um ... er ... this is ..." and with a resounding crash, the phone landed on the floor. "Hello? Hello? Are you still there?" yelled Georgina, scrabbling for the receiver. The line was dead. *Oh shit! He'll think I'm a nutter!* It hadn't crossed her mind that he probably had no idea who had called him. Looking back, she realized it was the first time she could remember thinking how important his approval of her was.

She rang again, and after a weird and strained conversation, they agreed to meet.

They did a week later, three days before she left for Germany. For the first time in her life, she had many positive things going on, and she wasn't sure what to focus on. The reunion was monumental, something she'd dreamed about for years, but she knew she had to focus on the next four months because the report the university received from the Bundesbank would be a major determining factor in her degree and her future. She couldn't afford to blow that.

The meeting with her father was pleasant but strange. It was naturally strained at first, but gradually, after an hour, they started to relax and learn about each other. There were huge differences in their lives and many questions that needed to be answered, certainly on Georgina's part. They both accepted it would take time, but they had at least taken the first step.

# CHAPTER 12

## Grown-Up Love

THE GERMAN PLACEMENT LASTED ABOUT fifteen weeks; she found it valuable in helping her in her major subject. Those she worked with were very accepting, and she made friends in the bank and outside.

She graduated several months later with a well-earned 2–1 and felt fantastically lucky when she was offered a position with Bundesbank in Germany. She'd applied for the position while there. She'd been based in a small town on the Ruhr River near Mulhiem, and she felt good that the officers at that branch were impressed enough to invite her to return. She would be able to resurrect the friendships she'd made. Her friends Claus and Helga Leihmann had insisted that if she got the job, she was to stay with them for as long as she wanted.

Another of her friendships was with Mike Grantley, an army officer who banked at the branch and who came into the branch nearly every day until she agreed to go to dinner with him. He was with the Royal Corp of Transport based at BFPO headquarters in. Munchengladbach but working from the Mulhiem barracks. They'd become inseparable in the four months she was there, and it was another reason she was so pleased to be going back. She's missed him terribly but had been comforted by weekly letters and frequent phone calls. While she'd had occasional relationships in university, none of them had been serious. She believed Mike was her soulmate.

Georgina received the letter of confirmation from the bank stating her terms of employment, when they wanted her to start, her salary, and the necessity of her becoming fluent in German in six months.

Within thirty minutes of receiving the letter, she'd rung and left a message for Mike saying she'd be back in days. She was elated! At last, things were starting to go her way again. A great job offer, a relationship with all the makings of a long-term commitment, and an adventure. She finally felt in charge of her own future. All thoughts of her father were in the background.

The phone rang about an hour later. "Darling, its Mike. You got it then?"

"Yes! Isn't it wonderful? They've offered me a twelve-month renewable contract at the Oberhausen branch. I'm going to book the ferry for Thursday. What are your plans?"

"I'll be off duty on Friday at four. Where are you coming into?"

"Zeebrugge. I'll drive down. I've spoken to Claus and Helga. They're happy for me to stay with them until I get something sorted. Why not come over on Friday night?"

"You're on, sweetheart! I can't wait to see you again. You have no idea how much I love you!"

Georgina smiled. "Oh yes, darling, I think so. And you know just how much I love you too. It's going to be wonderful. I'll call you when I get to Helga's."

"All right, and drive carefully. See you Friday. Bye, darling."

Georgina had a lot to do including getting her work wardrobe together, but Zeebrugge was only four and a half hours away, so she didn't have to take all her personal stuff in one go. It wouldn't be long before she would make the return journey because Mike's brother, Raymond, was getting married in Worcester and they'd been invited as a couple. Mike had planned to drive over for the wedding and pick her up on the way, but they could make the trip together, their first official engagement so to speak. She just knew this was going to be a long-term thing.

Mike drove a large Ford Taurus estate car, so hopefully, they'd be able to bring the rest of her things on the return trip. She was hoping to have an apartment by then because she hoped Mike would be staying with her more often than not.

She scurried around for the next few days, saying her good-byes, doing last- minute shopping, and making sure her car was okay. After a hectic thirty-six hours, Georgina was on her way to Dover to catch the 11:00 p.m. ferry to Zeebrugge. She planned to get to Mulhiem around 8:00 local time, allowing for breaks en route for coffee. She knew of a great service area at the Dutch/German border at Venlo that had pastries to die for.

She had an uneventful drive down to Dover and took her place in the queue waiting to board. As ever, she had arrived early, almost an obsession of hers. She'd arrive early for meetings, dates, even casual lunches with friends. People would say, "Let's meet between one and one-thirty," and Georgina would panic if she didn't get there before one. She had a ridiculous feeling of satisfaction by being early. Having been advised to get to the port one hour before departure, she was there at ten to nine. She was at the front of the queue and felt good about that.

She drove onboard, parked, and took the metal stairway to the forth deck to the restaurant. One of the disadvantages of getting to Dover at 8:50 p.m. meant she had left home at around 6:00 a.m.; she was ravenous. One good thing about P&O ferries was the excellent smorgasbord they served; she chose from fish, pasta, cheeses, meats—so much to choose from. The rumble of the engines grew louder. She was beginning a new chapter in her life. Everything for the last few days had been such a whirl that she hadn't realized what all this meant. For the first time in her life, she had her own plan. She was free to do as she wanted—make decisions about her father and about Mike—and if she made the wrong decisions, she had only herself to blame.

In Zeebrugge, she concentrated on driving on their side of the road and drove through Belgium into Holland and then into Germany, 245 miles in all. She stopped in Venlo for pastries, which were as good as she had remembered. She set off again with a bag of pastries for her friends and Mike.

She thought about what the meeting with Mike would be like. She hadn't seen him for about five months. They'd exchanged regular letters and spoken on the phone at least a couple of times a week, but she couldn't get the thought from her mind that maybe he had cooled off since she'd left. She had no rational reason to think so, but it was in her makeup to not get too excited just in case.

But her sensible head told her a different story. He had been excited on the phone when she told him she was coming back. She'd told him briefly about her father, but she hadn't expressed too much of her inner self to him as she wasn't overly comfortable doing so on the phone. And she wasn't sure what her inner feelings actually were. She was hoping that after a long chat with Mike, her mind would become clearer. One of the things she loved about Mike was that he was a considerate listener. Even with the little she'd allowed herself to divulge to him, he'd shown a gentle interest and let her offer her feelings as well as the facts.

Georgina pulled up at the apartment block where Claus and Helga lived at about 7:30 p.m., a half hour ahead of schedule. She was unloading her car as Claus came out.

"Liebling! You're here! You made good time. Let me help you." He gathered up all but two bags and hurried into the four-story building in a traditional part of Mulhiem. Most of the buildings had been built before the war, and while Essen had suffered a lot of bombing because of its industrial nature, Mulhiem had missed most of that though it was only about twelve miles away.

It was the end of June, and the trees lining the strasse were in full leaf; much of the pink blossoms that had adorned them in May had been blown away like confetti. It was a picturesque area and only a short walk into town.

Claus spoke very good English, having learned it at school and then again while studying engineering at Düsseldorf University. Helga, a very petite, almost Scandinavian-looking girl, had learned English at school but had gone straight into her father's dental practice as a nurse and had seen no need to continue with the language.

"You are so welcome to our home. We will enjoy so much you and Mike of course to stay with us." Claus beamed and put his arm protectively around his wife. "Helga too has been practicing, haven't you, mein Liebling?"

Helga smiled and broke free of Claus's arms to hug Georgina. "We love that you come, and you must not go soon." She looked at Claus for approval; he and Georgina were laughing.

"No, I will not go soon if you wish." She hugged Helga and smiled at both. *What good friends they are.* She had been introduced to them by Claus's brother, Jochem, a few months earlier when he had invited her and a friend to a party he and his wife were holding to celebrate her birthday.

Jochem, who worked at the bank as an investment advisor, had befriended Georgina and introduced her to his lovely wife, Anna. They were about twenty-four; they had been childhood sweethearts since they were twelve. They had married against their parents' wishes when they were eighteen. They were determined to prove their parents wrong; they finished their education and had gained very good degrees, Jochem's in banking and Anna's in accounting.

They lived in a small but beautifully furnished apartment about three miles from town. Anna obviously had an eye for design. Their apartment wasn't overfurnished, but she had found some wonderful pieces at secondhand sales. It was all in such good, classical taste that one would never know it hadn't all been matched professionally.

They had decided on no children until they were thirty, hoping that would have given them time to develop their careers and be able to continue them later.

Claus and Helga had been married some ten years; they were in their early thirties. She'd had four miscarriages; they had almost determined not to have children (unless one came along of course) and live life to the full.

Claus had started an engineering company soon after finishing university and had been lucky (or "at the right time in the right place" he would say, knowing it was the wrong way around) to gain several contracts from the government. Things were going very well for them.

While Georgina was considerably younger than them, she fit in with their philosophy of life and had immediately felt comfortable with them all. While language was a bit of a problem with Helga, the other three were more than able to converse on most levels. She and Georgina had, however, promised each other they would help each other because language wasn't a problem just for Helga.

Part of Georgina's contract was that she would take German lessons and become good at the language in six months. It helped that Mike was fluent in German; he was on his third tour of duty in Germany, and the language was second nature to him then.

Georgina joined in the merriment of the moment, but she was tired and nervous about Mike arriving the next day. *What will be will be* she convinced herself.

About ten, she excused herself and went to bed. There was the threat of a headache coming, and she wanted to be fresh for the next day. "Sleep well, schatz," Claus told her. "Rise when you wish. You must be in good form for Mike."

*No pressure then!* She was sure they would fall into each other's arms as soon as they set eyes on each other, but as was always the way, she mentally prepared for something less. *Oh stop it! Don't be stupid. Get some sleep. It'll make tomorrow come quicker.*

# CHAPTER 13

## *Live Together? Really?*

AFTER A RESTLESS NIGHT, SHE awoke about seven the following morning to the sun shining through the windows and bird songs emanating from the avenue of trees. Her headache hadn't lasted, and her mind was clear. She lay in bed feeling decadent, just enjoying the smells and the sounds coming through the window.

She dozed off again. She awoke with a start and saw it was 9:25. *It doesn't matter. I'm here on my own. Who's to know?*

She put on her matching floral satin dressing gown and slippers and found Helga, also in a dressing gown, at the table, reading *Das Spiegel*, the national German paper.

"Guten Morgen, mein freund." Helga smiled. "Heute ist ein guter tag fur sie, yah?"

"Oh yes," said Georgina, "a really good day. Why are you not a work? Is all okay with you?"

"I take 'oliday. Is this right?"

Georgina laughed and gave Helga a hug. "Yes that's right. You have ein 'oliday."

They ate breakfast and spoke a comical mix of English and German, happy in the knowledge their friendship could overcome the language barrier.

After maybe an hour or so, she excused herself, and strolling back to her bedroom, she gathered her things and headed for the bathroom. After a luxurious shower, she emerged with a feeling of peace and anticipation of Mike's arrival.

Claus returned from work around 4:30 and opened a very pleasant white wine they'd tried the previous evening. "So we start tonight now!" He laughed as he poured four glasses.

Georgina was confused. *That won't be very cold when Mike gets here.* But there came a loud knock at the door. *Claus has brought a friend home with him.*

Claus said, "Won't you welcome your man then?"

She looked down the hallway toward the front door and saw Mike in uniform and carrying a huge bouquet of gorgeous flowers.

"That fooled ya! Got off early and didn't stop to change! Hey, Helga, wie geht es? Blumem fur dich." He put down the bag he had slung over his shoulder and headed for Georgina, passing a stunned Helga on the way and almost throwing the flowers at her.

"God, you smell good," he murmured in Georgina's ear as he picked her up and hugged her so tightly she thought she'd burst. "Just as I remember! I haven't been able to do a thing all day. I've been going crazy!"

All her worries melted away with this welcome. She couldn't have asked for more from him. "God, darling, it's so good to see you! I wasn't expecting you for hours." She realized Claus and Helga had made a tactical withdrawal and were conspicuous by their absence.

And so the evening continued with a delicious meal of mussels Helga prepared and several bottles of beautiful, crisp, white wine. Georgina and Mike looked at each other knowing exactly what the other was thinking. Mike started to yawn. Laughing, they made their excuses, saying it was time to turn in. They took two glasses and a bottle of Piper champagne Mike had secreted in the fridge earlier. This was all to the amusement of their hosts, who looked at each other knowingly and smiled.

The rest of the evening was all Georgina had hoped for and more. All her worries and insecurities diminished as she just gave herself again and again to the joy and rapture that was her love, Mike. It was as if they'd never been apart.

They rose unsurprisingly late the following day. They were completely on their own. A note on the table informed them that Claus and Helga would meet the two lovebirds at a Balkan restaurant in town at 8:30 that evening.

*How sweet of them! They've given us space to get reacquainted.* But it was as if they'd been apart for only a day or so—no uncomfortable silences, no awkwardness.

"So, sexy, what's the plan for today? Don't worry if you haven't made any. I have some ideas." Mike chuckled as he put the filter in the coffee machine. "What say we take this and some croissants back to bed and work on a plan of action?"

"You're going to be a bad influence on me I can see." Georgina laughed. "But no, I hadn't made any plans."

The morning rolled deliciously into the afternoon. They sauntered from the bathroom having spent a luxurious hour or so (which actually took longer than planned) to the bedroom, reveling in each other, two people head over heels in love.

"I've made some plans for tomorrow," Mike said while shaving. "I hope you don't mind."

"That depends what they are," Georgina said in a mock-serious voice she realized she wasn't very good at. "I'm not going stock-car racing if that's what it is."

Mike laughed. "As if, my darling, as if. Seriously, I've been doing a bit of legwork this last week knowing you were coming back, and I think I've found us a gorgeous garden flat near Oberhausen. I know you'll love it. I did! We don't want to stay here too long, do we? It's available right away. If you like it, we could move in next weekend."

Georgina was blown away by Mike's comment. She knew she had to get an apartment, the nearer to the bank the better, but she hadn't thought Mike would move out of barracks and in with her. She didn't know why she hadn't considered it an option, but she supposed that was due to her insecurities about Mike's commitment to her. Their reunion had been more that she could have asked for; she hadn't dared think any further. She had thought she would get an apartment and Mike would visit and stay over weekends maybe, but live together? Wow! She hadn't dared to go that far. *Is this what I want?* She'd never had to make a commitment to anyone before. *But why not? I love him, and he obviously loves me.*

These thoughts were buzzing through her mind when she realized Mike was in the doorway watching her dry her hair. He wrapped his arms around her and nuzzled her neck. "Um, have I said the wrong thing, darling? I assumed that was what you wanted too, sweetheart. I didn't mean to rush you. Please don't think that. You can take the apartment for yourself, and I could come weekends. Would you rather do that?"

*Oh shit.* Georgina melted under his touch. *It's make-your-mind-up time. But why shouldn't it work? And if it doesn't, what's the worst that could happen? I could stay there on my own. Here they come again, those doubts.* She lacked confidence in herself to make it work though he was promising his undying love. *Trust him, you silly bitch!* These thoughts took no more than three seconds. She turned around in his arms and looking into his eyes, whispered, "No, love, it's not the wrong thing at all. It sounds idyllic!" But as if she felt she had to bring things back to reality, she said, "But let's see if we like it first."

"So you're not totally adverse to us shacking up then?" he asked, laughing and still holding her close. "'Cuz I think we've got the best chance in the world of making a bloody good life here, don't you?"

*He wants me to commit. Why wasn't I expecting this?* "Mike, sit down a minute." She took his hand and walked the few steps to the bed. She sat and patted the space next to her. She smiled and ran her fingers gently down his face. "No sweetheart, I don't think I am, but we haven't even discussed this. Please don't think I don't want it as much as you because I do, but it's a surprise. I didn't realize you felt so strongly. Yeah, I know what you're going to say. We've chatted over the phone about a hypothetical future, but this is real, babe! I suppose I thought you'd want time to get to know me again."

He took her face in his hands. "Georgina Annabel Frazer, you are without a doubt the best bloody thing that's ever happened to me! I want this more than anything. I've never loved anyone or missed anyone as much as I have you, and that tells me not to let you go." He kissed her face and forehead gently. Easing her up from the bed, he pulled her closer. "I want us to get married, have kids, and do all the stuff married people do. I know it's sudden to you, but it's not to me. I've been thinking about it ever since you went back to Blighty."

Georgina couldn't believe what she'd just heard. Yes, she had quietly hoped Mike was the one, but she hadn't actually considered what that would mean. *Married? Me?* She supposed it wouldn't be the end of the road. After all, she loved him, and what was more important to her than to have a family of her own that no one could ever take away?

She took his face in her hands and looked into his eyes. With tears in her eyes, she kissed his face gently—first his eyes, then chin, cheeks, and lips. "Mike, I love you so very much. If you're sure it's what you want, then yes, let's do it. When can we see the apartment?"

# CHAPTER 14

## *Decision Day*

THE REST OF THAT DAY passed in a haze. Once she had accepted what seemed to be the inevitable—that she would live with Mike and marry him—she realized how happy she was. Every now and then, she'd catch a glimpse of herself in a mirror or window and saw her grinning face. Mike was moving around the apartment humming. As he would pass her, he'd nonchalantly touch her hair or arm. God, it was wonderful to feel so loved!

At around 6:30, they started to start to think about getting ready to go out. They sort of started. It took a bit longer than usual to get dressed. They simply weren't able to leave each other alone.

Dressed in casual clothes, they headed into town and arrived at the restaurant at about 8:20, a few minutes before Claus and Helga got there.

"Well my friend, how did it go?" Georgina heard Claus ask Mike while they were at the bar.

"Absolutely bloody fantastic. She's up for it. I think she's agreed to marry me!"

"Hey, you guys!" Georgina called out with a laugh. "Is this a private conversation or can anyone join? What do you mean 'She's up for it'?"

"Ah, Georgina, you should know he's been planning this for weeks," Claus said. "He's dragged Helga and me to many apartments to see if we thought you'd like them. He's a very happy man tonight."

She felt more secure knowing his desire for them to live together hadn't been a spur-of-the-moment thing. He'd obviously wanted it and had taken the two of them into his confidence. *But the sod hadn't even hinted to me about it over the phone!* She'd have to remember he was good at surprises. *To the future!*

The evening was a great success. The Balkan food, a choice of several wonderful, peppery rice dishes and pork steaks, was delicious. Mike bought a couple of bottles of Moet to celebrate the couple's good news.

Toward the end of the evening, Mike and Claus left the table, and Helga and Georgina had an opportunity to speak to each other.

"So my friend, you will be happy, yes?" Helga asked. "He loves you very much, you know."

"Yes, I believe he does. Have he and Claus been planning this?" asked Georgina, already knowing the answer.

"Not the planning … but Mike, he come to us for help with some things. You will see, I think. They come. Look!"

Georgina saw Claus and Mike weaving their way through the tables. Mike looked decidedly guilty as he produced from behind his back a present beautifully wrapped in gold, shimmery paper with pretty decorations, gold and silver ribbons that cascaded over the side, and a big bow on top. He (or someone) had spent a great deal of time and effort on the preparation, and Georgina was assuming this was what Helga had alluded to.

"Uh, darling, um, I thought you might like this," he said as he handed her the present.

"What else are you going to surprise me with today, Mike? I don't think I can stand anymore," she said as she took the present, which was about a four-inch cube. "This is too pretty to undo. I think you've had a hand in this, Helga, am I right?"

Helga looked a bit shifty. Her smile said it all.

Georgina gingerly undid the ribbons, almost not wanting to spoil it, but as the ribbons came undone, she lifted the lid and saw folds of a silver, silky material.

"Careful now. Don't want to tear it," Mike said with a laugh.

She very carefully separated the folds of material and found another box hidden underneath. *The bastard! He took for granted I'd agree. Maybe he knows me better than I thought.* She opened the second box, and there sparkling up at her was the most beautiful diamond and emerald ring.

"I hope you like it, sweetheart. If not, we can always change it."

For the second time that day, Georgina shed a flood of tears. "Oh Mike! It's exquisite! Oh my God! It's the most beautiful thing I've ever seen!"

Mike gently took the ring out of the box, and taking her hand in his, placed the ring on her finger. "So my darling, insecure, beautiful Georgina, please say you'll marry me and soon."

She gasped, "Oh yes, darling, of course I will."

# CHAPTER 15

## The Daughter Act

THUS BEGAN A WONDERFUL, EXCITING chapter in Georgina's life, one she had always hoped for but had often wondered whether it would ever be. Would anyone actually want her? She didn't have too good a track record. First, her biological parents didn't want her, and then the Frazers … Here, she was proving she was indeed worthy.

She and Mike moved into the lovely apartment the following weekend and set about putting their personal touches on it. He had been right. It was in a lovely, old part of Oberhausen near the river and was ideal for them. She could walk to the bank in less than fifteen minutes, and Mike could get to camp in about twenty-five minutes.\

The owners had decorated the apartment beautifully. German style tended to the dark with large patterns, but this wasn't like that all. The hallway and lounge were painted in a very soft and fresh lemon shade. The larger of the two bedrooms was a pastel lavender color, with a voile type of curtains that let enough light in to make the room shimmer. The smaller bedroom would be used as a study, but it had a sofa bed for guests. It was on the first floor of an old, four-story building, and it overlooked a garden lovingly tended by the elderly couple in the apartment below.

The small balcony off their bedroom wasn't much bigger than a Juliette but big enough for a small table and stools. The railing were black wrought iron with gold tips. Georgina enjoyed having the French windows open and feeling the soft breeze.

She was to start work at the bank on August 1, so she had about three weeks to settle in. Mike took ten days' leave toward the end of the month because they had to travel to the UK for Raymond's wedding. Georgina would bring more of her stuff over then. By the time things got back to normal and they both had to go back to work, everything was in its right place, and they felt like an old married couple.

She'd put to the back of her mind the situation with her Father except to drop him a line about her job and address and the news of her engagement.

Her first days in the bank were very intense; she had to come to grips with so much. She was reintroduced to everyone but still had a job remembering all their names and those of people who hadn't been there when she had earlier.

While everyone was very friendly, she knew she had to learn the language fast to become accepted as part of the already established team. She also needed to get back to the UK again. While they had gotten a huge percentage of her things at the end of August, there was still a small amount of knickknacks she'd left with Mrs. Wetherby. She and Mike made arrangements to go the first week in October. She also thought it might be a good time to meet up with her father.

But before that, she knew she had to fill in some gaps for Mike. He deserved to know some of the history of the girl he was marrying. He had been talking about setting a date for the wedding. They'd tentatively decided it would be a quiet affair in the new year, so she had a bit of time.

One evening a few weeks prior to the trip, she and Mike had dinner on their balcony that overlooked the garden. It was a magical evening. The smells from the garden were intoxicating, as was the Western Australian Chardonnay.

When they'd finished eating, Georgina took a deep breath. "Mike darling, can I talk to you for a minute?"

"Of course, love. What's the problem?"

"No problem, sweetheart, but there are things about me you need to know."

She started in not about the whole childhood thing, though she knew she'd have to at some time, but with her adoption, the letter from the Salvation Army, and the meeting she'd had with her father.

He listened and occasionally touched her hand and murmured encouragement. When she finished, he moved closer to her and put his arms around her. "You poor baby. You shouldn't have to have kept all that to yourself. Don't worry, sweetheart. Of course we'll see him and the family if that's what you want. Maybe it'll be easier for you if I'm there—not so heavy."

She felt a huge weight lifted from her shoulders having finally talked to someone about it. But the rest would have to wait. She hoped Mike wouldn't think badly of her for not telling him sooner, but one thing at a time.

She telephoned her father the next day. While the conversation was still a bit stilted, she explained about Mike and asked if they could meet the family the weekend they were in the UK.

"Of course you can visit. You will stay overnight, won't you?"

That took Georgina aback. She wasn't sure she was ready for that much yet. She thanked him and said that because of having to get back to Germany, they'd just come down on Saturday for the day.

"More than okay, m'love. We'll be looking forward to seeing you."

He sounded pleased. One hurdle overcome.

They arrived in the UK late on Friday and drove an hour before checking into a small hotel Mike knew of just outside Portsmouth.

Saturday arrived. After breakfast, they started the drive to Devon to meet her father and his second family. He had told her he'd been married to Margaret for over fifteen years and had four children, three boys and a girl ages seven to thirteen.

She'd been trying to put the dates together—her birth date, the year of her adoption, and the story he'd told her briefly when they'd met a few months back. It didn't seem to fit, but maybe as time went by, she'd make more sense of it.

He had been very convincing when he told her at their previous meeting that he had told his family about her and that they were very excited to meet her. She found that difficult to believe. Surely, a child from a previous marriage would upset any family dynamic no matter how stable it was. But she had nothing to judge this by. She decided to take his word for it.

It was with considerable trepidation that they set off on the journey. She was glad Mike was with her. His presence would maybe defuse the awkwardness she was sure would arise.

It was only a two-hour journey from the hotel just off the A27 at Portsdown Hill, and they arrived as planned just after 11:00. Having turned off the main road, they came across the village. It was a typical English chocolate box that exuded a sense of peace and tranquility. The houses were all set back in beautifully manicured gardens. The lovely, quaint church was surrounded by cedars. The river estuary sparkling in the late summer sun enhanced the picture.

After a few minutes of driving around, they found the house, and pulled up onto the drive. It was a large, imposing, rambling, old place with beautiful wisteria where earlier in the year hundreds of colored heads would have hung over the front door. At that time, the twisted stems clung to the stonework like a spider's web just waiting to shoot back into life in a few months. The house appeared to be several hundred years old and looked as if it should have been a listed building. She was surprised to see that the roof wasn't thatched as were other houses in the area.

Mike, who was undoing his seatbelt, had a strange look on his face.

"Are you okay, love?" she asked.

He put his hand on hers. "I'm fine, sweetheart. Honestly. It's just all a bit strange not knowing what to expect or what sort of reception we'll get."

She was reassured that he had reservations as well.

"Come on then, boy, let's do this!"

They got out, she straightened her clothes, and they started up the flower-lined drive to the house, passing a lovely array of colorful and well-tended plants. The deep porch flanked by benches led to a once grand and imposing oak door that then looked very old just like the house. It wasn't the most welcoming of entrances.

They worked the old-fashioned twist bell that rang somewhere in the house. Shortly, they heard running footsteps. The door was flung open by a child of about eight or nine who was chomping on a piece of toast.

"Hi! You must be Georgina. And who are you?"

"Hello there yourself. I'm Mike, Georgina's fiancé … well, boyfriend."

"Okay. Did we know you were coming too?" he asked with a mischievous grin.

"Is that our guests, young David? Bring them in then. Don't leave them standing on the doorstep."

Georgina recognized her father's voice. They followed young David into a huge entrance hall with a tall grandfather clock that commanded pride of place on the facing wall. To either side were large portraits. One subject looked particularly ostentatious—a gentleman in what looked like an ermine gown, a judge maybe, but not someone to be trifled with.

Georgina's father came through a doorway followed by a rotund woman dressed in a floral apron and sporting a huge, red-faced smile.

"Hello, my love," said her father. "And you must be Mike. I'm very pleased you could join us. This is Margaret, my wife, er, I suppose, your stepmum. Hadn't thought of that, had we, Mummy?"

"No, but I'm more than happy. You can call me anything you like. Hello, dear. It's lovely to meet you after all this time, and you too, Mike," said Margaret with one of the most welcoming smiles Georgina had ever seen. While she had initially had her hand outstretched, she was obviously happy to hug both of them. Georgina immediately liked her; she had such an open, happy face and seemed to glow from within.

"Come on through to the kitchen and meet the rest of the tribe."

They were led from the hall through a huge lounge and through another door that was so low Mike had to duck under the frame. They entered a large country kitchen with an enormous farmhouse table around which were seated the "tribe." "These are our children. David, whom you've met, Philip, Alan, and last but not least, Sandra. Kids, this is Georgina, your sister and her friend Mike. Say hello then."

There were mix of mumbled hellos and hi yas from the children, who looked unimpressed and even bored. Georgina felt a bit uneasy at the children's reception; she'd had reservations all along about how they would take to her. And she could understand their reticence. For so long, they'd apparently lived a perfectly normal life with a mum and a dad, and suddenly, they learn they're not a family of six but seven! She wondered if they'd known about her for some time or if they'd learned about her only recently. *Oh well. It won't be long before we'll be on our way back.*

Lunch was a mammoth event—an enormous joint of beef, Yorkshire puddings, and every vegetable you could think of. There was of course a lot of general chitchat, but Georgina sensed an undercurrent of unspoken conversation between the children and to a certain extent her father. Maybe it was that they thought they'd had this visit foisted upon them.

Margaret on the other hand did her utmost to make them feel part of the family. There was no difference in the way she spoke to Georgina and Mike and the way she was with the others. She wasn't involved in the eye game going on between the four kids and their father.

The meal ended. Georgina helped clear the table and took the plates to the kitchen, where Margaret was loading the dishwasher.

"That was a lovely meal. Thank you so much," said Georgina.

"I'll second that!" piped up Mike. "Don't get too many roast dinners like that in Germany."

The kids asked to be excused one by one. They didn't go out of their way to join in any conversations their father had tried to start and would occasionally mutter a reply, but Georgina sensed their attitude was, *What's all the fuss about? You're nothing to do with us.*

The afternoon wore on. The only person in the room seeming to be completely natural was Margaret. She didn't stand on ceremony at all. She chatted about the village and the school she taught in occasionally as a substitute teacher. She seemed genuinely interested in Georgina's job and where they were living.

Georgina's father was making heavy work of starting conversation, and it was becoming a strain for all concerned, so after a while, around 4:30, Mike announced they were sorry to break up the party but had to leave. Georgina could have hugged him.

The kids had long ago disappeared upstairs and were summoned to say good-bye. They thundered down the stairs; The two older boys extended their hands while the others shifted from foot to foot in embarrassed silence. "Say good-bye to your sister," said their father. It was more of an order than a request.

Margaret, sensing the uncomfortable atmosphere, hugged Georgina and kissed her on the cheek. "It was lovely to meet you at last! Don't be a stranger. You're more than welcome any time." She hugged Mike. "And that means you too." She smiled.

The kids looked at her in amazement. They hadn't expected their mum to behave in that way, and just seeing her beaming confused them totally.

"Yeah, good to see you," mumbled Phillip. "See you again I expect."

He and Georgina exchanged surreptitious glances that spoke volumes. Alan just stood at the bottom of the stairs with a sullen frown.

"Come on boys, be nice," said their father as a stern instruction.

"'Bye then," said Alan. He turned and went back upstairs.

They took their leave, promising to keep in touch and to come again soon. They made their way to the car in silence until they were in the car. "Thank Christ that's over!" breathed Georgina with a sigh of relief. "I shan't be doing that again for a while."

"Oh come on, darling, what did you expect? They're kids! They've had their dad all to themselves for all this time, and now all of a sudden, they have a big sister. The oldest boy's the worst, and I guess the others just follow him. He has a huge chip on his shoulder. He's always been the leader of the pack up to now. You've knocked him off his pedestal."

Georgina knew he was right. She recognized a potential bully in Philip in the way he looked at the others and the way they deferred to him. It was just like the kids at school. There was always a leader, someone who seemed to have right of passage in any area, even in the minds of others.

"Let's go back, babe. I've had enough of family life for today," Georgina said despondently.

"You're on," said Mike as they drove away. It took about fifteen minutes to get out of the village and back onto the main road. They gathered speed and headed out of the county. "Soon be home!" said Mike.

They reached the hotel around 10:30 having stopped at a pub near Fareham for a meal. They went straight to the room, neither of them saying much, and within thirty minutes, they were in bed.

"Night, darling. Sleep tight. Love you," whispered Mike as he snuggled into Georgina's back and kissed her neck. "Don't let today upset you. You don't need their approval, you know."

"Yeah, you bet. Love you too," said Georgina, desperately trying not to let Mike see she was in tears. It was easy for him. He didn't understand she *did* need their approval.

# CHAPTER 16

## Lover vs. Friend

AFTER A LEISURELY BREAKFAST AND an equally leisurely drive, they arrived at the port of Dover just after one o'clock and drove aboard the ferry.

Their conversation had been sparse on the drive, and it was the same on the ferry and the drive back to Oberhausen. Neither felt like talking. They knew the topic of the visit was bound to come up, and neither was comfortable with that for separate reasons. They didn't want to encroach on each other's thoughts.

Georgina had naively been hoping their visit would be the start of a fairy-tale reconciliation between her and her father and her only family. But the sensible part of her said it would take time because they were strangers linked only by DNA. But the emotional part of her wanted it immediately.

Mike approached the situation a lot more logically than did Georgina. He wanted it all to work out for her sake. If it took that to make her happy, there would be no discussion—he would do whatever was asked of him. But he understood the situation. He knew what she wanted and what she was hoping for wouldn't happen overnight. His thoughts were about her father. He couldn't understand how Georgina's father could possibly imagine that his kids and wife would roll over and accept it all as if it were an everyday occurrence. While the wife appeared to be very receptive—and he supposed that was because she'd known this was going to come up for some time—the kids were a different matter.

He had recognized a budding alpha male in the oldest boy with the others following his lead. Not necessarily because they wanted to but because he was such a forceful personality that it made for a quiet life. He'd unfortunately seen examples of this in his squadron in the army, where a single squaddy could convince several other members of a troop to commit acts of aggression on the rookies. They couldn't or wouldn't see that they were being manipulated, but they still ended up taking a proportion of the blame for whatever prank they'd been encouraged to get involved in by the alpha, who didn't mind taking his share because it proved him to be the leader.

The only problem was when such alphas met a similarly minded person who threatened their positions in the pack; it was watch out for the fireworks. Mike could see that happening with Phillip and the others, but more to the point, he could see the similarity in Phillip and his father. This was the only explanation that made any sense. The father had given no thought whatsoever of how this introduction of Georgina was going to affect anyone else; he had thought it was a good idea, so he did it.

*God knows how it'll end up*, Mike thought. He could foresee horrific problems in the future that he'd be unable to say or do anything about. He also realized there was a huge chunk of Georgina's life she had still to tell. He assumed he'd hear about it when she was ready. At that point, that was more than okay with him.

Back in Oberhausen, life returned to normal. Georgina was taking lessons in German through the bank and with Jochem, who came to the apartment every Wednesday evening while Anna went out with her friends. He and Georgina would converse, and he would correct her pronunciation. She was determined to master the language.

Mike helped as much as he could, but she was being taught textbook German while he had picked up conversational German on his own.

He was more than able to make himself understood and spoke in the guttural dialect of the area, which convinced Germans he was a native. While no one had said anything to Georgina at the bank, she felt at a disadvantage at not having a full understanding of all going on around her.

They were planning the wedding for the eleventh of January and had decided on a registry marriage in Mulhiem with a few of their closest friends. They also decided not to invite their families.

Christmas was rapidly approaching, and the German holiday season had a feeling different from that of England. Towns and villages came magically alive with traditional oompa bands playing everywhere. In the evenings, the shopping areas glittered and sparkled with beautifully lit garlands. Colorful markets everywhere sold wooden tree decorations and garden ornaments as well as hats, scarves, and gloves in traditional Christmas patterns. The smell of glu wein, a warm cinnamon and red wine offered as a wonderful warming drink for shoppers, hung in the air.

They were to spend Christmas in Germany with Claus, Helga, Jochem, and Anna in a traditional German Christmas. Saint Nicholas visited them on Christmas Eve, and they exchanged presents.

On Christmas morning, they went to the magnificent, old church that stood majestically in the alt stadt of Mulhiem. It had withstood any effort to bomb it, and it made a superb centerpiece for the town. They sat in old, worn, wooden pews at the rear of the church and watched as the congregation, extended families, fill the rest of the church. It almost looked rehearsed; everyone knew exactly where to sit.

The bells stopped ringing at 9:00. Georgina estimated there were more than two hundred in the congregation. Twenty or so angelic boys and girls robed in deep-red cassocks, surplices, and white neck ruffs formed the choir. Their singing accompanied the organ with a sweetness she hadn't heard for a long time; it brought back memories, and she lost herself in the familiar music. The service was mostly in Latin, but even though they couldn't understand the words, the meanings were obvious and were the same the world over as were the hymns.

As they left an hour later, she felt a wonderful, warm feeling of togetherness. The rest of the day was spent as ever eating, drinking, and enjoying the friendship of Claus and his family.

They decided to go to the UK on boxing day. There were Georgina's friends to see in Southampton, and they were going to Worcester for a couple of days to see Mike's family. Georgina had met some at Raymond's wedding but hadn't gotten to know them other than just to say hello, so it would be interesting. Apart from the two days at the wedding, Mike hadn't seen his family in about eighteen months. He was preparing for a wedding none of them was invited to and to a girl they'd never really met.

They traveled via Zeebrugge again and arrived in Southampton after a rough crossing of the North Sea in a winter storm of torrential rain and gale-force winds. They had been invited to stay that night with her old friend, Janey, and her brother, Johno. They arrived tired and irritable late in the afternoon only to be told there was a party that night with quite a few of Georgina's friends from university and some of the people she'd worked with at the pharmacy and at Marks & Spencer. Just what they needed!

Johno showed them up to their bedroom, where they were thankfully left to their own devices for an hour or two while Janey did some last-minute shopping.

"God, I could bloody well do without this," groaned Mike, still feeling rough from the journey and in a foul mood. He'd barely managed to be civil to Johno, who appeared to be a bit the worse for wear. "That bloke's a real prat, isn't he?"

Georgina thought it wisest to ignore the comment about Johno. "Me too, love, but we've got no choice. Janey's gone to a lot of trouble to find all my old mates." She swung her legs off the bed. "Come on, let's make the most of it. Do you want a Resolve? It'll help the old stomach to settle. I'm having one."

Georgina went into the kitchen and made tea. As she carried it and the Resolve back to the bedroom, she had a strange feeling. She's been at her lowest when she became friends with Janey and had much to thank her for, but she had moved on, away from Janey and everything she stood for. While terribly grateful for the friendship, she wasn't sure they had enough in common to maintain it. Mike's comment highlighted it.

She entered the bedroom and heard Mike singing in the shower. "Feeling a bit better, love?" she called, laughingly realizing he wouldn't hear her over the noise of the shower and David Bowie's "Walking on the Moon." She put the tea on the dressing table, dropped her robe, and joined him in the en suite bathroom. She slid the shower screen back and slipped into the shower, wrapping her arms around him as he faced the wall, letting the steaming hot water run over his face.

"Hey, what's this? Can't a man have a shower in peace?" He laughed.

"You know you don't mean that, my darling. I'll leave if you want me to."

"Come here, you witch." He pulled her close. "I do feel better. Don't you?"

Quite a while later, they emerged from the shower. As Georgina wrapped her hair in a towel, Mike went over to the dressing table and sipped his tea. "This tea's cold, bitch! Can't you even get that right?"

With a smile, he ducked the hairbrush winging its way across the room.

"Okay, I'll make another!" Chuckling, he left the room.

Georgina heard him moving around the kitchen and then voices. Janey and her brother were back. She had dressed and done her hair by the time Mike came with tea.

"What took you so long?" she asked while sipping the piping-hot drink.

"Janey wanted to know if you were okay and had met up with your dad. I filled her in, okay?"

"Sure. Saves me doing it."

They had to admit the party was a lot of fun. Georgina enjoyed showing off her man and her ring. She was pleased they'd stayed, but the next day was the trip to Worcester and meeting the clan Grantley.

They were in good form on the drive up though it was absolutely chucking it down again. Both the A34 and the A43 were awash with so much water on the road that the journey took longer that it should have.

They arrived at Mike's sister Pauline's house about two and a half hours later than they'd planned, and that was the start of a disastrous weekend. The family couldn't understand why they were getting married in Germany and why no one was invited.

"Because you'll bloody well take over just like you're fucking doing now," shouted Mike, trying to be heard over the cacophony coming from the rest of the house. His face white with rage, he shouted at Georgina, "Come on, babe. We're getting out of this dump." They grabbed their stuff from the bedroom and drove to the ferry.

That was a side of Mike she'd never seen before, and it wasn't a good side. Blood was pulsing through the veins in his temples. He looked as if he would explode. "Now you know why I don't go home," he spat out through gritted teeth. "What with your lot and mine, we are *so* going to stay in Germany."

They arrived in Oberhausen on the third of January, which gave Georgina just seven days to get ready for the wedding. But Helga and Anna had been doing much in her absence, and she was happy it was all in capable hands.

The days flew by, and Saturday the eleventh was upon them. Mike had stayed in Jochem and Anna's apartment, placating Georgina's demand that she was not to see him until the service.

"Total twaddle," said Mike to Jochem as he knocked back a wonderfully large Asbach brandy. "But what the lady wants the lady gets, eh?"

The wedding went off without a hitch on a crisp morning; the temperature was around minus six degrees. The sun was shining brightly; the photographs, when they appeared a couple of weeks later, were of an obviously happy but a cold group of friends.

# CHAPTER 17

## News to Impart

G EORGINA SUCCESSFULLY PASSED HER LANGUAGE exam with two weeks to spare. She enjoyed her work at the bank. When Mike had to leave for an exercise with his squadron in February for four months, Georgina spent a lot of time with Claus, Helga, Jochem, and Anna and several other colleagues from the bank. Her circle of friends had grown tremendously as her German had improved. They respected her for the speed at which she had reached her level of fluency.

The bank had initially agreed to a twelve-month contract, but after about seven months, Georgina was advised they were more than happy with her work and would renew her contract in August.

When Mike returned from his exercise, he seemed a bit distant to Georgina. He had written only twice a few lines saying it was all hush-hush but would see her soon. They'd spoken a few times on the phone, but again, it had been very brief. She'd chatted on about work and their friends, but he seemed distracted. While he was reasonably attentive when he got back, he wasn't overly so. She had expected their return celebration to be considerably more, shall we say, physical than it was. It was her first experience of him returning from exercise, so she put it down to the fact he'd just spent four months with his mates and had almost gone back to the single life by default.

In July, with summer having arrived well and truly and temperatures above twenty-five, she had a spell of sickness and took a few days off from the bank. She and Mike put it down to the humidity and the stifling heat. There was no air-conditioning in the bank or in the apartment—nowhere to get cool air. However, in August, Georgina realized it wasn't the humidity that was making her feel sick and dizzy. Missing her second period was a bit of a clue.

Mike had remained distracted since his return, but Georgina thought it had to do with his selection to be promoted to captain. She knew he was under pressure and had to present the right image, but she'd never seen that side of his work before and didn't know how to handle it.

And he'd started drinking more—so it seemed to Georgina. Several nights a week, he would come off duty at four but wouldn't return home until close to midnight. The day she had been to the doctor's and learned she was nine weeks pregnant was one such evening. Mike had called to say a pal of his was over from Paderborn and he'd be late. Such occurrences were starting to worry Georgina. She knew about the strong drink ethic in the army, and the officers' mess was always full of married men (and women) who didn't particularly want to go home, but she couldn't believe Mike fit that category.

"Okay, love, but I need to talk to you urgently."

"Yeah, right, but it'll wait?"

"Looks as if it'll have to."

He rang off, and Georgina burst into tears. This wasn't how it was meant to be. She'd imagined a candlelit table, soft music, and her telling Mike, "We're going to have a baby, darling." He'd jump to his feet, sweep her up in his arms, and cry with happiness. She knew her hormones were totally up the creek and told herself, *Don't be daft. He'll be happy. You know he will.*

She stayed up until after midnight before she turned in. She heard the key turn in the lock about 2:15. While relieved Mike was home, she didn't want to have one of the most important conversations of their married life with the drunk who'd just fallen over the chair in the hall and was staggering into the bedroom. She pretended to be asleep.

"Hello, my little daaarling." He was slurring his words. She smelled his beery breath. "Wanna give the ol' man a cuddle?" He fumbled under the duvet until he found her slightly enlarged, tender breasts and started squeezing them hard. He moved his hand down her stomach and let it rest just above her pubic hair. She stayed perfectly still, hoping he wouldn't feel her trembling.

"Come on, sweet pea, I really could do with a fuck right now!" His hand moved to her mound. His fingers were looking for a way in. She shifted away and turned onto her belly. "Oh well, fuck you then," he growled. He rolled over and was soon fast asleep.

Georgina rose at about 6:45 and hurried to the bathroom due to the morning sickness that had haunted her for the past month. Mike, oblivious to everything, was fast asleep in the same position he'd been all night. She had her shower and felt better after a glass of milk and a piece of toast, about all she could manage to keep down those days. She assumed Mike was on a rest day and so left him where he was.

She wanted to be so happy about the baby, but she desperately wanted to share it with Mike. She was sure he'd be happy too if only she could tell him.

"Telephone for you, George," Myra called out from the office that adjoined Georgina's. "I think it's Mike."

She picked up the phone, and before she could speak, he screamed, "Why the hell didn't you wake me, you daft bitch? You've made me late for duty."

"Just a minute, you! It was you who came in totally pissed as two-thirty this morning!" she hissed into the phone, hoping no one could hear her. "It's not my job to get you out of bed and off to work. I've got enough problems of my own in the morning, but I don't suppose you've noticed. You've been coming in pissed so often I'm surprised you can find your way home half the time!" She was infuriated. *How dare he talk to me like that especially at work!* She'd never mentioned his drinking before because she knew it was part of the army way, but enough was enough. He'd never lost it like that before. She felt threatened, vulnerable.

"All you had to do was wake me up! I've never not got into work. I don't know what your fucking problem is!"

"We need to talk, Mike. There's going to be some changes soon, and one of them is that you've got to be home more and cut down on the drinking. I need you to be home tonight. I mean it!" She hung up, shaking with rage.

She tried to concentrate at work but found it difficult to get the conversation with Mike out of her mind. She was unusually pleased when the end of the workday arrived. She made her way home hoping against hope Mike would be in straight after duty, about 4:40. But the afternoon turned into the evening. At 11:00, she realized she was being punished for trying to tell him what to do. Because of the lack of sleep she'd had the night before, she had to sleep or be useless at work the next day.

She wasn't sure anyone at work had heard any of the conversation or had guessed there was anything wrong, but it was so important that it didn't affect her position. She wrote Mike a note. She tore that up and wrote another. Then another. She ended up with,

Hi Mike,

I'm sorry you weren't at home this evening, but I'm sure you were enjoying yourself with your friends. I on the other hand sat here looking at the meal I'd cooked for you watching it ruin. It was unfortunately your favorite, spaghetti carbonara, and it's now in the bin.

You might wonder why I was so insistent you come home. It was because I had some news I hoped you'd be as happy about as I am. I'm pregnant! Our baby is due early March. Please don't wake me when you come in. Maybe you could spare me some time tomorrow?

Night night,
Georgina

The next morning, Georgina woke to find the other side of the bed as it had been when she had turned in. Mike hadn't come home at all. She was going crazy. *Was he in an accident? In a fight? Or run off with another woman?*

She called the guardroom and spoke to Ben, a young lance corporal who had been in Mike's troop. "Hi, Ben. It's Georgina Grantley. Have you seen Lieutenant Grantley recently?"

"Oh hi, Mrs. Grantley. Not recently. He was here when I came on duty last night at ten. It looked as if he and his mates were going downtown. Is there a problem?"

"No, nothing to worry about. He's obviously stayed over somewhere too pissed to come home."

"Oops! Someone's in the shit then." Ben laughed conspiratorially.

"Absolutely not, Ben. I'd rather he did that than drive. Catch you later."

She hoped Ben would believe her. She made a drink. Her morning sickness seemed to be easing off at last. After a shower, she had another drink and some toast and tried to get herself in the right frame of mind for work. She had an important client coming in that morning, and while she'd prepped the file the day before, she'd need her wits about her to get the full investment he had access to.

# CHAPTER 18

# Spots on the Leopard

GEORGINA GOT BIGGER AND BIGGER as the months wore on. So did the cracks in her marriage. Mike would spend more and more time at the barracks usually because he was too drunk to make it home after extended sessions in the officers' mess. He took very little interest in the baby or in Georgina. On the occasions when he deigned to come home, he would sit sullenly watching the television or invite friends for a party. If Georgina commented on that, he'd say, "You don't want to come out looking like that, do you?"

Christmas came and went with little or no family time but with four of his fellow officers invited to stay over the period. Georgina was expected to cater to them all. David, a young second lieutenant from Leeds, and Solomon, a recently divorced captain from Fiji, could see what was going on and tried to include her in the festivities. They also gave her a hand with the clearing up, but that caused Mike to yell drunkenly, "Let her be. She's all right, You're okay, aren't you, darling?"

"You're being a fucking dickhead and a prat," said Solomon on Boxing Day, looking at his friend in disgust. "What's with the attitude? She deserves better than this."

"No she doesn't," slurred Mike, taking a huge swig of brandy. "She's the one got knocked up. I didn't want the bloody sprog!"

That did it for Georgina. She burst into tears and yelled at Mike, "That's not what you told me in May, you bastard! It was you that said, 'Don't worry about the pill, darling. A little one would be fun."

As she fled for the door, she heard, "We all say things we don't mean when we're pissed."

By the time the baby was due, Mike had worn out his welcome at the officers' mess. He was being treated with disgust by many of his fellow officers, including those he used to call his friends. No one wanted to stay all night drinking with him, and a one- man piss-up wasn't much fun even for him. That seemed to bring him back into line. When David was born in March, he was reasonably receptive to the little fellow. He'd cut down the drinking considerably and came home rather than drinking at camp. But Georgina viewed this change with skepticism. She waited for the excuses to start again. They did.

After about six months, just after he'd returned from a brief exercise in Sweden, he was quickly turning back into the drunk he'd been prior to David's birth. It seemed to coincide with a new intake of new officers, and of course, they hadn't experienced any of his previous antics.

During this time, Claus and Helga had watched from the sidelines, worried about their friends but saying nothing. Mike had managed to upset them terribly with drunken visits to their home (without Georgina of course) in which he would maul Helga and sneer at Claus, making reference to the fact that they weren't able to have children. "What you need is a proper bloke," he'd slur at Helga, grabbing her around the waist and pulling her to him. "Why don't we give it a go, eh?"

"Please, Mike, I not want to do this." Helga would wriggle away from him as best she could but was no match for Mike's groping hands.

Claus wasn't in the room when that episode started, but on coming in and seeing what Mike was up to, he pushed Mike away from Helga and against the wall. "You go near my wife again, you little shit, and I'll put you in the hospital! I don't want to see you anywhere near here ever again, you bastard!"

"Truth hurts, don't it?" Mike laughed as he slipped from Claus's grip and moved toward the door. "Don't forget, Helga. Anytime!" He was still laughing as he left the apartment. Claus followed him down the hallway. "You're not man enough," Mike said. "Come on then, pretty boy. Let's see what you've got." He sneered at Claus, who was white with rage.

"Claus! Com zuruck, bitte, bitte," screamed the sobbing Helga, pulling at his arm.

Mike left the two of them trying to comfort each other.

They had told Georgina about this episode, and she was of course appalled at Mike's behavior. Though Claus and Helga had assured her they in no way held her responsible, she was so embarrassed. Their friendship unfortunately suffered, and she saw less and less of them once the baby was born.

She had planned to take about six months off from work, but because of the situation with Mike, she felt she should give up work for the time being, and thankfully, the bank was very accommodating. They extended her maternity leave to twelve months and cut her pay to one-third. She was more than happy with that; she thought that in twelve months, things would be back to normal.

She spent her time looking after little David and began to socialize more with some of the other officers' wives, one of which ran a kindergarten. Some of the women knew of Mike's exploits and were supportive of Georgina. Others kept their distance, not knowing what to say. She felt sidelined; she took the friendship offered by the few at face value and made the best she could of her time as an army mum.

David's first birthday came and went. She had decided not to return to the bank. While they were saddened by her departure, they made it clear she could be reemployed whenever she wanted to.

Mike's behavior had improved a bit over the last month or two; she assumed it was due to one of the wives she was friendly with, Sally, speaking to the SAAFA woman at the base, SAAFA being the army version of a welfare office. Georgina was surprised one afternoon when the wife of the commanding officer, Mrs. Morrison, visited her.

"Hello, my dear. I hope you don't mind, but I was visiting Carole across the way and thought I'd pop in for a cuppa. You don't mind, do you?"

Georgina knew that Carole had been poorly after having had a baby and that Mrs. Morrison had a reputation for being kindly and concerned about her husband's officers and their families.

"No of course not! Please, come on in," said Georgina, smiling. "The baby's just gone down, so do you mind the kitchen?"

"That will do fine, love. How are things with you? Everything all right now?"

Georgina wasn't sure what she meant by now. *What has she heard?*

"Yes, we're fine, thank you. David's starting to walk, and he's into everything!"

"That's good. And … er … has the trouble with Mike sorted itself out?"

*God! What does she know? Who's been blabbing?* "I'm sorry, Mrs. Morrison. I'm not sure what you mean."

"Georgina, everyone in the mess knows what Mike's been like for the last year or so. The CO's had a word with him a couple of times, but he seems to be on a collision course to disaster. It's been noticed that you have continued to act appropriately throughout, and you are to be admired for that. It can't have been easy."

*Christ! They've been laughing at us behind our backs.* "No, it hasn't been easy, but it really is just between us."

"I'm afraid it stops being just between you two when Mike's work starts to suffer." Mrs. Morrison looked uncomfortable. "Did you know SAAFA wants him stood down and booked into a rehab unit?"

"What? Why wasn't I told for God's sake?"

"Because up to now he's refused any help. It seemed pointless worrying you any more than you already were."

"You said up to now. Does that mean he's agreed to it?"

Mrs. Morrison smiled and patted Georgina's hand. "Yes, that's the good bit. He's finally agreed. We're sending him down to the unit at Paderborn. He asked us to tell you he was on maneuvers. My husband agreed but asked that I come to tell you the truth. We think it's a pride thing with Mike, but in a way, that's good. Otherwise, he wouldn't care. Do you understand?"

# CHAPTER 19

# So This Is How a Single Mum Feels

FOUR MONTHS PASSED, AND GEORGINA and the little boy got on with life. Nothing really changed; everyone acted as if Mike were on secondment and carried on as normal.

Mike sent the occasional letter, being very vague about the "maneuvers." Georgina would write about David's antics and all the normal things expected. She was happy to go along with the façade if it meant Mike could come back without being embarrassed.

One sultry evening in July, she had decided to take David to some friends she'd made at the hospital. They were sitting in the garden drinking cool white wine as their boys were playing with a couple of sit-on toys.

Matthew was just a few days older than David but wasn't as advanced. At fourteen months, David was walking and had been for a couple of months and was therefore into everything. He was communicating well for his age and had started using his potty. Matthew, however, wasn't walking yet and didn't have the interactive skills David had.

Vicky, his mum, was a lovely girl. They'd hit it off well in the hospital. She was from Bolton, and her husband, Mike, had recently been promoted from staff sergeant to sergeant major. This was a huge boost for them; he'd almost been promised a officership in the next couple of years if he kept his nose clean.

They were considerably older than Georgina and Mike. She had been trying for a baby for all their married life, just over twelve years, so Matthew was a miracle child to them and was cosseted and cuddled endlessly. If he wouldn't sleep, they'd wrap him up, put him in the carry cot, and take him out for a drive until he fell asleep.

Vicky and Georgina were chatting merrily about everything and nothing—the new CO who had arrived the previous week, the last party at the officers' mess, coming trips to the UK, and such. Vicky asked, "So when are you guys going back home? They haven't seen the baby yet, have they?"

"I don't know. It depends on Mike's maneuvers. I don't want to go on my own 'cuz I've not had that much to do with Mike's family. Don't forget we're not like you. We've been married only two and a half years, and I haven't any family to speak of."

She surprised herself as that came out of her mouth. She glanced at Vicky to gauge her reaction. They'd never really talked about each other's lives in the UK except that Georgina knew that Vicki's Mike was one of five brothers. She knew that because they'd been to see the baby along with all the grandparents.

"Oh how awful," said Vicky. "I don't know what I'd do without my lot. They can be a pain in the butt sometimes, but it's good to know they're there. Do you think you'll go when Mike gets out of Paderborn?"

Georgina stared at her, mouth open. *Shit!* The barracks were like a bush telegraph, but it had never crossed her mind that everyone knew about Mike. She looked away but not before a tear fell.

"Oh my poor darling!" cried Vicky. "Go on, have a good weep! I bet you haven't since they took him away, have you?"

Georgina sobbed in disbelief. Mike had been away for about eleven weeks, and she'd carried on pretending he was on maneuvers. Nobody had said anything when she'd shopped in the NAAFI or when she had to go to camp for some reason. *How stupid can I be?* The officers would close ranks, but the wives would just chatter. Because she'd been working and spoke fluent German, she hadn't felt the need to mix with the other wives. She imagined they thought of her as standoffish, but she hadn't minded. Until then.

She brought herself back to the present and looked at Vicky, who was patting her hand. "Come on, love. It'll do you good to talk about it."

Georgina looked at the two boys playing, completely unaware of what was going on. "Yes, I'd like that."

# CHAPTER 20

## Closed Ranks

THREE WEEKS AFTER THE GARDEN exposé, Georgina received a phone call from Mrs. Carter, the new CO's wife.

"Hello there, my dear, I do hope you don't mind me calling you. As you know, one of my little jobs is to take care of the welfare of our soldiers and their families. I was with Mrs. Morrison last week, and she brought me up to speed. How are you coping?"

"Oh you know, not too bad, thank you. Do you have news of Mike? How's he doing?"

"Well my dear, that's why I'm ringing actually. He seems to have turned the corner and is responding well to the treatment. Colonel Carter asked me to invite you to dinner on Thursday. Do you think you can make it? Bring little David of course. He can sleep in one of our rooms if he gets tired."

Georgina was confused. *Why does Mike's CO want me to come to dinner especially after saying he was doing well?* "I suppose I can, but I don't understand why, Mrs. Carter."

"We need to discuss with you Mike's reintroduction into real life. He's been through a lot, you know, and it will be difficult for him. We want to make sure you're ready for him to come home."

Georgina's blood started to boil. *What about me?* She'd given up a great job, had the baby, been humiliated by her husband and some of his drunken fellow officers, and was in a strange country with no family or anyone to turn to. Add to that the humiliation of knowing that everyone else knew her business while she had toed the party line as she was required to do. But she knew it would be no good saying any of that. The army looked after its own, but she was not its own.

With a sigh, she said, "Thank you. That's very kind of you. What time?"

Thursday dawned a beautiful, sunny August day—clear, blue skies. It was the fifth, only two days from her twenty-fourth birthday. She went into David's bedroom and lifted the happy cherub from his cot. "Hello, my little darling. How's Mummy's little soldier today?"

"Mum, mum, mum, dink, dink," the chap chattered. He had a vocabulary of his own, but only about 10 percent was decipherable.

"Yes darling, Mummy will get you a drink. Shall we take that nappy off first?"

"Nap-nap, nap-nap," he chuntered.

That was the normal morning routine, and while sorting out the little boy, Georgina's mind went to Mike. He'd missed so much of David's first year. He hadn't seen him take his first steps or heard him say his first word or feed himself. And he'd be home soon.

There were two parts to her thoughts. The first part was the hope that Mike was back to the wonderful guy she's met nearly four years earlier. She wanted to see him playing on the floor with David while she cooked dinner. She wanted to hear him come through the door and be happy to greet them with big hugs. She wanted to curl up beside him in bed and feel his gentle touch on her body, which by then was crying for attention. She wanted to feel his breath on her neck and his gentle kisses.

But the second part kept coming to the surface—the drunken slob groping her in the darkness. The aggressive bully making fun of her in front of his pals. The man who had once wanted a baby but as soon as he was born totally ignored him. Yes, he'd missed David's first year, but he had deserved to.

They had a fun day at the park playing on the swings, and they had an impromptu picnic by the little stream. "Mum mum. 'Ook! duc ducs."

"Yes darling, aren't they pretty? Lots of ducks. Lady ducks and daddy ducks."

"Daddy duc? Daddy?"

*How ironic. His father will be here, and already he's saying "daddy."*

She checked the time. It was near two. She scooped up the lad. "Right then, little man. Let's go have a shower and put on clean clothes, shall we?"

David's smile and chuckle melted her heart. "No matter what, my little darling man, Mummy will always be here for you."

# Chapter 21

## The Return of the Wanderer

"Good evening, Mrs. Grantley. Isn't it a beautiful one," gushed Mrs. Carter. "And you've brought that handsome little chap with you. Isn't he like his father? Look, George. Here's Mrs. Grantley with a mini Lieutenant Grantley. Isn't he absolutely gorgeous?"

Georgina and David were shown into the lounge where the CO was sitting and holding a big glass of what looked like Scotch.

"Well, Mrs. Grantley, how good of you to come and grace our table."

About an hour later, after what seemed to be interminable small talk, dinner was served. They put out a wooden highchair for David. She fastened him in, hoping he would behave. He often objected to highchairs for some reason, perhaps because of the straps, but he was being the perfect baby.

"Well, Mrs. Grantley—Look, may we call you Georgina?"

"Yes of course," she said, surprised they had asked.

"Georgina, as my wife advised you last week, we're pleased Mike will be coming home soon. I'm sure you share our joy. It must have been very difficult for you."

Georgina looked at them and bowed. "Yes," she mumbled into her napkin. She took a mouthful of food, enabling her to stall a bit. "It has been tough, but I think the worst thing was finding out that most of his fellow officers and their wives knew more about what was going than I did."

"Well my dear," the CO said with a sickly sweet smile on his face, "unfortunately, these things have a habit of getting out into the public domain."

It was almost a closing statement. He finished his meal with a flourish, put down his cutlery, wiped his chin with a white damask napkin, and sat back.

Georgina knew that whatever she said would be futile. He would always come down on the side of his men regardless. She thought it best to let him have his say. After he rambled on a bit, he stopped excusing himself and the actions of the other and suddenly changed the tone of his voice.

"Okay then, let's get a plan together, shall we?" He stood and retrieved a manila file from a table. "Now then, Mike'll be coming home on the, let me see, ah yes, the ninth. That's right, isn't it?"

Georgina nearly dropped her glass. "The ninth? Of this month? God, that's only five days away! How am I meant to get ready in that time?" She panicked. *What will happen? What will he be like?* It struck her that she was scared of what the future would bring and scared the past would return. Something else struck her—she was alone with no exit strategy if it all went tits-up. She was out of the banking world. *If I end up on my own, how will I manage?* She realized the CO was still talking. "... about six days leave to acclimatize himself, so he'll come back on duty on the sixteenth, okay?"

That was that. All settled. No discussion. No time to get used to it. *He's back!*

Georgina made her way home that evening with a sleepy boy snuggled close to her. She was in a daze. What should she do to prepare? What would she say to the other wives when they asked about Mike? Should she let on she knew that they knew?

Georgina's twenty-second birthday came and went with hardly anyone noticing. Claus and Helga came over in the evening for a drink, and she told them of Mike's return in four days. She was comforted when they voiced the same concerns she had. "Don't forget, schatz," Claus said as they stood to leave. "If you need help, you must call, yes?"

"Oh it'll be okay, I'm sure," said Georgina none too convincingly.

"Without the drink, he'll be the Mike we all fell in love with."

These words stayed in her mind for the next four days, but she awoke on the ninth in fear and trepidation. She performed the normal duties of the day as if on autopilot. David of course was his normal chatty self running around the house and leaving toys in his wake. Georgina clung to this element of normality on a day that was anything but normal.

Mike was expected to arrive around 3:00 p.m. That of course gave Georgina plenty of time to build on the anxiety she had woken up with. But just before 2:00, as she was feeding David, she heard the key turn in the lock. She jumped up and managed to knock the dish all over her and the floor. *This is not how it was meant to be!* She had planned that the little chap would be ready for his afternoon sleep soon, and that would give her and Mike time to talk.

In walked Mike beaming as if he'd just returned from the shops. Georgina stood there covered in tomato sauce and holding David, also covered head to foot in food.

"Hi there, darling. Glad to see you were expecting me!" He beamed and came toward her arms outstretched. "God, I've missed you two. And there's the little chap! Hello, pal!"

David looked from his mum to Mike and back to Georgina. He started to cry, burying his spaghetti-covered face in her top.

"Don't worry about him. He's a bit clingy these days," she mumbled, shaking. "How … how are you, Mike? Are you … um … better?"

"Me? I'm fine, darling. You've nothing to worry about on that score. Three months' abstinence would cure anyone. But God, I've missed you! Can we do something tonight, something special? How about the Balkan?"

"I've missed you too, darling, but I didn't know what … what to do, get a baby-sitter or whether you'd just want a quiet night in."

"For fuck sake, babe, I've had enough quiet nights in. Let's celebrate! Why don't we ask Claus, Helga, Jochem, and Anna over? Let's have a party!"

"But I don't understand, love. Are you allowed to drink? I thought—"

"Yeah right! If you or they think I'm never going to drink again, you've got it wrong I can tell you! But don't worry, darling. They taught me how to handle it, so I can drink, but I can handle it now. Find someone to look after the lad. I'll make some calls."

He left the room. Georgina hugged David, rooted to the spot.

After cleaning up David and putting him down for his nap, she returned to the kitchen to clean up the mess. She heard Mike on the phone in the lounge. "Yeah, I'm back … You gotta be joking! … Come on. It'll be a laugh … Yeah, she's up for it."

He was on such a high. She assumed it was a reaction to having been shut away for three months. He obviously needed to make sure his pals were still his pals.

She reluctantly phoned Julia, a girl who lived around the corner and had baby-sat for them many times. "Yes, Mrs. Grantley, I can come. What time shall—"

"About seven-thirty."

The rest of the afternoon was weird. Mike was elated; it was as if nothing were wrong and the last three months hadn't happened. He had reached several of his friends who had agreed to come out for the meal, but neither Claus nor Jochem had agreed to come. Georgina wasn't surprised; they were finding it difficult to forgive the vulgar, drunken Mike who had been apparent over the previous six months or so.

Georgina had met them all while Mike was away, and they had told her she was more than welcome but Mike was a different matter. Claus had voiced concern about whether rehab had cured him. Claus and Helga had told her that if she was worried about him, she could stay with them.

She had dismissed that, saying she was sure he'd be fine, but it was great comfort to know she had somewhere to run just in case.

Julia arrived at 7:25, and they were ready to leave. Mike had settled down a bit and was being reasonably normal; Georgina's hopes were rising. Maybe it would be okay after all.

David had gone down about seven after Mike had joined then at bath time. He played with the little chap and even got him out the bath and into his PJs. It helped Georgina to no end to know the two of them were bonding again. The little boy had eventually snuggled up to his dad and went straight to sleep, obviously feeling more secure than he had done initially.

"He's asleep, Julia, for about ten minutes now. If he wakes, just give him some warm milk in his cup. I've left it on the side. Is that okay?"

"Yes, Mrs. Grantley. He'll be fine, I have some studying to do, so I won't even need the TV on."

"We'll be back around eleven. Is that okay?"

"That's fine. I don't have class until midday. Have a good time."

Georgina and Mike drove into Mulhiem to Eah Passa, their regular Balkan restaurant. They got there about 7:45. Georgia spotted four of Mike's officer friends at a table on their own. Georgina thought that was odd, but she supposed that as it was such short notice, they couldn't get baby-sitters.

"Mike you old bastard! You made it back!" was the cry they were greeted with.

Georgina tried to hide because the restaurant was full mostly with Germans, and she knew some of her clients from the bank often ate there. She'd been away a while, but she prayed no one recognized her.

The evening went great for Mike. He and his mates reverted to their previous behavior, and Georgina felt superfluous. She was concerned about the amount of beer and schnapps he was putting away. Surely, rehab was meant to suppress the desire to drink, and a fair amount of self-restraint was needed. She didn't think Mike was an alcoholic, but she knew that once he'd started drinking, he wouldn't stop.

She was right. By 10:30, he was hammered. She tried to prize him away from his pals. "Darling we have to get back. Julie needs to get home."

"Oh for fuck sake, you go! I'm got some more catchin' up to do."

"But Mike! Please come back now. It's your first night."

She might as well have been talking to the wall. He wasn't budging, and his pals weren't any help.

"Aw, you go on, Georgy. We'll make sure he gets back okay."

That didn't give her any confidence. They were all shitfaced; she knew better than to argue. She went to the front and asked Pieter, the manager, to call a taxi. She should have gotten the car keys from Mike, but he would have started again on her if she'd even mentioned it. It wasn't worth it.

"Pieter, can you please make sure Mr. Mike doesn't drive? I can't get the keys off him. Maybe you could try?"

"Yes, Mrs. Mike. I do that. He not drive. Don't worry."

The taxi pulled up. She looked over her shoulder and saw Mike in full flight laughing and joking with the waitress. He hadn't noticed she'd gone.

Back at the apartment, she thanked Julia. "Any problems?" she asked.

"No, Mrs. Grantley. He slept all night. No drink, nothing. I looked in on him twenty minutes ago, and he was snoring." Smiling, she accepted thirty marks from Georgia and said good night.

Georgina shut the door behind Julia and thought about sliding the bolt but didn't. She went into David's room and saw him snoring away. She tiptoed out of the room and went into her bedroom. She had no idea when Mike would come home or even if he would. She thought about phoning the CO but decided against it. Maybe she was overreacting. Maybe it was just Mike blowing off steam.

She cleaned her teeth and got ready for bed. It was 11:30, and she was shattered. It had been a stressful day she wanted to put behind her.

Sometime later, she wasn't sure when, she was awakened by an obviously drunk Mike stumbling against the furniture. She lay on her side facing away from him and pretending to be asleep, hoping he'd just fall into bed and pass out. But she was not so lucky. He got his clothes off somehow and got into bed. He put his hand on her shoulder and started slobbering on her neck.

"Come on, baby. Daddy's been away too long. Show Daddy you still love him."

She tried to move away, but he wasn't having any of that. "Come on, Georgy. Daddy needs some lovin'."

The smell of drink on his breath was so horrendous it almost made her sick. He used all his force to turn her on her back and started to mount her. Unlike most men, alcohol didn't affect him in the normal way. If anything, it made him harder. She tried to move, but he was too strong for her, and crying, she realized she had no option but to let him rape her, exactly what it was.

When he'd finished, he laughed. "There's a good girl. Daddy's home."

Georgina lay still, crying softly. Her fears had been justified. He hadn't changed. The detox had been a waste of time. She knew her marriage was over. She had to get away before he really hurt her or worse, David.

# CHAPTER 22

## There's Only One Option

O VER THE NEXT THREE WEEKS, she made her plans. Desperately trying to keep out of Mike's way, she would spend time with Helga, who had taken time off work to stay with Georgina. She was able to make phone calls from there and speak to SAAFA without Mike being aware.

She had been lucky enough to know one of Mike's fellow officers who absolutely despised the way Mike had behaved. He made it known in a subtle way that if necessary, he'd drive Georgina and the baby to the UK. He could take leave at any time.

He also had some friends stationed in Marchwood, near Southampton, who would put her up. She found it difficult to believe she had such a friend. He had been emphatic, and God, she needed a friend. She was terrified Mike would find out. She knew she had to make a clean break, get away once and for all. Her dreams seemed so far away at that point. It was only three years earlier that she'd thought she had the perfect solution to her need for family life.

The forth of September was the planned date. Dave Whatts had arranged time off, booked the ferry, and told his pals when they would arrive. Mike left the apartment that morning at around 6:30 a.m., calling out his normal "See ya" and slamming the door behind him.

As soon as Georgina heard the car pull out of the carport, she showered and pulled David's and her clothes down from the shelves. Joyce, her neighbor who was in on it, had been holding four big suitcases at her place for Georgina, so just before 8:00, Georgina knocked on her door. "All ready then, love?" Joyce asked.

Joyce was about forty; her husband was due to retire in a few years. This was their forth tour in Germany, and she knew all the tricks. She had seen so many army marriages fail, the majority to drink. She'd been more than willing to help, having heard the drunken Mike coming home in the middle of the night for so long.

"Yes, I think so. I just hope he doesn't find out. Dave said he'd be here about eleven. I want to get as much done as I can before David wakes up."

"Do what you need to do and then come round to me, okay?"

"Thanks, Joyce. You're an angel." Georgina gave her friend a hug.

She packed as David, a late sleeper, was still down, which she was thankful for. True to form, about twenty past nine, the little fellow stirred, climbed out of his bunk, and came to the door, bleary-eyed and tousle-haired. She thought about how gorgeous he looked. His hair was all matted at the back, and he stood, rubbing his eyes. "Hi, little man. That was a big sleep. Do you want a drink, sweetie?"

"Mumma, dink pease! Dadda?"

*Oh Lord, here's the first of many lies.* "Dadda's gone to work, sweetie. See him later." She warmed some strawberry milk in the microwave to take the chill off. She handed him his cup, and he drank a good swig. Grinning, he said, "Stawby mumma. Tank u."

She had almost finished the packing; she just needing to put some toys in a separate bag but hadn't wanted to disturb him while he slept, so she had left that for last. It took only took about ten minutes to finish off. She dragged the bags to the door.

She gave David a good breakfast and bathed him. She dressed him in his dungarees and sweater. It was about ten-fifteen when she was done. She took David round to Joyce's.

"All done, love? Come in and have a cup of coffee. You've got a bit of time."

The doorbell rang at about five past eleven. Dave was at the door. "All set then? Where's the bags? I'll take them to the car."

Good-byes said, Georgina made her way downstairs with little David and got into the car Dave had loaded tidily. She strapped the little one into the car seat and got into the front seat. Looking at Dave, she said wistfully, "That's the end of that. Let's go."

# CHAPTER 23

## *Thank God for Friends*

THEY ARRIVED IN MARCHWOOD LATE that night after an uneventful journey. They pulled up to the house of Dave's friends. The front door opened, and out came a young, thick-set chap with his blond wife following close behind.

"Hi you two. Get your arses into the house. We'll bring the stuff in. Hello, little man. My, you're a smart boy, aren't you!"

Dave unhooked David's seatbelt and passed him to Georgina.

"Go on in, love. We'll bring the stuff."

The little boy had slept most of the way from the ferry. Once he got his bearings, he enjoyed the attention. Georgina was too tired to argue. She walked into a lovely, warm house smelling of freshly cooked food, but she desperately wanted to sleep.

Everyone was in from the car, and introductions followed.

"This is my mate, Doug, and his wife, Elles," Dave said. "And guys, this is Georgina and David. It's okay, love. They know what's happened. You can stay here as long as you want. Elles is looking forward to speaking German with you. She's from Duisburg, and this prat doesn't speak the lingo."

Georgina broke out in sobs. "I don't know how to thank you … You don't know me from Adam, and here you are opening up your home. I'm so sorry."

Elles flung her arms around her. "You mustn't cry, liebling. We're your friends now. Dave has told us about Mike. We won't let him find you."

Elles took Georgina's hand, and the three of them went upstairs to a lovely, large bedroom with a little bed in the corner all made up and ready for them. David was looking about and beaming at Elles. "What a beautiful boy you are," she said, holding out her hands to him.

"I don't think …" Georgina didn't finish her sentence. David was leaning toward Elles's outstretched arms. *Well I'll be damned.*

"Look, Georgina, here is for you. Let me help you. There are your bags. Let's get the little one into bed, and then you come down. Only if you want to, though," she added quickly as she saw Georgina's tired look.

"Would you mind very much if I just stayed here and went to bed? We can talk as long as we want tomorrow."

"Of course. This is your home. You must do as you wish. Night night!" She passed David to Georgina after kissing his forehead. "Night night, little one."

Georgina undressed David and got him into the bed. He was quiet and subdued, and within minutes, he was asleep. She undressed and climbed into bed. *God, this is wonderful.* She turned on her side facing her son, and within minutes, she was also asleep.

# CHAPTER 24

## Number Two on the Way

G EORGINA WAS MADE VERY WELCOME at Doug and Elles's house. She couldn't believe total strangers would open their home to her. She had repeatedly tried to thank then, but all they would say was that Dave was a lifelong friend for whom they would do anything. Dave had left the following day but not before making sure she knew she could contact him any time.

September ran into October, and Georgina had managed to find a pretty little flat in Portswood, an area she knew reasonably well from her uni days. Doug and Elles wanted her to stay longer, but she needed her independence. She'd had some luck in that the flat was in a house, and Sally, who rented the ground floor, had offered to look after David. She had a child of her own and considered it no problem and more income. Once Georgina had settled in, she began to believe she could manage on her own.

She had been to several interviews and had within a week received three job offers. While they were not of the caliber she was used to, she had David to think of, so she accepted a position as a cashier's clerk for a printer whose offices were close to her flat. She was to start the tenth of October.

However, fate hadn't finished with her. She hadn't be feeling very well since she'd been at the flat, but she'd initially put it down to stress.

But when she missed her second period, she panicked. One of the first things she'd done once getting the flat was to register with a doctor. She got an appointment for the next afternoon.

"Sally?" she called quietly the next morning.

"Hi Georgina. Got a problem?"

"Not really, but I have to go to the doctor's this afternoon. Would you be able to keep David for me? I don't think I'd be much longer than an hour."

"Of course, m'dear. Lucy will be glad for someone to play with."

Georgina couldn't have hoped for a more willing and convenient baby-sitter. She'd never had to consider leaving the little chap with anyone else except for the odd trip to the shops, so she had had serious reservations on the matter.

Having said good-bye to David around two, she walked to the surgery. It was actually a waste of time; she knew she was pregnant. It could only have been the night Mike had raped her. She'd managed to resist his attentions after that, saying she was sore from when he'd forced himself on her.

After a brief examination, the doctor confirmed her worst fears. She was eight weeks pregnant and due the tenth of May. She had no idea what to do. She supposed she ought to tell Mike but wondered if he would care. Or was it something that might change him? She couldn't see how she could manage on her own with two children. This was not the way she'd planned her life. She seemed to be careering from one disastrous situation to another. *Oh how the Frazers would laugh.* Their premonition about her not making anything of herself was coming true.

She made her way home pondering her next move. She let herself in and was greeted by David, who came charging down the hallway. "Mumma home!"

"Has he been okay?" she asked Sally.

"Oh my dear, he's been fine. He and Lucy are great friends already. He's adorable. When do you start work?"

*Oh shit! The job! How long will I be able to work? Will they tell me not to bother if I tell them I'm pregnant?* She also worried about being able to stay in the flat with two children.

"Next Monday. Ah …. I need to make a call. See you later, okay?" She swooped up David and fled upstairs.

She made cheese on toast for David's tea, bathed him, and got him to bed early. She needed time to think. She stood the chance of being thrown out of her flat, which wasn't big enough for her and two children. She could apply to the council for housing, but that would more than likely put her in one of the awful-looking tower blocks where the council put what it termed as problems—misfits, junkies, criminals … and unmarried mothers. *I really can't. I'd die!*

That was the housing problem. As for work, she considered telling them the first day that she was pregnant and would need several months off starting maybe in March. *That'll go down really well.* She was sure they'd tell her not to start at all or would employ her until she needed time off and not take her back. Either way, she'd have no income. She supposed she could go to the army and get money from Mike, but she didn't think that was right; she was the one who had left.

The future was gloomy. There was another option, but as dire as her situation was, she couldn't bring herself to consider it not for religious reasons but because she considered it killing.

And then there was the last option, which terrified her. She could go back to Mike. But maybe he wouldn't have her back. How more humiliating could that be? *Would he punish me for leaving? Make my life hell? Could I stand that? Christ, what a mess I've made of everything. The Frazers were right. I'm a failure.*

# CHAPTER 25

## Humble Pie Doesn't Taste Good

S HE DECIDED TO TEST THE water. She wrote to Mike about being pregnant rather than phoning. If he wasn't interested, she didn't want to hear that firsthand. She also told him she was sorry for having left when he needed her the most. She played down the time he'd spent away and expressed her hopes he was better. She sent him a photo of David playing in the park near the flat. He'd grown so much over the last three or four months that he wasn't a baby anymore.

She realized that she was going back—if he'd have her—for all the wrong reasons, but she couldn't see what else to do other than live on her own with two kids in a multistory block of flats in a crappy area with no money and no job. If she swallowed her pride and went back to her former life, she'd forgo happiness but gain a decent home and money, which would be infinitely better for the children. She knew she'd have to put up with Mike's behavior, but if she knew why she was there and didn't try to resurrect the romance they once had, she believed she could cope.

She started her job and decided not to tell her employer anything for the time being. They were all very friendly and seemed to be a good team. She'd worked out that she might not need to tell them about the baby if she was heading back to Germany.

She would normally get home around 5:45, and after picking up David from Sally and with as little small talk as possible, she'd rush to check her mail.

About ten days later, there it was. She recognized Mike's heavy scrawl and panicked. *What if he tells me to fuck off?* She got the little lad into bed and took the unopened letter to the lounge. She looked for the umpteenth time at the envelope. She wasn't sure even then what she wanted it to say. If he rejected her, she'd *have* to manage on her own, but she didn't think she'd be able to cope. *Open the bloody thing!*

Hi, Georgy,

I was so pleased to get your letter though it was a great surprise. I was devastated when you left, you know that, don't you? … blah, blah, blah … wonderful news about the new baby … blah, blah, blah … sorry I behaved like a beast … blah, blah … I'll come over and get the two of you.

So that was it. He'd come over and pick them up, and they would go back to how it was. But at least the kids would be safe, and that's the only thing that kept her convinced she was doing the right thing. She just hoped she'd be able to put up with whatever he slung at her.

*Think of the kids.*

# CHAPTER 26

## No Change

LIFE SETTLED DOWN GRADUALLY. GEORGINA, Mike, and David lived in the camp in a spacious, four-bedroom house. She didn't want to face the other wives, so she kept to herself as much as she could.

The pregnancy went along fine, and it appeared Mike had conquered the demon drink. He'd still have the occasional night out with the guys but usually rolled in around midnight. As she got bigger and sleep started evading her, it was agreed he'd sleep in the spare room on those occasions.

Sex was an issue, however. Georgina did her utmost to find an excuse. On the rare times she had to succumb, she just wasn't able to relax, and Mike, in fairness, seemed to understand. It seemed he put it all down to the pregnancy. He'd roll over and say, "Night night, darling. Don't worry. It'll be okay when the baby's come."

The one big downside was the constant visits from the CO's wife. She took it as a personal responsibility to make sure all was well in the Grantley family. Maybe it was because they felt guilty about the previous episode or wanted to be there for early signs of it happening again.

Georgina felt she was doing her duty when she called to greet her with a smile and the assurance all was fine. Georgina hoped another family would go into crisis and take the pressure off them.

Anthony was delivered in RAF Wegburg on the last week in April, and Mike was the perfect new father. He came to the hospital the first night with David in one hand and a huge bouquet and a balloon in the other. "Here we are, little guy! Here's our mummy and baby brother. Look! There's Anthony."

"Mumma, me see Anney?" Georgina and Mike laughed at David's try at Anthony.

"There's a very clever boy, David. Can you say 'Anthony'?"

"Yes mumma, I did! Anney."

The name stuck for about two years.

Georgina and the boys settled in, and Mike spent at least six months of the year on exercises in Norway and Sweden.

In November, Mike went back to normal duties, and Georgina was finally getting back to a routine. David was around two and a half, and Anthony was about seven months. Both slept as soon as they were put down and through the night. With Mike around, Georgina could take care of personal stuff she'd neglected. A letter she'd been putting off for ages was one to Dave. After all he'd done for her, he deserved an explanation. She wrote to him about the situation, Anthony, and the apparent change in Mike. She mostly thanked him for helping her when she most needed it. She also wrote to Doug and Elles explaining why after all the dramatics she'd decided to return to Mike.

Then came the most difficult letter. She hadn't had any contact with her father for over a year and hadn't seen him since she and Mike had prior to the wedding four years earlier. She was very selective about the story she told. She said the reason she hadn't seen them was that she and Mike had moved to a different camp (that eliminated the need to tell him about their split), and she told him about the Anthony, which explained why they hadn't been back to the UK. She painted a rosy picture of her life. It was still important to her that he was proud of her and approved of her life.

If she asked herself if she was truly happy, she would have had to have answered no, but considering her options, she accepted that happiness was a small price to pay. Mike certainly wasn't the man she'd fallen in love with, but she had a home, nice furniture, enough money, and a certain amount of respect due to Mike's rank of captain.

She'd renewed her friendships with Claus, Helga, Jochem, and Anna though they still wouldn't accept Mike. But she and the boys visited them when he was away.

They came to see her occasionally. They'd spend happy Sunday afternoons in the enclosed garden that included a patio table and chairs and a barbecue. Claus was a brilliant cook—barbecue was his domain. Even Jochem wasn't allowed to intrude on the cooking space. They regularly feasted on beautifully seasoned chicken, burgers, sausages, and fish, which all tasted better barbecued. And what he did with bananas and cognac was out of this world. The boys enjoyed all the attention and were usually spoiled rotten with new toys every time anyone visited.

Christmas was a happy time. Mike, on duty over the holiday, stayed in camp, which left Georgina and the boys free to go over to Claus and Helga's for Christmas Eve and Christmas Day. Again, the boys had presents lavished on them, and Georgina enjoyed it more than if Mike had been home because there was always an undercurrent. He would have invited single officers or those whose families were back in the UK over, and she would have ended cooking for a crowd and putting up with the drinking. When that happened, she'd go to bed and leave them to it. Most of the time, Mike would drink until the early hours and collapse in the spare room. That was the compromise—he didn't bother her and she didn't bother him.

In the New Year, Georgina received a letter from her father. He'd been wondering why she'd not been in touch. She read that as disapproval and determined to write more often. He painted a wonderful picture of his family life—nothing specific, just what the kids and he and Margaret had been up to.

He did, however, go into detail about a trip he'd made to Biafra on behalf of the Save the Children Fund. He's been asked to go to help set up a supply route for food to the villages. She was obviously meant to be impressed, so she decided she would be. She was coming to understand there were things in life that were expected of her, prices she was to pay for the rest of her life.

He was keen for her and family to come to Devon. He said they'd love to meet her boys. He included a check for £40 for belated Christmas presents for them. He also suggested she phone them for a chat. She smiled. *I don't think so.* She didn't discuss the letter with Mike. She wrote back explaining that they hadn't any plans to return to the UK anytime soon but that she'd certainly let him know when they were.

# CHAPTER 27

---

## *Lies, Lies, and More Lies*

SPRING CAME ALONG WITH BOTH boys' birthdays six weeks apart. It was a busy time for Georgina. Anthony was only a year old, but David was three, and she'd arranged a big party for him.

The day of the party arrived, and she had much to do. Helga took the boys to the park so Georgina could prepare. She had invited about twenty-four children of Mike's fellow officers. The 3:00 party was being held in the officers' mess. The catering was to be done by the mess, but the decorating and the preparation for the games fell to Georgina. Mike had promised to be there, and Helga was to bring the boys at 2:45.

All went so well there was even time for lunch and a drink at the bar before Helga arrived. True to form, she arrived with the boys both clutching new toys—surprise surprise. "It's David's birthday after all, and I must not leave Don out of the presents, yes?" she smiled as she hugged the little chaps.

Mike walked into the mess. "Hello, stranger! It's been far too long!" He approached her and leaned in to kiss her.

"No! Stay away from me!" she spat out. "Never come near me! You are not our friend!"

Georgina was stunned at the venom with which Helga spoke. She knew after all the shit had come down last year that she and Claus had said they would never have Mike as a friend, but she had imagined they would at least be civil if they met. But there was nothing civil going on at that time.

A teary-eyed Helga said, "I'm sorry, Georgina. I cannot stay here with Mike. I'll call you tomorrow. I hope you have wonderful party. Bye bye, boys, see you soon." She hugged and kissed the boys and left.

Georgina was stunned! She wished she had gone after her friend, but all she could think of was the boys and the party and the way Mike had approached Helga as if nothing had happened.

"Christ! where did that come from?" He laughed as if he had been surprised at the outburst. Surely he must of known he wasn't going to be her most favorite person. He had apparently accepted that Georgina and the boys would spend time with them, so he'd spend time with his pals drinking.

This was an incident that should have alerted Georgina to Mike's changing attitude—there was a total separation of their social life, and they accepted it. Mike would stay out at nights and come home drunk. On a few occasions, he tried to force himself on Georgina, but because of her previous experiences, she knew how to get out of the situation; her physical agility versus drunken advances also helped.

They'd completely stopped communicating. While there wasn't the nastiness there had been before such as the humiliation in front of the other officers and the slagging off, he had no consideration for her and the boys. She was happy when Mike said he was going to Rheindahlen to run a training course. "Not sure how long it'll be love. Depends on the intake."

She didn't know if he was indeed running a course, but she didn't care. And the other wives weren't laughing at her; she was regularly invited to coffee shop chats. Luckily, the boys didn't witness much of what was going on as most of the unpleasantness occurred while they were asleep, but David was certainly picking up on the mood in the house when his father was there; he'd sometimes cuddle up to Georgina not saying a word but obviously looking for security.

Georgina started to feel really unwell around this time. She was suffering constant back pain that even copious amounts of Paracetamol didn't seem to touch. It continued unchecked for about two months before she saw the medical officer in camp. She left the boys with one of her neighbors, Chris, who said, "Take your time, Georgy. They'll be fine. Give yourself a break. Go shopping, spoil yourself. You deserve it."

Georgina loved looking after the boys but missed having adult conversations. "I could actually do with getting some bits from town."

"Go!" Chris said laughing.

After lunch, she dropped the boys off with Chris and took the tram to the camp. She got there at 2:00 and smiled at the lads at the gate as they waved her though. "On your own, Mrs. H? What have you done with him? Left him at home with the kids?" They laughed, knowing Mike would do anything rather than stay home with the boys.

Their comments amused her as he had told her he was on training exercise in Rheindahlen. "I wish! No, he's away with C troop up at HQ," she said with a smile. She wanted them to believe she couldn't care less about the game he was playing.

"Oh yes, that's right," the young sergeant said. "I forgot."

As she walked toward the medical center, she heard them laugh. She had to pretend there was no doubt in her mind he was training. If it became apparent he was playing silly buggers again, she needed to be the innocent party.

Captain Marshall, the camp MO, greeted her with hand outstretched. "Georgina, how nice to see you. It's been, oh, maybe a year?"

"Yes, Mike. When I had Anthony."

"A right little bruiser if I remember rightly. What's he now? Twelve pound something? He came out about three months old, didn't he?" He chuckled in a friendly, fatherly way. He was maybe in his late forties, stocky, with little hair left. His wife had died of cancer a few years earlier. He had chosen to stay on, dismissing the option of retirement. "What would I do with myself for God's sake?" he'd exclaimed when they chatted the previous year. "I can do more good here than wandering around the garden like a sad old git."

"How are you doing, Mike?" asked Georgina softly, "Is it getting any easier?"

"Yes, m'dear, it is. I'd rather be here than anywhere else. The kids don't need me, they're too busy off enjoying themselves, so here I'll stay until they kick me out. Anyway, what can I do for you today?"

She explained the pain and occasional nausea, and he examined her. He thought it was a urinary tract infection and gave her a prescription for antibiotics and Debendox for the nausea. "If it doesn't get better after this, come back. Don't leave it any longer than a week."

They said their good-byes, and she headed to the CO's office. She was determined to clarify what Mike was up to. Colonel Carter was at his huge desk smoking a pipe and rummaging through a mound of papers as she gently tapped on the open door. "Er, excuse me sir. Can you spare me a moment or two please?"

He looked over the top of his horn-rimmed glasses that looked about to fall off his nose. "Why Mrs. Grantley. How nice to see you. So glad things got sorted out with you and young Mike."

"Well sir, actually, they're not. He's being a … well sir … a complete arse at the moment. I wonder sir, can you tell me when he's due back from HQ?"

"What on earth do you mean an arse? I've spoken to him only last week, and he assured me all was well. And what do you mean about HQ? He's on leave!"

He must have registered the look on Georgina's face because he stood, came around the desk, and helped Georgian, who was swaying, into a chair. "Oh my God, Georgina, I'm sorry! I believed him when he said it was all okay. When did he tell you he was away from?"

Georgina was surprised at her feelings. She had her suspicions, but having them confirmed made her angry. *Where is the bastard?* "Well sir, he left in civvies on Sunday night. He said he was driving to HQ to start an induction exercise and would be there a week or maybe more depending on the intake numbers. I asked if he was going to be able to get back at the weekend, and he said, 'I don't expect so.' It didn't cross my mind to question it until the lads at the gate said they thought I'd left the kids with him as he was on leave."

Colonel Carter perched on the edge of his desk, and rubbed the back of his head. "I don't believe it. The prat! Has anything like this happened before?"

"I don't think so, sir. I've never thought to question him on his movements. To be perfectly honest, if I had, he'd have gone mad!"

"Okay my dear, try not to worry. I'll see if I can find him. Has he taken his car?"

"Yes sir, the BMW."

"Are you okay? I have to go to a bloody meeting, but stay here if you want. Do you want a cup of tea?"

"No thank you, sir. I'm fine. I'll go and leave it with you. Is that okay?"

Her lasting memory of that meeting was of the enraged colonel's veins standing out on his neck. Mike's actions were against every rule in the book; she had the comfort of knowing the consequences would be laid totally at his door. Or so she thought.

She made her way down the stairway and out of the building and headed toward the gate. She was pleased that the lads on guard duty were talking to officers as she passed them. She gave them a casual wave and got on the next tram to town.

She picked up her prescription and aimlessly wandered into Neckermann, a huge departmental store in the center of town. She was still in a bit of a daze and feeling numb. As she was walking around the departments, not really looking at anything, she heard, "Hi, Georgina!"

"Oh Anna! I'm so sorry. I couldn't see you. Shall we have a coffee?"

Anna looked at her watch. "That would be great. What have you done with the boys?"

"I left them with a neighbor for the afternoon. I had to go to camp."

"That's great. You need time for yourself even though they're lovely boys. Jochem and I were just saying we hadn't seen you for too long. You must come!"

"That would be brilliant, actually. How about we do it this weekend? I don't think Mike will be home. Even if he is, I'd rather not be there."

"Oh poor Georgina. What's he up to now? You must leave him, you know."

That was the last straw. What with the meeting with the CO and then Anna's outburst, Georgina couldn't contain herself. She burst into tears.

Anna put her arm around Georgina. "What is it, schatz?"

Georgina sobbed, not caring they must have appeared a peculiar couple wrapped in each other's arms, one sobbing and the other trying to comfort her.

"You must come back to the house. We can talk there, yes?" Anna wiped tears from Georgina's face. "Can your friend look to the boys for a while longer?"

Georgina panicked. "I must get back to the boys!"

"But Georgina, your friend has them. Let's phone her."

Anna guided Georgina to the phone booth. "Georgina, call!"

Chris had told her to take her time, but she'd phone her just to make sure. She was subdued. "I'm so sorry, Anna. If I can, I'll come with you. What shall I tell Chris? Will you drop me off later?"

"Of course. My car is behind the market. Jochem will be home soon. We'll have dinner and take you home."

Georgina sighed. It would be good to talk to them and not worry about what she said or if it would get back to camp. "Oh Anna, yes please. That would be wonderful. You just don't know how good it'll be to talk."

Chris confirmed she'd be happy to feed the boys tea and if necessary put them to bed and sit with them until Georgina got home. "I told you to take your time! We'll be fine."

# CHAPTER 28

It's the Kidney's Fault

THE NEXT FEW DAYS WERE a nightmare; Georgina didn't hear anything from the CO, and of course Mike hadn't come home. The pain in her back was getting worse. The tablets weren't working because she'd vomited three or four times, but she just put that down to stress. She's completed the course of antibiotics expecting some relief at least. Chris had been great; she'd taken the boys when she could so Georgina could rest.

On the weekend, she and the boys visited Anna and Jochem. He was so good with the lads, letting them climb all over him and carrying them around one under each arm yelling and screaming. "They want to go to the park, Georgina. That okay?"

"Of course, Jochem, if you're sure you can cope!"

Jochem's kind act gave Georgina and Anna peace and quiet. She knew she shouldn't drink while taking painkillers, but she had gotten to the stage of *Sod it!* It was a beautiful, warm day, and they were barbecuing later, but then, with the sun cascading through the windows and warming her face, she could almost forget all the crap going on. Except for the constant ache in her back.

They chatted about her situation with Mike and her options. Georgina was relieved to voice her fears to someone who wasn't involved with the army. She was so aware of her previous escape and what and who had been involved. But with two boys, doing a runner again was out of the question.

"Georgina, you're not well enough to travel let alone start up again on your own in England. How would you look after the boys if you're ill?"

"Oh don't be silly, Anna. I'm fine. The pills should start working soon. I've taken them for five days. The MO thinks it'll clear up soon." But she knew the pills weren't doing any good.

"Shall we have another glass, Anna? Is there anything we must do for the barbecue?" Georgina strolled over to the wine and began to fill her glass. Without any warning, she let out a yell, and the bottle crashed to the floor. She clutched her back. "Jesus! That hurts!" She doubled up in pain.

"Georgina! What can I do? Shall I call the hospital? The medical officer?"

That was the first of several similar episodes over the next few days. Georgina knew she had to get back to the MO as soon as possible. She had said no to getting medical attention at Anna's, and they'd taken her and the boys home, promising to see her the next day. While she was settling into bed, they went next door and spoke with Chris, who assured them she'd look after the boys and keep an eye on Georgina. She had a key, she told them, so she'd be able to get the boys to bed and look in on her.

Georgina knew something was very wrong but wasn't too keen on finding out what. She had enough crap to deal with.

On Monday, she called the MO. "Hi, Mike. Georgina Grantley. You said to call you if I had a problem. It's gotten worse. Can I get up to see you soon?"

"Of course, Georgina. Can you get up this afternoon? Maybe your husband could bring you up."

"Not much chance of that, Mike. I haven't seen him for more than a week."

Mike didn't answer. She could hear him breathing. He obviously hadn't known what had been going on. She was glad the CO hadn't said anything, but she would have to come clean when she saw him. *Christ! I have to go all over it again.*

She took a taxi to the camp that afternoon because it was a more comfortable ride than the tram. Her back wasn't too bad, and it hadn't gone into spasms since the previous night, so the short walk didn't cause her too much of a problem. She arrived at the medical office at a few minutes to two hoping she would be able to go straight in and not have to sit on the most uncomfortable chairs she'd ever known in the waiting room. Even with a broken leg you'd want to stand!

"Georgina, come on through." Mike held the door open. "So tell me what's been happening."

She told him about the pain when lying down and the spasms that had sent her sprawling to the floor. He examined her back and her side. He took her temperature and blood pressure.

"Look, love, I think it's best we get you to the hospital at Wegburg. I think you have kidney stones. We need to get an X-ray done ASAP. Paul Sheridan, the urologist there, is a friend of mine. He's good. Where's Mike? And where are the boys?"

She told him the story of Mike's escapades. He took it all in.

"Oh for God's sake, Georgina. I'm so sorry. We should have seen this coming."

"Why should *you* have seen it coming? Was he coming to see you?"

"No love, but we had a responsibility to him and you to keep an eye on things when he came home from Paderborn. He told us everything was fine with the two of you, and he was very convincing. We all believed him. He's a bloody good liar!"

After the consultation, she rang Chris. "Chris, I'm so sorry, but Mike wants me to go up to the hospital … Yes, now. I'm so sorry. Are you okay for a while? Mrs. Carter will call you and arrange something more permanent if I've got to stay in."

Her friend's "Don't worry" and "They'll be fine" put Georgina's mind at ease.

Mike arranged for Georgina to go by ambulance to Wegburg Hospital. "Mrs. Grantley? Ready when you are," the driver said.

The trip took just over an hour. The last time Georgina had ridden in the back of such a converted Land Rover was when she was in labor with Anthony. *I'm not sick! I just have kidney stones. What's all the fuss about?*

Mike had obviously phoned ahead. Upon arrival, she was taken straight to the urology department. "Mr. Sheridan's expecting you. He'll see you shortly," said a young naval nurse.

RAF Wegburg was a large, tri-military hospital staffed predominantly by QARANCs (Queen Alexandra Royal Army Nursing Corps) with a few naval and RAF nursing staff. It looked after the BFPO officers and troops and their families. It never seemed busy, unlike hospitals in the UK, maybe because it was run under military supervision.

"Mrs. Grantley, please come in." A tall, tanned officer stood in the doorway. "I'm Captain Paul Sheridan. Captain Martin called me a while ago. He seems concerned. If I may, let's just have a look at the area of concern. If you'd just sit on the edge of the couch please?"

She took off her jacket and climbed onto the exam couch. He lifted her blouse at the back and put the very cold stethoscope on her. When he's finished, he wrote something on his pad and took her blood pressure and temperature. "Thanks, Mrs. Grantley. I need to send you down for an X-ray. We need to see what's happening with your kidneys. If you'll just go with the nurse. Thank you. And try now to worry."

She got the feeling he wasn't the sort to chat, so she picked up her jacket and scrambled off the bench. "Er, thank you, Captain Sheridan. Do I come back here?"

"They'll bring you back, dear," he mumbled, his head bowed over his desk, engrossed in his writing.

She followed the nurse down the corridor, their footsteps clicking on the marble floors. In a few minutes, they reached a seating area for the X-ray lab. "This is Mrs. Grantley, Trisha. Captain Sheridan wants it done ASAP."

"There's several people waiting, Jen. I'll do my best," Trisha said.

"Soon as, or he'll be on my back. You know what he's like."

Twenty minutes later, the nurse said, "Mrs. Grantley, sorry to keep you waiting, but we're ready for you now." She smiled at Georgina and motioned for her to follow.

"When was the last time you ate anything, Mrs. Grantley?"

"Oh, er … maybe this morning about ten, I think. Cup of coffee and a couple of biscuits. Is it a problem?"

"No, it's just better if you haven't got a full stomach. So no lunch then?"

"No, nothing."

"That's fine then."

They entered the X-ray room. "Will you take your clothes off down to your underwear and put on one of the gowns? There's a little cubicle over there."

The cubicle was the size of a single shower. She struggled out of her clothes and into the gown, which was to be done up with ties in the back, but they were missing. She left the cubicle clutching the back.

"Need the bra off please," came a comforting male voice from behind a screen.

"Sorry," said Georgina, turning and knowing her back view was awful. She removed her bra and went back out.

"Hi. Mrs. Grantley, is it?" asked the technician from behind the screen.

"Yes, that's right."

He walked out from where he was flipping switches at a console and smiled at her. "Can you give me your date of birth please?"

"Twelfth July 1950."

"That's good. We have the right client then. Can you climb up on the bench please and lie flat on your back?"

Georgina did as she was instructed first on her back and then on both sides. She was asked to sit up while he injected her with orange dye that apparently "would just feel a bit weird." He had been right about that. It was as if hot water had been poured into her head. It was one of the weirdest feelings she'd ever had.

After he'd done all the necessary tests and X-rays, he told her to get dressed and wait outside until she was called. She did that for a good hour before the nurse she'd seen earlier came back. She went to the desk and asked for the prints. The receptionist nurse handed her a brown envelope and smiled. "Bye, Mrs. Grantley. Good luck."

She waited in the urology department until Captain Sheridan opened the door of his consulting room and smiled. "There you are. Sorry. Come in. That took longer than I'd hoped. Are you ok?"

She stood, smiled, and walked to the door. She was suddenly racked with stabbing pain in her back. She stumbled and was saved from crashing to the floor by the doctor. "I've got you. Let's get you on the couch." With a firm but gentle hand, he eased her onto the examination couch and put a pillow under her head.

"Well that was good timing eh?" he said with a smile as he smoothed the hair from her face. "If I needed any more evidence as to your symptoms, I couldn't have asked better than that. Let me give you an injection to ease that pain." Taking out a syringe and a small phial, he drew the contents and flicked the tube. He hitched her dress up a bit, swabbed a spot on her thigh, and gave her the injection.

"That should work quickly, dear. We need to get you down to the ward. I'll check on the bed situation. The nurse is just outside if you need anything. Here's the cord. Just tug it if you feel sick, okay?"

Georgina nodded feebly. She felt awful. She didn't care what he was doing. Not much of what he had said had sunk in. All she wanted was for the pain to go away.

Sometime later, she felt a gentle hand on her arm. The young nurse said, "Hi, Mrs. Grantley. You've had a bit of a doze. Best thing for you. The morphine tends to have that effect. How's the pain?"

Georgina tried to find the pain; it was as if she didn't know where to look for it. "Um ... okay I think," she stuttered, confused as to what was happening.

"Captain Sheridan gave you morphine. Do you remember falling?"

Georgina nodded.

"He went to sort out a bed for you, and when he came back, you'd passed out. He's been back and checked you out. He told me to stay until you came round."

"Er, where am I?" slurred Georgina.

"Oh sorry, I thought you'd got that bit. You're on Delta Ward, RAF Hospital, Wegburg. You came in this afternoon with kidney trouble. Ring any bells?"

# CHAPTER 29

# *What a Welcome Home*

GEORGINA WAS DIAGNOSED WITH RENAL colic and kidney stones. The doctors gave her medication but warned that it was likely to recur. If it became too much of a problem and she wasn't able to pass the stones, she might have to have an operation to remove them. Meanwhile, she was to drink at least four pints of water a day, apparently the only thing that would hold the colic at bay.

Since she'd been more *compos mentis*, she had been constantly asking everyone where her boys were. She'd been told, "Don't worry. They're fine." The CO's wife had visited her on the second day and had done her best to put Georgina's mind at rest. The boys had been placed with another officer and his wife while she recovered.

"Why couldn't they stay with Chris, my neighbor? And where the hell's Mike?" She burst into tears. The nurses asked Mrs. Carter to leave. "Georgina needs rest."

Two days later, it was decided she could return home as long as the MO kept an eye on her. Georgina couldn't wait to see the boys, and she felt able to manage on her own because the wonderful painkillers they'd prescribed were keeping the pain at bay.

The ambulance pulled up at the house around 3:00, and as she was helped out of the ambulance, she heard whoops and yells and saw two little boys charging down the path. "Mummy! We're here!" It was such a relief to see them. She didn't know what they'd been told and had worried they thought she'd just left them.

"Be careful, boys," came the wonderfully familiar sound of Chris's voice. "You don't want to knock Mummy over, do you?"

"Oh darlings, Mummy's home. How are you? God, I've missed you!"

She stooped and wrapped her arms around them. Seeing that she was still a bit unsteady on her feet, Chris scooped up Anthony and took David's hand. "Come on, boys. Let's get Mummy in the house."

Georgina followed them in. The driver was close behind with her coat and bag. "You okay, ma'am?"

"Yes. Thanks again. I'll be fine now that I'm home."

Chris helped her settle on the sofa and went to the kitchen to make tea. The boys climbed on her lap and chatted away about where they'd been and what they'd done. They seemed to have enjoyed themselves and weren't at all upset about her absence. But David wrapped his arms around Georgina's neck and said, "I cried, Mummy."

That tore her up! *Poor little mite!* She couldn't understand why they hadn't been left with Chris. They would have been completely at home there. She'd have to ask Mrs. Carter if Chris didn't have the answers.

Chris came with tea for her and Georgina and strawberry milk for the boys. "Okay, boys, sit here. There's milk for you and some cake."

The two boys scrambled off the sofa, sat on the floor at the table, and tucked into their favorite drink.

Christ handed Georgina a very welcome cup of tea. "Bless you, Chris. This tastes so good. Tell me what happened."

"It was so stupid! After your call, I settled the boys down, and they were just playing. They had no idea what was going on. They thought they were staying with me 'cuz you'd gone out. I was going to bathe them and get them ready for bed when that cow Mrs. Carter turned up. She said they'd kept you in and she would take the boys to some officer's wife as she was registered as a 'foster parent.' I told her it was daft because the boys knew me and I was more than happy to have them for as long as necessary. The silly old bat wouldn't listen. She insisted I dress the boys and pack a bag for them. She left with them. Mind you, this was about eight o'clock. I asked who was having them so I could go see them, but she wouldn't tell me."

"Haven't they found Mike yet?" asked Georgina. "This is all so bloody stupid. How can they just take the boys and not tell me? What if I'd been in longer?"

"Don't worry about it now, love. You're home now and on the mend we hope."

She looked at the lads contentedly chomping on cakes Chris had baked for them. They hadn't come to any harm. But was the camp doing anything to find Mike? If he'd been a normal dad, none of this ridiculous situation would have happened.

The MO called the day and reiterated the need for Georgina to keep drinking the water. "It's nature's flush, m'dear. I'll see you in a couple of days."

Chris was an absolute brick. Every morning, she'd knock and let herself in with the key she'd insisted Georgina give her ages ago. She'd make sure all was well with Georgina, dress the boys, and take them to her place or the park. Georgina was grateful because she wasn't able to pick the boys up or dress or bathe them due to her pain.

One of the times when the boys were off somewhere with Chris and Georgina lay on the bed, she heard the key in the door. Assuming it was Chris, she called out, "Hi guys! Back already?" Silence. "Is that you, boys?"

"No darling, it's me!" After some sixteen days away, Mike turned up as if he's left that morning. He climbed the stairs and sauntered into the bedroom, slinging his bag onto the bed. "What's up, love? Having a quick nap? Where are the lads?"

Georgina had no idea what he did or didn't know. *Has he been in touch with camp? Did they somehow find out where he was and told him to come home?* But by his questions, it seemed he was unaware she'd been ill. Either that or he was a very good liar.

While still weak, she managed to pull herself up on the pillows and said quietly, "Where the fuck have you been? Do you have any idea what's been going on here? More to the point, do you fucking care?"

He frowned. "You know where I've been. Up at the training school. Where the fuck do you think I've been? And why are you in bed! Get up! I need some grub."

His outburst made it blatantly obvious that he'd not spoken to anyone at camp and that they hadn't found him and sent him home. *Had they even tried? Or had they just closed ranks to protect their own?*

"Mike, don't make it any worse than it already is. I know you haven't been in Monchengladbach. The CO and everyone else thought you were on leave. I don't care where you've been, but maybe you'd like to know that while you were wherever you were doing whatever you were doing, I've been in the hospital and the boys were fostered out to God knows who on camp. That's it, Mike. I've had it. I can't take this anymore. Once I get the all clear from the doctor, I'm leaving with the boys."

Mike frowned and headed downstairs. She heard the chink, chink of ice going into a glass. "Do you hear me, you bastard? No more!"

She gingerly eased herself off the bed and pulled on her dressing gown. She was appalled at what she saw in the mirror—dark circles under her eyes, a grey hue to her complexion, and her hair an absolute mess. A thought fought its way into her mind: *Why would he want to stay with me? Can I really blame him?* But she heard another drink being poured. *This is not my fault! This isn't down to me.*

She made her way downstairs to the lounge door. A totally unconcerned Mike sat on the sofa with drink in hand. He hissed, "You'd better just fuck off then. But don't think for one second you're taking the boys. You're not fit to look after them. Look at you, sleeping in the afternoon, palming them off on a neighbor. No, Georgy, you can go if you like, but the lads stay with me. And don't try to get the camp on your side. They'll listen to me, trust me!"

He looked confident, even arrogant. He nonchalantly returned to his drink. Georgina couldn't imagine anyone taking his side against her not after this last lot of antics. She felt that the CO was furious with him, but she didn't have a clue about what to do next. She knew she wasn't fit enough to have a row with him, so she went up to her room and shut the door. She perched on the edge of the bed and stared into space. *None of this makes sense. What happens now?*

About half an hour later, she got an answer. She heard the front door slam. She went downstairs and found the house empty.

# CHAPTER 30

## No Other Choice

THE NEXT FEW DAYS WERE a blur. The MO came and gave her an injection of some sort, and the CO's wife arrived full of bustle and planning what must be done. Mike was coming and going but taking extreme care to avoid her. He came one lunchtime and took the boys, but Georgina was seeing everything through a fog.

The MO came back, and she was taken to the hospital. A different doctor looked after her. All she knew was that the pain in her back was very dull. The nurse would occasionally give her an injection that would send her into the fog again.

Once, she thought she remembered Chris coming to see her, but she was confused because the boys weren't with her. "The boys. My boys … Where … with you?"

"No, Georgy, I'm so sorry. They're not with me. Mike won't let me have them, the bastard. Christ knows why. What the hell does he think I'll do, kidnap them?"

A week later, Georgina was able to get out of bed and was surprised that there seemed to be very little pain. The doctor was pleased to the extent that he told the accompanying nurses on his rounds that she could probably go home soon.

*Great. What am I going home to? Do I even have a home?*

At least she was thinking rationally; she felt clear of the drugs.

As if to answer her questions, Mrs. Carter arrived. After the normal niceties, she looked seriously at Georgina. "Now then, my dear, we have to make plans, haven't we?"

Georgina didn't know what plans she had in mind, but she was sure she wouldn't like them. Mrs. Carter had that sort of face—very intense, concerned, headmistressy.

"You've given us all a scare you know, dear. We just hope we can put things right so that nothing like this ever happens again. That's what you want too, isn't it, dear? It's obvious you and Captain Grantley can't carry on the way you've been doing, isn't it?"

She didn't wait for a reply. "So we all think it will be best for you if you return to the UK. You can continue to get treatment as and when you need it, and you'll be better off with your family, won't you?" It was of course a rhetorical question.

"What family? I … I don't know what you mean."

"Now come on, dear, Mike's told us of your parents and brothers and sisters and that you'd be more than welcome to go there for as long as you want."

Georgina stared at her, jaw open. "That's absolute rubbish, Mrs. Carter, and Mike knows it. I hardly know them. I've met them only once!"

Mrs. Carter frowned and put her head to one side as if trying to think what to say next. "Well, no matter. Whatever the situation is, we all know you can't stay here, don't we. We'll make all the arrangements for—"

"When do we go then, and how do we get back?" Georgina desperately tried to take charge of the situation, but she was sure there was more to follow. Were they kicking her and the boys out of the quarter? Did she have to pay her own travel, because that was going to be a problem as she had nothing in her own name. Everything had always been in joint names.

"Sorry dear, you're saying 'we'? What do you mean exactly?" Mrs. Carter shifted uncomfortably in her chair. "We'll make the necessary arrangements for your travel, but that's all."

Georgina remembered Mike's threat. "You mean mine and the boys travel of course," she said quietly, preparing herself for what was coming next.

"Oh no, dear. The boys will stay here with Captain Grantley until he makes other arrangements for them in England. It's perfectly clear that you're not well enough to look after them properly, isn't it. You must surely see that."

*They can't possibly mean to send her away without the two boys. They're the only good things left in my life! They can't do that! Please, God. This is so unfair!*

"We will get you back to the UK at SAAFA's expense, and after that, I'm afraid you must return to your family. It's entirely up to Mike what happens to the boys. I believe he's going to take them to the UK to his family in the first instance. You must discuss with him what happens after that. But first, my dear, you need to get whatever medical treatment is necessary. If we're asked to answer to the UK Social Services, I'm afraid we'll have no option but to acknowledge your health problems and your obvious inability to look after the boys when you're ill."

Georgina was in utter panic. It sounded that it had all been arranged by Mike. The whole camp knew what he'd been up to in spite of the fact that the CO had told her not to worry, that he'd get to the root of it all. The army was closing ranks without a doubt.

Mrs. Carter stood, brushed her skirt to remove invisible crumbs, and patted Georgina's hand. In a most condescending voice, she said, "It's all for the best, dear. We all just want you to get well. You understand that, don't you?"

The lasting image Georgina had of her was that sickly smile.

Georgina curled up in a ball and sobbed so much that she made herself sick. The nurse came into the ward and tried to placate her but to no avail. She lay there with all sorts of thoughts rushing through her mind. Was it her fault? What could she have done differently? It kept coming back to the same thing. *Yes, it is my fault. I should have never come back. I deserve it all.*

But to lose the boys? That was utterly wrong! Surely, they weren't allowed to do that.

# CHAPTER 31

## Alone Again

THE NEXT COUPLE OF MONTHS went by in a blur. Georgina's health was holding up due to the medication she'd been prescribed. True to form, the army had taken temporary joint custody of the boys with Mike, citing Georgina's ill health as her inability to care for the children in the absence of her husband.

She had been given about a week's notice to leave for the UK and was told she had to make her own arrangements once she was there. There was no way she could ask her father, so the only thing she could think of was Doug and Elles. She called them and explained the situation. They couldn't believe the callousness of the army's actions. They told her of course she could stay as long as she wanted.

She had gone through the motions the last days in Germany in a haze. She hadn't seen the boys. Every time she called the camp to find out where they were, she met a brick wall. She just couldn't believe they could do this legally. Mike had given her some money not out of generosity but because he'd been instructed to by the army, so she had enough to live on for a few months, but she'd have to get a job and a place of her own.

Doug has introduced her to a solicitor pal of his who'd given her some hope of overturning the army's decision, but he told her it wouldn't be easy. She'd have to prove beyond doubt that she was a capable and healthy mother. That became her main goal. Nothing would stop her. Or so she thought.

She stayed in Marchwood for just over five weeks, and after some interviews, she landed a job as a cashier in a furniture store in Southampton, about twenty miles away. She tried to call Mike and find out about the boys, but she got no reply from him. She called the CO and left several messages, none of which was returned. She called Chris, and while she was terribly upset about the way things had been done, she couldn't shed any light on what was happening. The CO's wife had visited her and told her she was no longer to be involved with "the situation." Chris's husband, Steve, had told her to stay out of it. "Nothing we can do now, babe," he'd said.

The commute to work was a nightmare. In a few weeks, she found a little bedsit about a mile from work. She made time to start planning what to do next. She'd promised Elles that she would visit them one weekend. She didn't want to slide back into the black hole of depression that had engulfed her for the first few weeks she was with them. She was so very grateful to them because there was no one else she could talk to.

She carried the burden of not knowing what she should do first, but she knew she had to prove to the authorities she was fit and able to look after the boys. Not being able to talk to her new friends at work was bad; she assumed that if they knew all about her, they'd condemn her out of hand. What mother would leave her children as she'd done? She had to keep it a secret; that meant inventing a story that excluded her boys.

The weeks rolled by. No contact from Mike or more important, the boys. As advised by Peter James, the solicitor, she'd written to Mike's family with her new address so they knew how to contact her. At his suggestion, she sent a copy of that letter to the Hampshire Social Services so they couldn't say they didn't know.

Peter told her that the most important thing to any court would be her physical, mental, and financial stability, so she registered with a doctor and booked an appointment to see him. Doctor Bowerman took all the details, and said he'd contact the medical office for her records. He asked her to return in a month as getting the records could take some time. He asked her what medication she was on. As she reeled them off, he looked at her quizzically. "You were being treated for renal colic and kidney stones?"

"Yes. And I think they gave me something for depression too, but I've finished those."

"And how do you feel without those pills?" he asked gently.

Georgina looked down. She felt she'd done something wrong. "I had only about three weeks' worth when I left Germany, and I knew I wouldn't be able to get any more for a while, so I … I started taking them less frequently. I was taking two a day in Germany, and then I went down to one a day for about a week, and for the last two weeks, I've been taking them sort of every other day. Is that okay?"

His expression changed. "My dear, you've done nothing wrong. I can't believe they let you to go cold turkey! But you did very well reducing the dosage. I couldn't have advised you better myself." He smiled and patted her hand. "I am, however, concerned that you're still depressed. Let me give you a prescription for some more that maybe you could take in the same way as you've done up to now. Let's call it a safety net, shall we? If you need anything at all, phone for an appointment. We're normally able to fit you in the same day."

That evening, she began to feel more positive. She enjoyed her job, and the people she worked with were friendly and not the least bit interested in her troubles. And the doctor seemed to be reasonably happy with her. Once he got her records, she could begin getting the paperwork together to present to the social services.

About three weeks later, she rang the doctor's surgery about her German medical records. They had. "Can I make an appointment with Doctor Bowerman?"

"Of course. All appointments are gone today, but tomorrow morning at nine?"

Georgina didn't want to be late for work the next day; one of the big bosses was coming down from headquarters for a visit. "Can't do the morning. What's the latest you can do tomorrow evening?"

"I could do any time after … say five-fifty? Any good?"

Georgina finished at 5:30. "Yes, that'll be great. See you then."

# CHAPTER 32

## How Dare He!

A PART FROM MISSING THE BOYS terribly, life wasn't so bad for Georgina over the next few months. She was signed off by the doctor, work was good, and she's even been out on a couple of dates with one of the guys from work.

He was the total opposite of Mike, not flamboyant in any way but a quiet, gentle chap. Alan had recently separated from his wife, and he's moved back into the family home in Winchester. Not the ideal situation, he said, but he clearly had a great relationship with his mum and dad.

Peter James had written to the social services on Georgina's behalf, and they were working at contacting Mike with regard to her seeing the boys. The best thing was that he had agreed to do all the work as a favor for Doug, but she was of course the beneficiary of such a generous act.

One Saturday in May, Georgina and Alan had planned to go to the theater in Southampton after work. She woke with a spring in her step and a smile on her face. Just as she was leaving for work, she met the postman. "Hi there. Anything for me?"

"It's Mrs. Grantley, isn't it? Yes, there's one here for you. Have a good day."

He handed her the letter. She was surprised to see Hereford and Worcester Social Services on the postmark. *That didn't take too long then.* "Thanks. I've been waiting for this," she said happily. She headed out of the gate and tore open the envelope.

> … Finally had contact … Apparently it didn't work out …
> Not able to keep them with him … away on exercise … no
> other option …
>
> Dr. Barnardos

*The bastard! The absolute bastard!* It sounded as if the family had decided they didn't want to look after the boys after all, and Mike had gone back to Germany. Somehow, the boys had been put into a Doctor Barnardos Children's Home. How could that possibly have happened when the family and Hampshire Social Services had had her address? She needed to call them straightaway and get her boys out of that terrible place.

She almost ran the rest of the way to work, tears stinging her eyes. As soon as she'd gotten her coat off, she spoke to Andrew Carluccio, the manager. "Andy, please, can I make some calls before I start work? It's really important … It's about … my boys." She burst into tears.

"Hey, Georgie! Come on, sweetness, sit down. Shall I get Alan? Want a cup of tea?" He hurried out the office obviously embarrassed and unsure what to do. He went to the loudspeaker. "Alan Porter, office please, straight away. Alan Porter."

Georgina sobbed alone in the office. *How could this have happened?* The solicitor pal of Doug's had sounded so positive things would soon be sorted. She'd done everything he suggested and had even gotten a letter from the doctor stating that in his opinion she was physically and mentally capable of looking after her children. There was also a letter from Elles saying that should anything happen and Georgina had to go back into the hospital, she would of course have the boys for as long as necessary.

But the one to blame was Mike. *The bastard! How could he just abandon them? They were his boys as well. It was if he didn't care what happened to them, that they were an inconvenience.* This was after he had made such a fuss about her not being capable and convincing the army the boys would be better off with his wonderful family. *How could they just let them go? For God's sake, there were enough of them!*

"Hey darling, what's up?" Alan walked into the office. "Andy said you're upset, but a bit of an understatement. Come on, tell me." His kindly face was full of concern and understanding.

"Oh Alan, I can't believe it. That bastard has dumped the boys. He's put them in a Barnardos home!"

"You're kidding! No, sorry, I can see you're not. But why? How? What about social services? They know where you are. Let's get on the phone and sort it out. Can you manage? Are you okay? Do you want me to do it?"

Georgina took a deep breath. "I'll call now. Can you stay with me please?"

"Yeah sure, of course. You got the number?"

She referred to the letter and dialed the number. It rang and rang. Georgina realized there wouldn't be anyone there on a Saturday. "There's no one there! What can I do?"

Alan, ever the logical one, said, "You'll have to hang on till Monday. I know it's not going to be easy, but there's nothing you can do now. Are you okay to work?"

*Christ. The last thing I need to do is smile and be pleasant to the customers.* But she couldn't afford to piss off the manager. "Yeah, I'll be okay. Just need a few minutes up in the rest room. Could you tell Andy please?"

"Of course. But … I know it's not that important, but do you think you'll be up to the theater tonight?"

Georgina had forgotten about their date. Maybe it would take her mind off the letter for a couple of hours. "Yeah, I'll be fine. But don't expect too much though."

The weekend came and went. Alan was a really good friend. He stayed purely to comfort her. Being a gentleman, he slept on the couch.

They left for work on Monday early to speak with Andy and get permission to make phone calls.

At nine, Georgina called Hereford and Worcester Social Services. "I was told … You've sent me a letter … My boys."

"Hold the line, please."

A new voice came on the line. "Child welfare. Can I help?"

"Yes. You sent me a letter saying you've put my two little boys in a home." She started to sob. Alan put his arm around her shoulder.

"Sorry dear, what name is it?"

"Grantley, Georgina. My boys are David and Anthony. They were sent to my ex-husband's family by the army because I was ill."

"Just a minute please. Ah yes. Georgina, isn't it? Yes, the boys were placed last week in the Malvern home by their father."

"But I don't understand. Why didn't someone call me? You knew where I was. My solicitor has kept Hampshire Social Services updated with my details."

"Mrs. Grantley, I think the best thing would be if you came to see us."

"It's a long way, and I haven't got a car, I'd have to come—"

Alan patting her arm and mouthed, *I'll take you.*

"I think a friend has just said he'd bring me up."

*Are you sure?* she mouthed to Alan.

He smiled. *Of course, silly!*

They took the next day off and headed for Worcester. She'd asked the person she'd spoken to the previous morning if she'd be able to see the boys, and he said he'd do his best as long as Georgina came to the offices first.

It was a quiet journey in spite of Alan's attempts to make conversation. She wasn't in the mood to talk. When they arrived at the council offices, the receptionist directed them up a flight of majestic stairs to a door marked Child Protection Services. Gingerly knocking on the door, Georgina poked her head in and opened the door wider. She and Alan passed into a large open office with at least a dozen people sitting in little booths.

A young man of perhaps twenty-five or so greeted them. "Mrs. Grantley is it?" He extended his hand. "Come over to my desk, will you? It's good to see you."

Georgina thought it was like a meeting with a banker, friendly and informal. But these people held the power to say if she could have her boys or not. *I better get this right.*

She and Alan followed the man to his desk, and he motioned to two chairs. "I'm sorry, but you are?" he asked Alan suspiciously.

"Just a friend. Mrs. Grantley had no way of getting here on her own. And we're well, good friends … you know."

"Yes of course."

Georgina saw his name on his desk—James. He shuffled some files on his untidy desk and found what he was looking for. "So Mrs. Grantley, you left the little boys in Germany with their father about four months ago as I understand it. Why would you do that?"

*Christ! He obviously hadn't been given any of the correct details.* Georgina explained everything—from Mike going to rehab, then going missing, then her illness, and finally how the army had taken his side and basically sent her home, having first taken a joint custody order out with Mike.

James shifting uncomfortably when Georgina started to cry. He made the odd "tut tut" while taking copious notes.

When she got to the part where the solicitor had sent what he believed to be sufficient documentation to the social services, he put his hand up. "Where did your solicitor send this information?"

"To Hampshire Social Services Child Care Department."

"Mrs. Grantley, why Hampshire? Why not us?"

Georgina looked at Alan and then to James. "Because when he phoned Southampton, they said in the first instance it had to go to them as I was living there. They said they would contact you and pass the paperwork on. Are you telling me you haven't got it?" She was panicked.

"I was given a list of what was necessary, and we've got it all, and there was some other stuff just to be on the safe side."

The look on James's face said it all. *What a bloody mess!*

"I think the best thing is for you to go with Mrs. Brown over there." He pointed to a matronly looking woman at another desk. "She'll take you to see your boys, and you can spend a bit of time with them, maybe get some lunch. While you're gone, I'll see what I can sort out with Hampshire, okay?"

*Okay? More than okay! I'll finally see my boys!*

"Mrs. Brown will have to stay with you at all times," he said almost apologetically. "They're in our care, you see."

"Yes of course. Can we go then? How far is it?"

Mrs. Brown was putting her coat on. "Hello, Mrs. Grantley. Can I call you Georgina? I'm Mrs. Brown. We'll go in my car. It's about forty minutes from here. I've got to sign out. I'll meet you in reception, okay?"

Georgina and Alan made their way down the stairs. Alan took her arm and squeezed it. "Not long now, love," he whispered.

"I wonder what they'll make of me. Will they remember me?"

"Of course they will, love. You're their mum. They'd never forget you." He was doing his best to comfort her and prepare her for the momentous meeting.

As they drove off, Mrs. Brown said, "Mr. Porter, I'll have to ask you to please stay with me when we get to Malvern. The boys need to be reunited with their mum first. Give them a while, and we'll go for some lunch. That okay?"

"Of course. No problem. This is Georgy's time."

# CHAPTER 33

## *Please! They're Mine!*

THE DRIVE THROUGH THE WORCESTERSHIRE countryside seemed endless, but in forty-five minutes, they pulled up to large, rambling, Dickensian house—terribly austere, not a place that would be very welcoming to children already traumatized by whatever circumstances had brought them there.

"Here we are, folks. Let's find the manager, Mrs. Hancock, an absolute darling."

They walked across the courtyard. The wind was howling around the building, making it seem even less friendly. The huge wooden front door stood open. As they walked through the doorway, they heard the lovely sounds of whoops and yells coming from the rooms on the next floor. They walked into an office beside the stairway and saw a rotund Mrs. Hancock at a tidy desk. A plant in the corner and photos on the windowsill gave the office an inviting look.

"Mrs. Hancock, I'm Mrs. Brown, Worcester Social Services, and this is Mrs. Grantley and her ... um ... friend. She'd like to see David and Anthony please. We thought we'd spend some time here and then go to lunch. Is that okay?"

"Hello and welcome, Mrs. Brown, Mrs. Grantley. Yes. I had a call from James in your office saying to expect you. The boys are upstairs in the playroom I think. Let's go and find them, shall we?"

Georgina could hardly contain herself. Her heart raced when she heard what she was sure was David's voice upstairs. She was close to tears. The expectation of seeing her boys for the first time in about five months was almost too much to bear.

Mrs. Hancock turned to Alan. "Alan, I wonder would you mind waiting down here for a while? Georgina needs some private time with the lads."

"Of course. You okay, Georgie?" He put his arm on her shoulder and gave her a peck on the cheek.

"Yes, I'm fine. You'll wait here then. Where are they? Upstairs?"

The three women walked toward the stairs. Georgina almost ran up them.

"Mrs. Grantley, please. Let me go ahead and get the boys. Will you wait here please, Mrs. Brown?"

It was almost a plea from Mrs. Hancock to hold Georgina back. Mrs. Brown gently put her hand on Georgina's arm and smiled. "Not long now, dear."

In less than a minute, Georgina saw two little boys come out of the playroom holding Mrs. Hancock's hands. "Now then boys, how about a big hug for Mummy?" She released them, expecting them to charge at Georgina. But that wasn't the case.

Georgina could hardly contain herself. She crouched on the floor maybe ten feet away from the boys and held out her arms. "David, Anthony! Oh babies, come see Mummy!"

But the boys didn't respond as she had expected. They looked at each other almost quizzically with an unspoken message. They moved as one toward her.

"Mummy? Are you okay? Where have you been?" asked David in a quiet voice. He took Anthony's hand. They slowly approached her. Suddenly, as if finally understanding the situation, they flung themselves at her.

"Oh my sweet, darling boys. I've missed you so much!" All three fell on the floor and cried inconsolably.

"Where you been, Mummy?" echoed Anthony, sobbing.

"Mummy, they said you left us," David said, his voice breaking.

"Oh my darlings, Mummy didn't leave you. She was just very poorly. But I'm here now."

"So we coming home with you now?" asked David in an usually quiet voice.

Georgina just looked at them. She would have to say no. *What will they think?*

Mrs. Hancock saw Georgina's turmoil and moved to the boys. "How about we all go to the family room? It's just down here."

That distracted the boys, and the moment passed. Georgina tried to stand with the boys clinging to her. "Hey come on, show me your toys then." She tried to hold back tears. Holding tightly to her bemused boys, they followed Mrs. Hancock to a very pleasant room with chintz curtains and an overstuffed sofa. She sat in the middle and patted each side for the boys to climb up.

Mrs. Hancock asked Georgina if she'd like a cup of tea. "Yes please, that would be lovely." She hugged the boys as if her life depended on it.

"And some milk, you two?" she asked the boys but didn't wait for an answer.

The tea and milk arrived, and the three chatted and hugged in privacy.

Maybe forty-five minutes later, there was a gentle tap on the door. Mrs. Hancock and Mrs. Brown were in the doorway.

"How about we have some lunch," said Mrs. Hancock. An unusual group of the two women, Georgina, Alan, and the boys went to a pleasant restaurant in town. Georgina, Alan, and the boys were at one table while Mrs. Brown and Mrs. Hancock were at another. The boys became more animated, talking over each other, telling Georgina about their friends, their bedroom, and the toys they played with. Neither mentioned their father or the short time they'd spent with his family.

They'd taken two cars. The meal came to an end. Mrs. Hancock stood up and with an apologetic look, said, "Okay, boys, we've got to get back home. Say good-bye to your mummy."

Georgina hadn't thought about that. Completely caught up with the joy of being with her boys again, she'd pushed their imminent separation to the back of her mind.

"Mummy, can't you stay with us, please?" cried David. Anthony threw his arms around her neck. "Don't go again, Mummy!"

She thought her heart would break. She cried inconsolably as she hung onto the two little chaps. "I'm so sorry, darlings, but Mummy will come back soon, I promise." *Please, just a little longer?* she mouthed at the two women.

"Sorry Georgina, we must go now. Come, boys."

The two boys were reaching for their mum as she and Alan walked to Mrs. Hancock's car, Georgina sobbing into Alan's chest. All she could think of was when she would see them again.

Mrs. Brown was talking most of the way, but Georgina didn't hear a word. Back at the office, Mrs. Brown asked, "Would you come up to the office, Georgina? We'll see if James has gotten anywhere with Hampshire."

Hanging onto Alan, she made her way upstairs. Her eyes and throat were sore. Her body was still wracked with quiet sobs.

"So Mrs. Grantley, Georgina, how was your visit?" James asked.

*What a bloody stupid question! What does he expect me to say? "Quite nice, thank you"?*

"I've been onto Southampton office, and they say yes they've got the paperwork a Mr. Jones sent in. It's been put on file, but they haven't done anything with it because of your accommodation."

Georgina frowned. "I don't understand. I answered all the questions and told them I had a place of my own."

"Yes but you see, the flat you've got … Apparently, it's no way suitable for you and the boys. You must see that. You'll have to apply for council accommodation, and you can't do that until the boys are living with you."

"Okay, so I'll take the boys and then apply. Is that it?" Peter Jones hadn't said anything about her needing a place from the outset suitable for the boys, but that had been before the boys had been taken into care. He thought it was going to be just getting custody away from Mike and the army.

"Unfortunately, it's … er … not quite that simple," James stammered. "You see, Barnardos won't be able to release the boys unless you have suitable accommodation, and social services won't entertain your application until you have the boys."

"What can I do? I can't afford a larger place. Why can't you talk to Hampshire for me? Please! I need my boys, and they need me!"

# CHAPTER 34

# Too Much to Ask?

RETURNING TO ANY SORT OF normal life was difficult for Georgina, and it was made worse by a letter from Barnardos saying that until the accommodation issue was resolved, they would ask Georgina to stay away from the boys, who were very upset after the visit. The home had decided it was "in their best interest."

She called the home several times but received the same response: "I'm so very sorry, Georgina, but they're really disturbed by it all. I'm sure you wouldn't want to exacerbate the situation now, would you? Why not write to them? We'll read the letters to them."

The gap widened. Social services wouldn't budge even after Peter Jones appealed to the local magistrate, and neither would Barnardos.

While Georgina enjoyed her job, it wasn't particularly well paying. She started looking at other jobs that would appear occasionally in the *Echo*, but none would have allowed her to rent a larger property.

A month or so later, she received a letter from Mrs. Brown at Hereford and Worcester Social Services saying they'd been able to place the boys with a foster family, which would be much better for them. Georgina wasn't sure how she felt about that. If the boys settled into this family, would they forget about her? Wouldn't it be even more difficult for her to get them back?

She spoke to Alan about it. He said, "Whatever happens in the future, darling, they'll be better off with these people. You know that's what David certainly needs, and at least they're together."

She knew he was right. On one occasion that she had phoned the home, Mrs. Hancock mentioned they were concerned about David; he was constantly disturbed, misbehaving, wetting the bed, fighting, and so on. Georgina had suggested she come up, but that, social services believed, wouldn't solve anything.

Months went by. Her relationship with Alan grew. When Alan suggested they rent a house together, she saw an answer to her prayers. *I've found a wonderful, sweet, gentle guy who helped me with the boys and who's suggesting we pool our resources.* He was fed up living with his parents, and her flat was small, particularly when he stayed over.

*Will I be able then to get the boys?* This was something she could see happening, but the first thing she had to do was to make sure she and Alan would get on and hopefully become more of a permanent arrangement. She knew she mustn't rush it and perhaps get it wrong again.

For the first time in a long time, she felt confident and comfortable in herself. Alan didn't make demands. He accepted her for what she was, and if she doubted herself over something, he was always there with encouragement. "You can do this," he'd say if she was getting nervous about something. She believed he was the kindest person she'd ever known. Nothing seemed to faze him. She began to think her future was looking up.

They moved into a newish house about twenty miles from the store, and everything seemed to be going well. After about a month, she and Alan went to the seaside for a weekend, and it was more than she could have hoped for. He seemed to take it as a stepping stone to a more permanent arrangement; he talked in loose terms about a holiday next year and so on. So when they got back from the long weekend, she decided to test the waters.

"I've had another go at social services last week. They still won't budge," she said casually while making tea. He didn't comment, engrossed in some football on the TV. "I have an idea," Georgina said tentatively. "You know the social services won't let me have the boys unless I have a suitable home for them, and the council won't give me a place unless I have the boys. If you and I are renting this, what if I went to Hereford and Worcester and said we'd have them as a family?"

She waited for a response. She walked into the lounge. Alan was engrossed in the game. *Oh God. He didn't hear me.* "So what do you think?" she nonetheless asked.

Alan turned to her with a look she'd never seen before. "Listen, love, come and sit down," he said in his gentle but firm voice.

"So you did hear me then."

"Yes darling, I did. Look, please don't hate me, and please don't let it spoil us, but Georgy, I'm not ready to take on a ready-made family. I had enough of that with Sharon. Her little one wasn't mine, but I ended up bringing her up for three years. I just don't think I'm ready to do it again."

Georgina could see he was close to tears. His ex had been pregnant when he'd started going out with her, and he'd taken her for all the tests and appointments. When the baby was born, he'd suggested they get married and he'd adopt the baby. She agreed, but within a couple of months, he was the one looking after the baby while she went out most nights. But his words still took Georgina totally by surprise. She realized she hadn't considered his feelings at all. She was still hurt that he wouldn't even consider what she was asking. *Doesn't he realize how important this is to me?* But again, she questioned her motives. *Did I agree to move in with him just so I could get my boys back?*

"I'm sorry love, but I'd rather say it now than go ahead with it and have it split us up later. That wouldn't be any good for anyone, especially the boys. They've had one dad do it. God forbid they get another."

Georgina was crying softly. She knew he was right. If she put the boys first, what she was trying to do was wrong. "I'll have the boys no matter what" was selfish. She had to accept that the best thing for the boys was a stable family, something the Townsends offered.

Over the next few months and into the next year, she maintained regular contact with them, and they sent photos on their birthdays and holidays and so on. Reports had come from Hereford and Worcester that David was a lot more stable and that the boys had settled into the local school. The Townsends had agreed to long-term foster care, so at last the boys knew what each day was to bring, something Georgina had to admit she couldn't offer them. But there was still the restriction on her seeing them.

While she heard what they were saying about the emotional stability of the boys being all important, it was very hard for her to come to terms with the fact she couldn't offer that stability, and she missed them so badly.

# CHAPTER 35

## So Much Love

ALAN CHANGED JOBS A COUPLE of months later and became a buyer for a large hypermarket. It was a good move as far as his career was concerned, and it gave them a very good social life, which they'd not had before. There was a dinner party or a barbecue to attend frequently at the homes of one or the other of eight managers. Georgina learned to accept a bit more every day that what she'd done was the right thing; she was reluctantly coming to terms with it.

Her health was holding up too, with only mild outbreaks of the kidney problem. And she enjoyed becoming part of Alan's family. They were totally committed to the others in the family, and there seemed to be dozens of them; Georgina felt accepted by them all.

They decided in February 1975 to marry the following November. Alan's mum was over the moon. She and Georgina spent time planning the wedding, and as things got ticked off the list, she would bustle about saying, "Right then. What's next?"

Eight or nine weeks before the wedding, Georgina had a couple of days when she felt ill and took time off work, but it didn't get any easier. Not saying anything to Alan, she went to the doctor. Her fears were confirmed. She was pregnant. She had no idea what Alan would say. They hadn't discussed a family, but on the other hand, they hadn't been using any protection, so he couldn't be totally surprised, she tried to convince herself.

Alan came home that night full of a meeting he'd had with a supplier and how he'd managed to get an exclusive deal on some new stock. After a while, he asked, "Sorry, love, I should have asked. How were you today? Still being sick?" He put his arm around her shoulder and kissed her neck. "Come on, sweetheart, we can have dinner a bit later, can't we?"

She smiled. "Yes of course, darling. I'd like to run something past you anyway."

They sat on the sofa. "So what is it, love?" he asked, gently stroking her hair.

She wasn't sure what reaction she'd get. *Here goes nothing.* "It's not been too bad today, but I thought I'd go to the doctor's anyway."

"Oh Lord, I didn't know it was that bad, love. You should have said!"

"You're usually gone by the time it starts, so you wouldn't have seen the worst."

"What did he say? It's not that bloody kidney again, is it?"

She took a deep breath. "No, it's not the kidney. But he did a bit of a test, and he knows exactly what it is."

Alan was clueless. "Oh Christ, come on, tell me."

"Okay, but can I just ask you something? Are you still going for the store manager's job in Telford?"

He laughed. "What on earth's that got to do with you being poorly?"

"If we have to move, I want to make sure I'll be able to help you, and if it's going to be in the summer as you thought, that could be a bit of a problem."

He was baffled. "What on earth are you going on about? Oh hang on. Are you … did the doctor tell you … Is that why you've been sick? Bloody hell, Georgy! Are you pregnant?"

Her eyes welled up with tears. "Yep darling, I am. It's bloody morning sickness! I'm about eight weeks gone. You don't mind, do you?"

"Mind? You silly sod! Of course I don't mind. It's brilliant, bloody brilliant!" He smothered her in kisses. "Oh my God! I'm going to be a dad!" He jumped up. "A dad! Can we tell anyone? I want to tell someone. What about Mum and Dad? Come on, we've got to tell them."

He took her smile as permission to do that. "Hey, Ma, How're you doing today?" He didn't wait to find out how she was. "We got some news today, Ma ... What? ... No, I'm not being transferred ... Listen, Ma! We're pregnant! Georgy's been to the doctor this morning. She eight weeks gone. Baby's due ... When babe?"

Georgina laughed and mouthed *June*.

"Ma, June. Isn't it great? At last I'm a dad!"

That evening, he walked around with a perpetual grin on his face, humming as he did the washing up and whistling as he put the rubbish out.

They sat on the sofa later that night, Alan with his arm around Georgina and stroking her hair. He became serious. "Hey Georgy, you know I couldn't be happier, don't you? I'd hate to think you're upset that I'm over the moon about our baby but I said no to having the boys. You do understand why I had to say that, don't you?"

Georgina smiled. "No, darling, I'm not upset. I suppose I've gotten used to it now, and I'm sure what I did was right for the boys. Okay, at the time, I thought it was the answer, but I realized I was being very selfish and almost using you. Not intentionally of course, but, yes, I accept what you said. Maybe if they'd have come to us, it would have split us up. We'll never know though, will we?"

A small part of Alan knew he should have said yes. But it could have led to resentment. He wondered if she would have wanted his child if she had hers with her.

Georgina said very quietly, "Darling, it's done! I still feel awfully guilty that we've got this, and they ... Well, they're not with me. But no, I'm fine with it. I just wish I'd hear a bit more often from the Townsends."

In the beginning, she'd received fairly regular letters from them and some photos, but as time went on, the contact had slowed. The last photo she'd had was of Anthony when he started school. Georgina was well aware she had to respect their wishes. They had taken on a lot and wanted to make their own family life without the worry of the biological mother butting in.

They sat in a comfortable silence for a while, each lost in thought. Eventually, Alan gently kissing her on her temple. "Fancy a cuppa, love? And then I'm ready for bed. All this excitement! I can't cope." He chuckled and walked into the kitchen.

"Yeah, love one, thanks. And yes, I'll join you. Best get plenty of sleep while we can, eh?"

# CHAPTER 36

# *Is This Really a Good Idea?*

OVER ALL THIS PERIOD, SOME four and a half years, Georgina was constantly aware of something niggling at the back of her mind. She knew only too well what it was and that she'd ultimately have to confront it. She hadn't spoken to her father in all that time. He knew nothing of the problems with Mike, the rehab, the aborted attempt to leave him, and her illness. Nor had she sent him any photos of the boys.

The last time she'd spoken to him was on the phone just before she went back to Germany. She'd been purposely noncommittal, not wanting him to know she wasn't the perfect daughter and that not everything in her garden was fabulous. She hadn't been ready for the emotional roller-coaster ride building a relationship with her father would undoubtedly turn into. But she felt secure enough to pick up from where they'd left off. She'd spoken to Alan about it, and while he couldn't comprehend the reasons for her father doing what he had, he was sympathetic to her needing to try to build on it again. "Whatever you need to do, love, I'm behind you."

She felt she needed to work out what she was going to tell him and what she wasn't. She needed to work out a time line so everything would fit seamlessly. But she had to keep asking herself why it was so important to her. It came back to the same thing—she needed his approval. She hated that this part of her had come alive again.

She felt comfortable with Alan. He'd accepted her warts and all. She didn't have to strive for his approval because she already had it, and she loved him for that.

She planned the call to her father with military precision. She practiced what to say if he asked an awkward question. She practiced how to skirt over periods of time. She practiced how to change the subject if he started digging where she didn't want him to. One day when Alan was at work, she dialed the number. "Jackson here." She was off.

About fifteen minutes later, she hung up feeling totally drained. She made tea and turned her attention to the list she'd written. There were ticks against all but two items on the list. She felt proud of herself. She was able to focus on the wedding, how she'd met Alan, and how welcoming and uncomplicated his family was. She was particularly pleased with that bit. And to top it all, not only had she asked him and Margaret to the wedding, she'd asked him to give her away, and he had agreed.

That would be the first outward display of family she'd ever really been involved in, and her thoughts were divided. On the one hand, she was proud she had a father to give her away; everyone would think they were just like any other family. But on the other hand, she was angry with herself for allowing it to be so important. She realized there was nothing she could do about such conflicting feelings, so the best thing was just to take out of the situation what she needed.

Alan came home from work about 6:00 p.m., and while she cooked, she told him about the call. He gave the "Oh wow," "Brilliant," and "Well done" comments and seemed pleased her father would give her away.

Plans for the wedding became more frantic as the day approached. Alan's mum was involved and loving every minute. Alan was the oldest son of two. She'd not been included in his brother Peter's wedding as the mother of his fiancée, Jen, had taken total control. If at any time she voiced a comment, "How about …" or "Wouldn't it be nice if …" she'd been ignored, so she had given up and let them get on with it.

Alan's mum was from a large family; she was the eldest of nine, and her parents were still alive. There were dozens of cousins, aunties, and uncles to invite as well as friends they'd made through Alan's new job. Georgina got on well with the wives and partners. The wife of the electrical manager was a gorgeous, long-legged, exotic creature with tremendous style and flair and had offered to do the wedding photos as a present. She'd worked in New York as a fashion photographer and enjoyed keeping her hand in, as she said.

It all seemed to be coming together. Georgina was happy and confident it would be a great day. If there was a small situation that had upset Georgina, it was that they'd been denied the right to get married in the Church of England. They'd approached three vicars of separate parishes where she'd sung in choirs, hoping they'd look favorably upon her and Alan, but each time the answer was no, sorry. This was apparently because both Georgina and Alan had been previously married. So faced with a registry office wedding or a different denomination, they had settled for the United Reform church in the village Alan had grown up in.

The morning of twenty-third of November dawned bright, crisp, and sunny. Georgina has stayed at Alan's parent's house for the night, glad for the peace. Dot was a sweet, kindhearted woman who made Georgina as comfortable as possible. When Georgina had arrived the night before, she was greeted with a big hug. "Now my dear, you just tell us what you need and we'll get it." Though Georgina wasn't particularly hungry, she had managed to tuck away a sizeable portion of homemade cottage pie.

Waking in the strange bed, she was disoriented. Once she'd worked out where she was, it hit her with a bang. *My wedding day!* The familiar morning nausea rose in her throat, but she made her way downstairs to Dot and Leslie sitting at the table. "Good morning, dear. How're you feeling? Excited I'll bet! Oh dear, are you okay, lovey? What can I get you?"

Swallowing hard, Georgina smiled. "Oh, it's just the usual, you know. Plus a bit of nerves I expect. Could I just have a piece of toast and some milk please?"

After the protestations of "Are you sure that's enough?" and "It'll be a busy day you know," she got toast and milk. In ten minutes, she felt a lot better.

At about ten, they heard a knock. Georgina was pleased to see the florist delivery girl holding the box containing her bouquet and the buttonholes. The day started.

The wedding was at 1:00, and her father was due at the house around 12:30. A few minutes past the allotted time, Georgina heard a knock on the door and Dot opening it. "Oh yes! She'll be down in a minute. Please do come in."

Dot ran upstairs and knocked gently on the bedroom door. "Are you ready, lovey? Your dad's here." She pushed the door open.

Georgina smiled at her. "Oh Dot, you look absolutely lovely!"

"And so do you, my dear. Are you ready to go down?"

"I'll put my shoes on and be down."

Smiling, Dot kissed Georgina's cheek. "I'll tell your dad."

A few minutes later, she left her room and approached the stairs. Holding her dress so as not to tread on it, she carefully started down. Her father appeared at the foot of the stairs. "Oh I say love, if I'd known you were going have a lay in, I'd have come later."

Georgina smiled at this attempt at humor and continued down the stairs.

And so she and Alan were married. It was a very happy and successful day. Along with her father, there was Margaret, who beamed all day, and David, the eldest boy, who was for some reason dressed in full military uniform and on crutches, having sustained an injury on the rugby pitch of all places. He'd recently joined the army and was enjoying everyone thinking he'd been injured in battle. And then there was the only daughter, Sandra, who spent the whole day scowling to show everyone she didn't want to be there.

After the ceremony, everyone gravitated to the community center, about a ten-minute walk from the church. The women of Alan's family had been working all morning to lay on a magnificent spread. It was an informal affair, and once most of the food was consumed, there appear a DJ, encouraging everyone to dance.

Just after that, her father approached her and Alan as they were dancing. "Listen, love, we've got to make a move. David's going back to Catterick Camp tomorrow."

With an uncomfortable embrace for her and a shake of Alan's hand, the family left, but not before Margaret gave her a big hug.

"Now don't you two be strangers! We haven't seen you for such a long time. You must come, do you hear?" She hugged Alan and kissed Dot and Leslie on the cheeks, thanking them for a lovely day.

By that time, David, Sandra, and her father were nowhere to be seen. The wedding party drew to a close. Alan and Georgina headed off for a short honeymoon in the New Forest.

# CHAPTER 37

## The New Perfect Family

OVER THE NEXT SIX MONTHS, Georgina got bigger of course. It wasn't a particularly easy pregnancy with her putting on about three and a half stone and being continually sick. At her thirty-six-week checkup, the doctor suggested that at the end of the next week she should go into Winchester maternity hospital for bedrest.

She took along an overnight bag and some take-home clothes for the baby in a delicate green; they didn't know if it was a boy or girl. There were four other mums in waiting in the little side ward. Over the ensuing days, they began to form friendships (that in a couple of cases lasted many years).

The eighteenth of June was Georgina's due date, but on the evening of the sixteenth, she went into labor. Jacqueline was born in the early hours of the seventeenth. She, as had been her boys, was big, weighing in at a bouncing ten pound two ounces.

They took the baby home a few days later and very quickly got into a routine. Alan was a great help even to the extent of getting up in the middle of the night if Georgina had had a tiring day. There was absolutely nothing he wouldn't do—changing nappies, bathing her, or taking her for a walk—he was in his element. Jacqueline was a good baby; she slept through the night at about six weeks, again much like the boys.

The summer of 1976 was terribly hot; it was difficult to keep the infant cool. Every chance they had, they'd go to the beach for the breeze.

Alan was promoted at work, and his friends were a great comfort to Georgina, who looked forward to adult conversation with the other wives. Some had children, so it became a routine of visits with the babies. Her friend Christine, a mum she'd met in the hospital, lived close by and joined the mums and babies group.

Alan and Georgina bought their first house around that time, a turn-of-the-century terraced house. They had tremendous fun over the next year putting their mark on it. It was a happy, cheerful house, and Georgina felt a peace she'd not had before. It was a feeling totally different from what she'd had with Mike and the boys. She felt comfortable with her own home and the regularity of Alan going off to work in the morning and coming home to her home-cooked dinner. There were no highs and lows to navigate; she was at ease and she could see no reason why it would ever change.

When Jacqueline (Jackie as she was then known) was just over one, Georgina became pregnant again, and they were more than happy to receive the news when they both went to the doctor after she'd missed two periods. However, as she'd also been having quite a bit of pain, she was afraid her kidneys were playing up again.

The doctor took some time to read her notes. "Okay, Mrs. Porter, let's see if there's anything unusual going on." After a bit of poking and prodding around her back and kidney area, he moved his examination to her lower abdomen. After some serious chin rubbing and an occasional "Umm" and "Ahh," he suggested she go to the hospital for a scan "Just to be on the safe side, Mrs. Porter. If you'll just pop your things back on, I'll make a quick call."

That wasn't how Georgina thought it would go, but Alan said, "Don't worry, love. He seems on the ball."

Unfortunately, his encouragement didn't take hold. She became even more anxious when the doctor returned and said, "Well then, that's all sorted. If you pop up to the hospital, the folks in the gynecology department will give you a checkup. I'm sure it's okay, but as I said, I'd rather be safe than sorry."

They drove the twenty minutes to Winchester General Hospital and made their way to the reception desk. "Hi there," said Georgina in a small, timid voice. "I've got to see someone at the gyne department. My name's Georgina Porter."

The woman checked her computer screen. "Ah yes, here we go, Mrs. Porter. If you go down this corridor and follow the blue line, you'll find it on the right."

They arrived at the department. Georgina went to the window and smiled nervously at the nurse. "Hi. I'm Georgina Porter. Doctor Timms said I needed to come for a scan."

"Oh yes, Mrs. Porter. Would you pop your things off behind the screen in that room and wait for us? We won't be long. If you'd take a seat out here please, sir."

Fifteen minutes later, she reappeared in the waiting room. "They were checking for the location of the baby, Alan. They thought it could be an ectopic pregnancy."

"What's that, darling? What's the result? Are you okay?"

Georgina smiled and sat. "God! So many questions! But it's all okay, love. An ectopic pregnancy is when the baby is growing in a fallopian tube, not in the womb. But it's not. It's where it should be. They say the pain is the kidney. Apparently, I'm not drinking enough. Simple, huh?"

After that scare, the rest of the pregnancy went normally, and Leslie was born in April. The only sadness was that Lesley, Alan's father, had passed away in October from lung cancer and never got to see her. They were more than happy to name her after him, which so pleased Dot.

Everything proceeded well. Alan's job went from strength to strength, and when Leslie was about nine months, the family moved to Newcastle upon Tyne; Alan's company had opened a store there. The girls were the apple of Alan's eye. He was so very proud of them, showing them off to anyone who stood long enough.

Georgina went about her daily life, looking after and loving her family. The only sadness was that she hadn't had any contact from the Townsends in some time. When she got a letter from Julie Townsend in May of 1979, she was surprised and worried something was wrong. She read the letter while the girls were in the playroom at the back of the house.

> Sorry about the shortage of letters … been busy … RAF life … We so love the boys … We'd really love to adopt them … Mike's kicking up … Could you come and see us? … I'll send the boys to a friend if you want.

A telephone number was at the top of the letter. It was all she could do not to pick up the phone straightaway, but she knew she must wait for Alan. But she did call him at the store. "What's up, love? Are you okay?"

"Yes, I'm fine. What time will you be home tonight? I've had a letter from the Townsends about the boys. Can you get home early?"

"I can make it about five-ish. Is that any good? I'll get Stuart to cover for me."

The day dragged. When Alan pulled into the drive, she was so eager to make the call that she rushed to the door. Jackie was saying "Daddy, daddy!" as she charged downstairs. He swept her into his arms. "Hello, little princess. What you been up to?"

"Playing with Leslie!" She hugged his neck. By that time, Leslie had made it downstairs, and Alan swept her up and nuzzled their necks.

"Off you go and play for a minute while mummy and I have a little talk." He set the girls down, and they raced off to their toys.

"Love, let's have tea and you can show me the letter. You okay, darling?"

"I think so. Actually, not sure, love." She went to the mantle for the letter, which she gave to Alan.

It appeared from the letter that the Townsends had approached Mike first about adopting the boys as he lived near them in Telford, but they'd received an extremely negative response from him along the lines of, "If anyone has my boys, it's me!" But he'd been to the social services, and they very sensibly told him, "No way."

Julie and Simon Townsend had had the boys at that time for some six years and felt it would be good for everyone if they were allowed to make the arrangement more permanent for everyone. Both boys had settled down. David was no longer being described as "disturbed," and Anthony was a healthy, happy chap. The term "stable environment" was one used by the social services and one that would go a long way toward them agreeing to this action.

"What do you think about it, love?" asked Alan.

"I'm not sure. My heart says it's too final. They won't be my boys anymore. I'll lose any rights to them. God, that sounds awful, doesn't it? I mean lose any chance of them ever being mine again."

With tears in her eyes, Georgina found it difficult to express her feelings. The guilt she'd felt every day for the past five years came rushing forward. She'd to all intents and purposes chosen her life with Alan over one with the boys, but she knew she'd done the right thing. *Stable* was the word that kept ringing in her head. *Could I have given them a stable life? No. Certainly not for some time anyway. But I could now, couldn't I? Should I have tried harder? Oh God, what a mess.*

Alan stroked her cheek. "Is this were I have to say sorry, love? It would or could have been so very different, couldn't it? Mind you, being very selfish, it's likely we wouldn't have had our girls, would we?"

"Christ, Alan! That really helps!" She sobbed, her whole body shaking. "That sounds as if I replaced the boys with our girls. Don't you think I feel guilty enough without you coming up with that little gem?"

She paced the room, sobbing. She couldn't clear her mind of the guilt. "I need to lie down. You sort the tea out, can't you? It's all done. I just need to think."

She must have dozed off. When she came too, it was dark. The house was silent. She went to the girls' room. They were asleep. Jackie was holding fast to the corner of the duvet and tickling her nose with it in her sleep, something she'd done since she was a few months old. And

Leslie was asleep with her two middle fingers in her mouth. *Nothing normal like thumbs for these two.* Georgina smiled.

That was when it became clear what she had to do. She had done the right thing for her darling boys. The Townsends had given them what she couldn't—security. The boys deserved a normal life. Their first years had been anything but normal. *What right do I have to take that away from them after all this time?*

She started down the staircase and saw Alan sitting in the dark.

"Hi, love," he said, coming to her. "You okay?"

She put her arms around his neck and kissed him. "Yes, love, I'm fine. I needed that. The girls are sound asleep. Thanks for taking care of the tea."

"The least I could do in the circumstances. So what conclusion did you come to? Or have you?"

She led him to the sofa. "I'm going to see the Townsends and give them my support. It's the least I can do for the boys. At last they'll have a family and the security they deserve, and no one will take it away."

# CHAPTER 38

## The Boys' New Life

THREE WEEKS LATER, GEORGINA PILED the girls, nappy bags, toys, and drinks into the car and headed down the A1 toward Worcester. Georgina had told Julia she wasn't sure how she would cope with seeing the boys, so Julie had suggested that the boys have a sleepover with a friend for the night.

They stopped at a Little Chef on the way for lunch and arrived on the outskirts of Hereford about 2:30. Julie had given her a full set of directions to her house, an RAF married quarter. Julie and Simon were cooks at the barracks.

Georgina got out and unloaded the girls from their car seats. She stood Jackie on the pavement while she reached in for Leslie. She heard, "Oh hi. You must be Georgina. I'm Julie. Welcome. Come on in."

She picked up Jackie and the nappy bag and walked toward the house through a little iron gate and past the neat front garden and into the house. She put Jackie down and turned toward Georgina "Firstly, look. My mate Jen was meant to be having the boys today and overnight, but she's got a bug. I'm afraid the boys will be home later when they come in from play. I'm so sorry. I know it's going to be difficult for you."

*Difficult? You must be bloody joking!* Her first thought was to bolt. Her second was that wouldn't achieve anything. She'd come all this way to help the Townsends finish what they'd unwittingly started the day they took the boys in.

The women sat, both a bit uncomfortable at first, but the girls were a great icebreaker. They seemed happy in their surroundings and were playing with the toys Georgina had brought.

"What an angelic pair," Julie said. "Just a minute. Let me show you something." She went to an old-fashioned bureau in the corner of the room. It had a roll top that hadn't had much use judging by the creaks and groans it gave off as she opened it and exposed a jumble. "Just a sec. I know they're in here somewhere. Yes!" She made her way back to the sofa with some photo albums and loose photos.

"Spot the resemblance then?" She laughed as she passed Georgina photos of the boys from maybe Jackie's age to recently. Jackie was the spitting image of David—the same coloring and face. Julie hadn't sent any photos for the past three years or so. When Jackie was born, Georgina saw she was identical to David in skin and hair color, but she had put the rest of the similarity down to the fact they had both been big babies.

"Can I see, Mummy?" Jackie had gotten to her knees and was scrambling up Georgina's legs. "Me too, Mummy!" Leslie said though she didn't know what she was looking at. It was surreal to Georgina.

The two women got down to the reason for the visit, and they soon agreed on a course of action. Julie was tearful; it obviously meant a huge amount to her and Simon. Of course, Georgina still had mixed feelings. It was without question vital to Julie, and Georgina accepted that it was the best thing she could do for her boys, but she still dreaded the finality of it all. She was giving up her boys for good. *Will they ever forgive me? What will the girls say years from now when the subject comes up? How will they ever understand why their brothers hadn't grown up with them?*

After they'd been there just over an hour, the door burst open and in charged the boys. They screeched to a halt when they saw Georgina and the girls. But that was because they hadn't known their mum would have visitors.

Georgina didn't know what to do. Jump up and hug them? Smile and pretend she didn't know them? She looked to Julie for help.

"Hey, guys, this is Jackie and Leslie. How about taking them to the park? Is that okay with you, Georgina? Sorry, I should have asked."

"Um … yes of course, but be careful, won't you? Girls, would you like that? I saw the park as we got out the car. There's swings, and a roundabout, and a climbing frame."

"That's my favorite," shouted Anthony.

"Come on then, let's go," said David. The quartet traipsed out the door.

Julie and Georgina chatted on at length about how things had happened and what the boys had been like when they got them. Georgina was saddened at how disturbed they had been. They were both angry and had had behavioral issues. But since being settled, most of this had calmed down. Julie described how they had to find a balance between understanding and discipline, a task she admitted Simon had been a lot better at than she'd been. But their school reports showed just how well they were doing. The women became very comfortable with each other and vowed to keep in touch.

Anthony burst through the door. "Come quick! She's stuck!"

Georgina and Julie jumped up. "What do you mean? Where's she stuck? Who?"

"The baby one. She went up the climbing ladder … I told her she was too little … She got stuck at the top. Well, not stuck. Just scared I think. I told her she gotta climb down backward, but she just keeps saying 'Stuck!'"

Julie and Georgina raced out of the house, through the gate, and across the road to the little park. Georgina saw swings, a roundabout, a couple of slides, all more suitable for a two-year-old than the ladder hoop Leslie had climbed. Going up was the simple bit, but coming down backward wasn't.

"Mummy, I stuck! Get me!"

She was obviously terrified, but it was amusing in a surreal way. Jackie and David were looking at her with a mixture of amusement and annoyance at Leslie, who had interrupted their fun.

"It's okay, darling. Mummy will get you down. Don't cry, sweetheart."

It was a simple matter to lift the little one down from the ladder. In seconds, she was tucked into Georgina's shoulder and sucking on her two middle fingers as she always did when she was upset or asleep.

After the excitement, everyone headed back to the house. Little Leslie quickly dropped off to sleep. Julie suggested she be put upstairs on the big bed for a well-deserved nap.

Julie made some tea. As Georgina sat on the sofa, Anthony just plunked himself down next to her. Georgina wanted to sweep him up and give him a huge cuddle, but she knew that was out of the question. She could feel his eyes on her.

"You used to be my old mum, didn't you?"

Georgina tried to speak, but nothing came out. She looked at Julie, but she was equally dumbstruck. Gathering herself and looking at Julie, who gave her the slightest of nods, she took a deep breath. "Yes, darling, I am. How did you know?"

David, who had been sitting at the table playing with a toy, jumped out of his seat, made a snorting sound, and stormed out of the room, slamming the door behind him.

"Don't worry. I'll go up to him," said Julie. "He goes off like this often. He'll be okay."

Georgina was torn between rushing up to David and staying with Anthony, who was much more receptive to her. But she realized it wasn't her place to go to David; Julie had to do that. She no longer had the right to rush to her children's side. Julie had been their mother for the majority of their lives. Georgina had given up any right to that title the day she chose her current life. She felt guilty as she always did when she thought of the options she'd had. But as always, she convinced herself that what she'd done had been for the boys.

# CHAPTER 39

## *Do the Right Thing*

THE DRIVE BACK WAS A time of soul searching for Georgina. The girls were asleep within ten minutes of getting in the car. There was nothing to distract her. She intended to drive straight through to save waking the girls. The five-hour drive gave her ample time to go over the day's events. She'd called Alan. "Should be about ten. I'm not going to rush."

Her head was buzzing. So much to come to terms with. She'd given up the boys. Should she have tried harder to keep them? Should she have turned down Alan's proposal because he wouldn't have the boys? Should she have contacted Julie Townsend when the letters and the school reports stopped coming?

The girls continued to sleep soundly. Georgina cried half the way home, grateful for the darkness and solitude. She drove the car up the drive close to eleven.

Alan was relieved. "Thank the Lord you're home. I was trying to imagine what you must have gone through. I should have come with you. I'm so sorry, love."

"I'm fine. Let's get the girls to bed. They've slept most of the way, but they'll need a pee."

They lifted the girls from the car, still in blankets, and took them upstairs. She sat Jackie on the toilet, and bless her, she peed but didn't wake up. Alan slipped a pair of night pants on Leslie, and within fifteen minutes, they were tucked up in bed totally unaware of any of the trip.

"Do you want to talk about it, love? You seem upset."

Georgina had always accepted that he was the master of understatement, but this! "Of course I'm fucking upset, you prat! You really have no idea, do you?"

He was stunned. She very rarely swore in front of him, and she absolutely hated the F word. He heading upstairs. "No need for that, Georgy. You're tired. Why don't we talk about it in the morning."

She was grateful for the reprise. She was sure that if they'd talked then, the resentment she was feeling would all be laid at Alan's door fair or unfair.

The girls slept in until just after nine the following morning, which luckily was Sunday. Alan took them downstairs for breakfast and got them dressed. He took a cup of tea upstairs to Georgina. "I'll sort them out and come back up. We can talk then, ok?"

"Yeah, why not," groaned Georgina sullenly. She's had very little sleep. She was struggling with the finality of her decision and was trying to make sense of it.

"So go on then, talk to me," Alan asked after having sorted out the girls and set them playing in the playroom. Confrontation was not his forte, and he would far sooner just quietly walk away from a situation rather than argue about it, but he knew this had to be faced. He put his hand on Georgina to reassure her, but that had the opposite effect.

"Well let's start with the fact that I've just agreed to give up my two boys forever! You'll never ever understand how that feels. I've had to come to terms with the reason I had to do it, because you wouldn't let me have them when I asked you. Just for a minute, can you imagine how that feels? The guilt?"

Her voice had started off level, but by the end of the statement, it was vitriolic. She knew in her heart that accusing Alan was completely unfair, but she was looking for a scapegoat. In his inimitable style, Alan looked at her stunned and didn't say a word. She snorted in contempt, walked into the bathroom, and locked the door.

Submerged up to her neck in hot, bubbly water, she realized it was the beginning of the end. She believed she would resent Alan for the rest of her life. Could she put it behind her? Did she want to? Was her relationship with Alan strong enough? She didn't know the answers. It never crossed her mind that Alan might have a say in it all as well.

# CHAPTER **40**

———— ✎ ————

## *Here We Go Again*

O VER THE NEXT COUPLE OF years, things went back to normal, whatever that was. The boys were never far from Georgina's thoughts, and the guilt was with her constantly. Some of the worst times were when shopping for clothes for the girls she would see things that would be nice for the boys. Birthdays and Christmas were always bittersweet.

They left Newcastle, Alan having been headhunted again by a company in Yorkshire. They found an unusually spacious house on the outskirts of town.

When Jackie was six and a half and Leslie was four and a half, Georgina started working again. The tiny Church of England school in the mining village on the outskirts of the town was threatened with closure if the number of students fell below fifty-four, so Leslie was invited to start school two terms early.

After a great deal of discussion, Alan and Georgina decided to hire a nanny for the girls. After several interviews, they settled on Mandy, a friendly, vivacious girl, the daughter of a lovely couple who were the wardens at the church affiliated with the school. She agreed to live in Monday to Friday and work from breakfast time until either of them returned from work. Finance was always an issue; they both earned good money but also enjoyed spending it. But like most young families, they were reasonably happy and accepted the situation as the norm.

Over the previous few years, Georgina's relationship with her father had progressed, and the four of them sometimes visited Devon, staying for a long weekend. Mandy would occasionally take the girls when Alan and Georgina were able to take a holiday on their own. It all let to the outward appearance of a perfect marriage.

Her relationship with her father was unusual. She was still desperate for his approval, so she and Alan portrayed an image of affluence and togetherness. Whenever they visited, Georgina would take a gift of some sort—maybe a jumper for Margaret, or a set of wine glasses, or a tablecloth and napkins. When staying for a weekend or Christmas, she would perhaps take a large joint of meat or a turkey.

During a November visit, her dad had hesitated to agree to their coming for Christmas. He told Alan they couldn't afford to have all the family down as it was a considerable strain on their finances. Alan, being suitably embarrassed, said, "Hey, that's fine, don't worry about it" and changed the subject.

A few days later, Georgina received a letter from her father that repeated the comments he'd made to Alan. He wrote that he and Margaret struggled from week to week on a limited budget.

*What absolute twaddle!* Georgina thought. Her father ran several companies and was always planning new projects with other businesses. He was also always buying high-end cars such as Daimlers, Jaguars, and Volvos. *And this thing about the two of us bragging about our financial circumstances. Doesn't he realize that's my way of saying, "Don't worry about me. I won't be borrowing money?" Obviously not!* Unlike the other four kids who, according to her father, were nothing but constant worries either being expelled from school or running off with his checkbooks to Europe. *Stuff you. Shan't be going there again for a while.*

A year or so later, Alan was promoted, which resulted in another move, this one to Nottinghamshire. The schools in the area were reputed to be not particularly good, so Alan and Georgina (but mostly she) put the girls in a public school in Mansfield. The girls didn't like the uniforms, particularly the hats.

But it was just papering over the cracks in the marriage. Georgina finally snapped a year or so later after a very difficult period of rows and constant bickering between the two. Not knowing what else to do, she packed her and the girls' stuff and went to her father's after a very humiliating phone call to him asking if they could come. He was so sympathetic that no one would have known they hadn't spoken in nine months.

That weekend was Easter, and so the girls were on holiday. Her father didn't know what to say, but Margaret was an absolute brick. She came into Georgina's room early on a Saturday and said in her soft, voice, "Come on then, dear. Tell me about the problems. That's if you want to of course."

Georgina poured out her guilt, resentment, anger, sadness, and most of all her fear of it going wrong again. They talked for hours and then again when her dad drove them to the beach and took the girls to play with the dogs.

At the end of the weekend, Georgina had come to a decision. She didn't want to go back to what she'd left; she wanted a good marriage. She knew the breakdown was mostly her fault. She resented Alan and had used every excuse to throw it back at him.

She went home with the girls after phoning Alan. She asked him if he was prepared to give it another go, and he had said, "Of course. That's all I want."

She determined to get the negative stuff out of her mind; she started to see a psychotherapist weekly. He encouraged her to talk about her feelings, going back to Germany, and especially about her childhood. He specialized in regression therapy; during some visits, that reduced her to floods of tears as she confronted every subconscious thought.

These visits had two results. The first was that she shed almost four stone. She was the lightest she'd been since having David. She was wearing a size twelve, down from an eighteen, and my, did she feel good! The second was that she became more confident, content, and willing to forgive. Or so she thought.

In November, once again came the all-too-familiar call to Alan's place of work.

"Hey Alan, my man, how's it going up there?" asked Steve, a previous manager of his who had left Savacentre several years earlier. "I need you, pal. I'm in Plymouth and could really do with a store manager down here. How's the job going? Ready for a change yet? I heard you and George were, um, having a few issues?"

"Christ!" Alan laughed. "Is nothing sacred?"

"You can run but you can't hide, not from me anyway! Come down. Let's work out a package that'll tempt you."

Alan got home that night around eight. The girls were already in bed, and Georgina was watching TV. "Hi, love. You okay?"

She smiled. "Hi to you too. Have you eaten?"

"I had something at Trowell. I had a call today from Steve. He's got a job going down in Plymouth. What do you think? It could be good for us, you know, a new start?"

And so they went down to Plymouth the next week, and as Steve had promised, it was a good deal. He's arranged a great package for Alan with a company house until they found something to buy. They put their house on the market and moved the first week of the new year.

Georgina, who had been working for a bank, put in for a transfer from the Midlands region to the southwest, but there was nothing available immediately, so she continued with the same team, traveling up the motorway on a Monday, staying in a hotel initially in Nottingham, and then when the next project came up in Leicester. They needed a new nanny as Mandy wouldn't move that far from home.

After many interviews, they found Trisha, a pretty, Plymouth girl who was happy to do the Mondays to Fridays. The girls took to her straight away, which eased Georgina's conscience as she was having to stay away for the whole week.

In October, they had a new audit to do in Luton, but she was assured at the end of this one she could transfer to the southwest. She enjoyed the freedom of the hotel life because she didn't have to play at making the relationship work with Alan, but she missed the girls terribly. She spoke to them every night and made sure the weekends were as full as she could possibly make them—the zoo or a day on the beach in Polperro. They seemed not to notice the atmosphere between her and Alan.

On the weekend prior to the start of the Luton job, they had been out on the moors. They'd had Sunday lunch at the Two Bridges Hotel, one of their favorites, a family-run, thatched-roofed property with fabulous food. They arrived home midafternoon. Georgina and Alan cleaned the two cars while the girls watched TV. It was a pleasant autumn day, which made the chore more palatable.

Georgina had to drive up to Luton on Monday, and Alan was heading to Manchester, so they both had long drives ahead of them. Georgina wanted to get away by 6:30, so she got up at 5:30. She crept into the girls' room and kissed them. "Bye, darlings, I love you very much. See you Friday." She met Trish at the bottom of the stairs. "They're still soundo. Alan doesn't have to leave until about seven-thirty, so have a coffee. Thanks for coming in early."

"No problem, Georgina."

Georgina picked up her case and suit bag and headed to the door. "Could you pass me my keys please, love?" she asked Alan.

"Where are they then? Not on the hook."

"They must be! I would have hung them up when I came in yesterday."

All three hunted for the keys for the next twenty minutes. Georgina was becoming frustrated. The thought of being late made her feel sick.

"Panic over," Alan called out. "You left them on the wall when you were out there yesterday. Good job it didn't get nicked!"

"Brilliant! Thanks."

Alan picked up her bags and walked down the steps. He opened the boot of the Ford Sierra and put the cases in. She got into the driver's seat and was about to shut the door when he leaned across her and fastened her seatbelt. "Calm down for God's sake. You're okay for time. Just take it steady."

"Yeah, thanks love. I'll call tonight. You're back home tomorrow aren't you?"

"Yes. I'll be leaving about four, so I'll be back with the girls before bedtime."

"Drive carefully, chat later, yeah?"

He kissed her cheek. "You too, love."

She headed out onto the A38. She'd calculated it would take about four and a half hours, so she'd make the midday meeting. It was still dark as she stopped for petrol about ten miles into the journey.

"You're out and about early, love," said the chubby guy behind the counter. "That's £44.38 please."

"Yeah, too early for me. Thanks."

She took her card and headed to her car.

# CHAPTER 41

## The Accident

THE EVENTS OF THE NEXT five days are totally unknown to Georgina, and so this account can only be as told to her later.

She rejoined the A38 at Ivybridge. She apparently built her speed back up to about seventy miles per hour. This was verified by a couple driving toward Exeter. They told the police that she had overtaken them on the hill through Rattery. She was several hundred yards in front of them when they saw her car take off and literally fly through the air. What had actually happened was that as she approached the bend, she hit full on a cow that had broken through the fence and wandered onto the road.

The report from the fire brigade who had to cut her out of the mangled vehicle was that just prior to impact, she must have pushed so hard on the brake that she broke the seat back, putting her in a prone position. They said this had saved her life because as the car catapulted front over back, front over back, finally coming to rest eighty feet into the field, she'd effectively become a sandwich between the floor and the roof of the car, which had compressed her.

The cow, all one point three tons of it, had been split in two. One half crashed through the sunroof, and the other penetrated the car, pushing the engine into the passenger floor. It took the firefighters close to an hour to free her unconscious body from the mangled wreckage. An ambulance rushed her to the nearest hospital, in Torquay, about twenty miles away.

The irony was that Alan was held up in the traffic jam that had built up due to the rubberneckers straining to see some blood and gore. *Sad sods*, he thought as he continued on to Manchester, not realizing Georgina was involved.

Four hours later, he arrived in Manchester. Chris rushed to him. "For Christ's sake, Alan! What are you doing here?"

"What the hell's the matter with you, Chris? You look like shite!"

"You don't know, do you? Bloody hell, boy. You need to get back to Torquay. Georgina's had a terrible accident. She's in the ICU!"

"What? Don't understand … She left just before … Oh my God!" He realized he'd driven past his wife being cut out of the car. He felt sick. Chris grabbed his arm.

"Get this guy a drink, someone! Now!"

Alan was quickly back on the M6, heading back the way he'd come. Four hours of terrifying thoughts and fearing the worst. He arrived at Torbay hospital absolutely shattered. He wasn't sure how he'd be able to cope with whatever was waiting for him. Just as he was about to enter, the door opened and out came a staff nurse who had just checked Georgina's vital signs.

"Mr. Porter, is it? Let's go into the office. I'll bring you up to speed."

Alan looked toward Georgina but allowed himself to be steered away.

The nurse gesturing to the chair to the side of her desk. Alan sank into it with emotions he hadn't felt before.

"So how is she? Will she be ok? What's—"

"Mr. Porter, let me get you a cup of tea. You look absolutely shattered." She put her head out the office door to catch the attention of a nurse. She closed the door and sat. "Mr. Porter, we've evaluated the injuries, and while there's quite a bit of work needs doing, she not in any danger. She's unconscious, but we've induced that. She needs to be kept absolutely still until we can operate. But we need your consent."

"What do you need to operate on? I need to see my wife now!"

"Mr. Porter, of course you can see her, but we need to get the OR prepped. Can we assume we've got your consent?"

"To do what? What damage is there?"

"She's suffered serious impact on the top right quartile of her body—her face, shoulder, arm, and right upper torso. She needs urgently an operation to put right the damage to her eye, cheekbone, and jaw. We think there could be damage to her airways, hence the urgency. She also needs work on her shoulder, arm, and spine, but I promise those bits aren't as bad as it sounds. But please sign the release so we can get started. The longer it's left, the more damage could happen."

He was in a haze but knew he had to agree. He hoped they had gotten it right.

"I'll sign, but I need to see her. Please!"

The release form signed and the OR notified Georgina was to be prepped straightaway, the nurse stood and motioned to Alan to follow her. "Don't be concerned about the tubes and stuff. It's just to keep her quiet and still."

Alan entered the room and stopped in his tracks. Georgina lay on the bed wired up to several machines, one of which was helping her breathe. Her face and head were bandaged. He saw bloodstains seeping through the dressing. Her right shoulder was encased in a plastic frame. She was motionless and looked so fragile.

"Mr. Porter, we need to prep her for the op. We need to get her down in about twenty minutes. You can stay, but I suggest you go home and try to get some rest. You look absolutely whacked. She's going to be out until at least midday tomorrow, and even then, we may have to sedate her to immobilize her."

Alan kissed Georgina's forehead. "Be well, darling. I love you."

He drove home in turmoil. *What shall I tell the girls? Should I call her father?*

Alan tried to make the following morning as normal as he could. He'd tried to explain to the girls that Mummy had had a bit of an accident and that they wouldn't have to go to school because they were going to see her in the hospital. He really wasn't sure what was best, but he'd called the hospital and had been told it would do Georgina good to hear the girls. She was still unconscious but in a natural sleep.

Alan had called her father the previous evening. They'd arranged to meet at the hospital restaurant at noon. Once the girls were dressed, they set off for Torquay. They arrived at the restaurant a few minutes ahead of time, and Alan ordered a drink for himself and the girls. He was struggling to maintain the appearance of normality; he knew he had to. Only the Lord knew what they were going to see.

Georgina's father appeared at the door. Alan stood. "Stephen! Thank you for coming. I … wasn't sure."

"But of course I'd come," Stephen said, shaking Alan's hand. "There's the little ones. Hello, you two. You've got a drink, I see. What about a sticky bun? What do you think, Daddy?"

Alan was glad to see the girls happy at the thought of a sticky bun. "Go on then. Thanks, Stephen."

The four eventually made their way to the musculoskeletal ward, where Georgina had been taken after the operation. Alan approached a nurse. "I'm Alan Porter. How's my wife?"

"Oh yes, Mr. Porter. You can go on in. She hasn't come round yet, but that doesn't mean anything. She's better off as she is for a while."

Alan approached the side ward with trepidation. He was glad Stephen had waited with the girls until he got there. He took the girls by the hand. "Look, girls, Mummy's still asleep. The doctor saw her last night, and they've made her comfortable. She's having a really big sleep. The nurse says she'll be asleep for quite a long while. But you mustn't worry about how she looks. There's a lot of tubes and stuff, but it's just to make her more comfortable, okay?"

The four walked into the room. Stephen gasped. The two girls started to cry. Georgina's head and face were swathed in bandages with a metal frame protruding from them. Her shoulder and arm were supported in a complete upper-body plaster cast.

She stayed that way for another four days, and Alan and the girls made the journey to see her every day. The girls chatted to their mum regardless of the fact she was sleeping. That made things more normal for Alan.

On the fifth day, she slowly came out of the coma. She opened her eyes and squinted due to the lights. She saw Alan and her girls. She cried.

The conversation was mostly between the girls and Alan; Georgina was popping in and out of consciousness due to the sedation. The days and nights passed in a haze.

Many days later, she was allowed home under the care of Mount Gould hospital in Plymouth.

Christmas came and went. Alan's mum came to visit and help with the cooking and so on. It was a distraction for the girls; it took some pressure off Alan.

As the weeks past, Georgina got stronger, became more mobile, and started getting involved in the day-to-day activities. Trisha came in, but she helped Georgina more than looked after the girls. They would go for a walk most days, which helped Georgina gain strength and confidence.

The HR director at the bank drove down from London to visit and assured Georgina they'd continue to pay her until she was signed off as fit to work again. That was a huge relief as her wages were more than 60 percent of their income.

Her father and Margaret visited a few times, as did Alan's mum, Dot. She insisted on doing the housework and said there was no need for the nanny. Alan assured her that Trisha gave a sense of normality to the girls, so Dot agreed to take care of Georgina.

While Georgina was recovering, she became aware of a difference in her mental state. While Alan had been very attentive and was great with the girls, she felt a distance had formed between them. She couldn't wait to get back to work.

# CHAPTER 42

## *Second Best?*

GEORGINA WAS DECLARED FIT TO return to work at the end of January and was finally able to transfer jobs within the bank. She was set to meet her new audit team on the thirteenth of February. The girls were settled in their schools, so all seemed fine.

She had to get back up to the Bristol branch office on the Monday morning, and as she didn't as yet have another company car, it had been arranged that one of her fellow workers would drive her. Alan was to drive her to Newton Abbot, where they would meet up with Nick, a guy who lived just outside town.

She started on the journey with considerable trepidation especially as she and Alan passed the site of the accident for the first time since, but she controlled herself and settled down. She changed cars, and after about an hour and a half, they pulled into the car park at 9:45, fifteen minutes early.

Leaving Nick to sort out some issue he had at reception, she took the elevator to the fourth floor and entered the meeting room, where four or five people were chatting and drinking coffee.

"Well hello there!" sang out one of them. "You must be Georgina. We've heard all about you. I'm Roz, and that's Jude, Nathan, Peter, and Simon." They all smiled and greeted her with outstretched hands.

"That's Jane coming in behind you, and there's Mike. And of course you've met Nick."

They had obviously been working together for a while as there was a pleasant air of familiarity in the room.

"Hello. Nice to meet you all. Is this the whole team?"

"There's three more joining us on-site, Taunton, but of course you know that," said Jude, a tall, willowy girl about thirty who was wearing huge red glasses.

"Isn't that where you live, Roz?" she asked.

"Yeah," she replied. "Bloody handy, actually. I live only about twelve miles from the hotel. But I'll be staying just in case you were worried, Georgina. We hear you like us all to stay."

The team had a busy few weeks, but they completed the project on time and to the client's satisfaction. Georgina had struggled at first; she got tired quickly, having spent the past five months with nothing to keep her awake but daytime TV. Working for twelve hours a day was a huge challenge, but she met it head-on. She wouldn't allow herself to do anything else.

The next location was to be Exeter. Two of the team were being seconded to another group working in the Midlands, so there were to be two new members joining Georgina's team. Their hotel was just off the M5 motorway at Exeter. While it was only thirty miles from home, Georgina wanted the team to stick together; there was so much after-hours work to do, and she wanted to keep her team's spirit up especially during the fractious times that arose.

The project intro meeting was to be held at the modern hotel on the outskirts of the town, their home for seven weeks. She checked out the bar and the restaurant prior to the team arriving and had a twinge of concern. The restaurant had only around sixty covers to the side of the bar. The guys had the habit of becoming a bit boisterous after work, and she could see they would have to tone down their antics. But the fact that the rooms were all ground floor around the grounds, she thought she could encourage them to let off steam in their rooms.

The meeting was due to start at 6:00 p.m. She made her way to the conference room, a small room with a huge table, making it difficult for anyone to get out easily. *Nothing like a captive audience!*

At 5:40, Roz arrived, followed closely by Simon and Nathan. Georgina had concerns about the amount of time those two guys spent together. While Nathan was footloose and fancy free, Simon was engaged to a strange, needy girl who constantly called him at the office as well as on his mobile. There were huge security issues there, thought Georgina. If Nathan was leading him astray, she could see it landing on her desk with the fiancée blaming her for letting him off his lead. It was sometimes like having kids. "You've had enough to drink" and "You had a really late night last night," she'd say to one or the other on occasion, but the last thing she wanted to be was an agony aunt.

It was time for the meeting to start. The team had arrived, including the two new members. One, Mervin, was a transferee from the north, and the other, Peter, was new to the job. He had a finance background but hadn't done auditing before. It was quite a stressful environment. She hoped he was up to it. Her results depended on a strong team, and she couldn't afford to carry anyone even if it was his or her first placement.

Georgina had one thing in her favor; she'd gained the reputation of being a great "buddy" leader. She'd make sure they all succeeded; apart from anything else, all their bonuses depended on it.

Introductions made, she got down to the project requirements, any issues anyone had, and the time lines. Afterward, they adjourned to the restaurant. A pleasant evening followed. The two new guys were fitting in well and were involved in the conversations.

After the meal, Georgina retired to the office to set up some files. She knew the team would be drinking well into the night, but she had too much to do and didn't want to be less than 100 percent in the morning.

The team was working together well, but Peter seemed to have some personal issues. He would often take calls as they were about to go to dinner. He would excuse himself and return in a different frame of mind. Quite often, he didn't join the conversation and would make excuses and head off to bed early. A couple of times, he'd asked Georgina if he could go home, about forty minutes away. She let him know she wasn't happy about it, but she felt it was important to him, so she agreed. He would return the following day and after a bit of a pep talk get to grips with the job.

Georgina liked the guy. He had a superb sense of humor and was obviously very bright. When joining the bank, part of the interview process was an IQ test, and she wasn't surprised to see he had scored 156, which put him at MENSA level. He would often return to the office after dinner rather than drink with the others. Peter and Georgina would do the work they needed to but also chat. They were forming a bond that was maybe stronger than just casual colleagues.

Once they'd finished their work, they would often talk about anything and everything. It would start as opinions on the news of the day, or bank protocols, or popular movies. But it soon became more personal. Peter opened up about his soon-to-be ex and his two teenage sons. Georgina talked about her accident and the change in her perception of what a good marriage should be.

The more they talked, the more obvious it was becoming to her that she needed to reevaluate her situation. It was almost as if the most important thing in her mind was *Don't accept second best.* Was her marriage second best? Alan was a solid, loyal guy she didn't want to hurt, but she realized she was hurting him by the way she was treating him. And a large part of her despised herself. She was coming to the conclusion that she'd been given a second chance. She knew she should never have made it out of that accident, and she felt it was almost her duty to make the most of the rest of her life.

She didn't think of Peter as anything but a great confidant, something she hadn't had for years, and she was sure he felt the same. But she felt his friendship might give her the strength to take action that would maybe become inevitable.

They were initially able to keep their friendship from the rest of the team. They would often meet for lunch or an evening meal if the others had decided to go into town. On occasion, Georgina would help him on an aspect of the audit that he was finding difficult, and that brought them closer. They began to leave as late as possible on Fridays and would return to the hotel on Sunday evening; that gave them time to shed the negativities of the weekend and enjoy a friendly evening with no chance of any of the team coming in.

The Exeter audit was drawing to a close on time and on budget. They were looking forward to the next job, in Cornwall, a county they both loved.

# CHAPTER 43

# *Friendships at Work*

THE NEXT JOB WAS GOING to be a twelve-week audit in two locations. The first five weeks were to be in Redruth, and the following seven weeks would be in Falmouth.

Georgina drove to Redruth on a Sunday, arriving late in the afternoon. It had been a lovely drive—brilliant sunshine and spring flowers. She had spoken to Peter the previous Friday. They had agreed to spend the evening together once she had set up the office.

The hotel was the biggest in the area; it had an indoor pool, gym, and a restaurant with a great reputation. The manager showed her the two adjoining rooms that had been allocated to them for the office.

"This is brilliant! We don't usually get such a setup," she told Brenda, the manager. "Can't thank you enough."

She brought in the office equipment from the car with the help of the young chap behind reception and made the two rooms work-friendly. They had phone lines, tables, fax machines, printers, computer lines, and coffee machines in both rooms.

After setting up, she made her way to her room conveniently just down the corridor. The majority of the team rooms were on the first floor, so that gave her and them a bit of distance, a good thing.

She showered. She looked forward to a pleasant, stress-free evening with Peter. She dressed in a very feminine dress of pale-green wool she'd bought that weekend and donned a pretty scarf. She made her way to the bar and ordered a gin and tonic. The bar staff were happy to make small talk. She was grateful for that; she needed the staff on her side if she ever needed special favors, which was always the case.

She was surprised at how much she was looking forward to seeing Peter. The weekend at home had been quite uncomfortable; she realized she was finding unwarranted fault with everything Alan was doing. It was as if she needed a reason to leave home early.

"Hi there, Georgy. Started without me I see," said Peter, who was smiling. "Missed you," he said softly and kissed her lightly on the cheek.

"Me too," she murmured, not pulling away. He put his arm on her shoulder. "I'll take this lot to my room and be right back. Do you know what room I'm in?"

"Okay, love. You're on the first floor with the others. I didn't move you. Don't want to make it too obvious, do we? Shall I get a table?"

"Sounds great. See you in a bit." He touched her cheek and headed to the reception desk. She was surprised at the strength of feeling. It was obviously not just her.

They enjoyed an intimate, enjoyable evening with good food, a delicious bottle of Chardonnay, and stimulating conversation. They finished the evening with a glass of port at the bar and took leave of each other.

Georgina undressed while glancing at the TV. Having attended to her bathroom needs, she slipped between the crisp sheets and found herself thinking about the evening. She and Peter were able to talk about anything. There was a synergy to their understanding of many of the subjects they covered whether news, work, or members of the team. They were able to discuss their personal relationships while not resorting to blaming Alan or Sandra, Peter's wife.

His openness was refreshing and stimulating. He had a quiet but intense intellect she wasn't used to, and she found that a challenge. He had an unusual depth to his emotions. Alan didn't enjoy confrontation;

if a conversation became uncomfortable, he would retreat to whatever was available—a paper or the TV. She saw in Peter a different approach. He would question opposing attitudes with an intense desire for understanding, which unfortunately led him and Sandra to argue. She was so concerned about what others were saying about her and Peter that she would fabricate lies to hide the financial difficulties they had been facing for the past year.

Georgina felt that Peter was becoming more than a colleague. This was not an easy realization for her on two fronts. First, such a relationship in a close-knit team situation could only lead to problems and was severely frowned upon by the bank. Second, she didn't want to have an affair; she wanted to make any decisions regarding her future without any other influences. But this wasn't going to be easy with her mounting feelings for Peter.

In the following weeks, the team came together as usual and the audit was running smoothly. They were due to leave Redruth in the next two weeks; the windup kept Georgina in the office late most evenings. She had to collate results and attribute these to specific members of the team.

She would return to Alan and the girls late on Friday evenings after having spent as much time as possible with Peter. Their relationship had developed further; he was coming to her room after the others had retired. Their lovemaking was amazing! So intense and passionate and yet tender and considerate. They enjoyed exploring each other with a frenetic enthusiasm as if they were in the throes of a first love. Peter always put her needs before his, which for the first time in her life resulted in multiple orgasms. She was in heaven.

She found herself shopping for new matching underwear, something she hadn't done for years. She paid more attention to her appearance more than usual and was wallowing in the joy of Peter's commitment to her. He paid her constant compliments; he was always attentive, caring, considerate and above all, romantic. He would leave her notes and post-its and send her flowers … And he had no compunction in affirming his feeling when with the rest of the team, who, by then were aware they were an item.

Georgina was very careful not to treat Peter any differently from the other team members; maybe she overcompensated by giving him a harder time than she did the others. He took it all in his stride, sometimes teasing her when they were in bed that she was a tyrant.

Things finally came to a head at home. She and Alan had sat down over the weekend and talked about the "problem." They both reluctantly accepted that it had gone past papering over the cracks; neither wanted that. She didn't think that what Peter and she had found had contributed in any way to her decision; it had made her realize how much she missed the closeness they used to have. The accident had been the catalyst that drove her to make the best of her life.

The conversation hadn't been easy, but true to form, Alan didn't put up an argument. He nodded and grunted as she did the hard work. One thing they agreed on was the girls, who had settled into the school very well and had many friends. They were very fond of Trisha.

She and Alan discussed what was best for the girls. If they came to live with her, she'd have to give up her job and its £40,000 salary and rent or buy a place big enough for them and a live-in nanny. But Trisha wouldn't move to Bristol.

Eventually, Georgina and Alan decided it would be kindest and more sensible to not uproot the girls. They should stay at the same school. Trisha was happy to stay on, and Alan was able to work his hours to suit him to an extent. Georgina told him she didn't want money from him as she earned considerably more; she would instead pay Trisha. He seemed to accept the inevitable. When she suggested they explained it to the girls, he just nodded and said, "Okay then. Up to you."

She didn't mention her feelings for Peter; she was adamant he wasn't the reason for her splitting up with Alan; it was more a consequence. And she didn't want to hurt Alan more than necessary.

They decided she would move out at the end of the Falmouth leg of the audit, about six weeks from then. If necessary, she'd live in a hotel until finding a place.

# CHAPTER 44

## Can't Help Myself

PETER'S SITUATION WASN'T QUITE AS diplomatically solved. He had been trying for some time (way before joining the bank) to extricate himself from his marriage, but Sandra was very good at playing the emotional blackmail card and would throw the two boys at him whenever he got to the stage of leaving. She wouldn't accept that her actions had driven Peter to the place he was.

She wanted to live the glamorous lifestyle their friends were living but hadn't worked out that they couldn't afford it. Peter had tried to keep up with the holidays, clothes, and parties but finally admitted defeat. Drowning in a mass of debt, he had declared bankruptcy, but she still couldn't understand why she couldn't have the finer things in life. And she had the boys thinking the same way. They constantly demanded the latest tech toys and gadgets; she would back up their requests, making Peter the baddy though he was trying to be the voice of reason by saying no to most such requests.

When it was time for Georgina to set off to Cornwall, she left the house with a heavy heart, having said a sad and emotional good-bye to the girls and Alan. While she was glad it was out in the open, she was aware this was the beginning of the end of her second marriage. *Am I doing the right thing for the girls?* While she would see them almost as much, she was leaving them with Alan. The only difference was that he doted on the girls, and they were certainly both Daddy's girls.

Once she had gotten away from the house, she started to cry, gently at first but increasing to uncontrollable sobbing. *Bloody history repeating itself.* She wondered why she couldn't be content with what she had rather than searching for something supposedly better. But back came the thought that she's had since coming out of the terrible accident—she'd been given a second chance at life. She felt duty bound to make the most of the opportunity. *But isn't that terribly selfish? Christ!*

What a decision. She just couldn't stay. She wasn't doing Alan or the girls any favors. The girls were constantly hearing their parents' rows and bitter comments and would slide off up to their bedrooms when they started up.

By the time she got to Liskeard, she felt so alone and desperate to talk to Peter. He offered what she needed at that time—a diversion, a place to hide, to pretend none of it mattered.

The road sign for Redruth was very welcome. *Please make him be there!* She turned into the car park and saw Peter's car. *Thank God.* She got out and opened the back to retrieve her things.

"Well hello there, you fascinating creature" came the familiar, friendly voice she had been longing to hear. "You made good time."

They hugged. Georgina desperately tried to hide her tears. "There wasn't much traffic. What time did you get down?"

Their small talk kept things almost impersonal. She checked in, and they settled her into her room. The hotel had been happy to let her have the same room each week, which made things simpler; she could leave a suit bag there over the weekends.

The plan was to finish that part of the project by Wednesday and go to Falmouth. That would give the team a chance to settle in to the office so they could hit the ground running on Monday morning.

Georgina suggested to Peter they meet in the bar at seven. She sorted out her room and got her papers in order for the morning meeting. She freshened up and slipped on her jeans and a new cashmere sweater. Running a brush through her titian-red hair, she smiled at herself in the mirror. She left her room and headed to the bar with a distinct bounce in her step. Some of the old hotel had been recently refurbished, but they'd very sensibly left the bar and the restaurant in their original elegant style.

She saw Peter perched on a stool caressing what looked like a large gin and tonic. There was another on the bar that he offered her. He had a huge smile. "Hi, Bave." That was his nickname for her. She had no idea where it had come from, but she enjoyed the implied intimacy.

"All done. I got some of the Wednesday close-down started, so we should be able to get on the way by lunchtime. How's your file looking?"

"Might need a bit of help on Tuesday winding up. You up for a late night?"

There was laughter in his voice but also some underlying emotion.

"What *are* you suggesting, sir? That sounds like a proposition to me! But I reckon I could fit you in."

The conversation was typical of their relationship—innuendo, satirical humor, and double entendres that were a mix of good humor, intellectual stimulation, and sexiness.

After enjoying the usual glass of port after the meal, they made their way to Georgina's room, and they continued to enjoy each other's company in the usual way.

They awoke around 6:00. Peter headed for the shower while Georgina enjoyed the coffee he'd made. She switched on the TV and propped herself up in bed to watch the news. The shower stopped. He emerged from the bathroom wrapped in a towel that really didn't do a great job in the modesty stakes.

They heard a loud banging on the door.

"Come on, love. Open there door. I've got the papers you want signed."

*Bloody hell! Its Alan!* mouthed Georgina.

If it wasn't so serious, it would have been comical. Peter was stunned. Georgina was madly gesturing to him to scoop up his clothes and get back in the bathroom. He did and closed the door.

Georgina pulled on her dressing gown and went to the door. "What the hell are you doing here?"

She had to step to one side as Alan pushed his way in. "You wanted these divorce papers signed, but as you made it seem so important, I wondered why you'd left them behind. You were obviously keen on getting back to work."

He put the envelope on the dressing table. "You can come out now, Peter."

Under the chair by the dressing table were Peter's size-eleven shoes.

Peter opened the door, still almost wrapped in the towel. "Alan, mate, sorry. We didn't mean it to work out this way."

"You got what you wanted. She's all yours. You're welcome."

Alan left. Peter and Georgina were painfully aware of what they'd done to Alan. Neither of them wanted to hurt him; neither had set out to let their feelings become more than friendship. It had just happened.

"I'll … um … head to my room," said Peter. Georgina was crying quietly. He dressed and slipped on the offending shoes. "I think you need some time alone."

"Oh God! What? Oh yes. See you in a bit."

He kissed her gently on top of her head, caressed her cheek, and left.

# CHAPTER 45

*A Great Result*

THE NEXT FEW DAYS WERE extremely busy. Georgina and Peter kept their distance, just meeting up in the office or in the restaurant with the rest of the team.

On Tuesday evening, the whole team met at the restaurant in an exuberant mood due to their success with the audit. Georgina left the party early with a glass of white she planned to finish in her room.

She slipped off her clothes, showered, donned a dressing gown, and watched some TV. She was still wired from the evening, and she wasn't sure how to play the situation with Peter. She didn't know how he felt because they had spent no time alone since Monday morning. She hoped to speak with him when they got to Falmouth.

She sipped the wine as she surfed the channels and had started to unwind when she heard a knock. It startled her at first, but then she realized it could only be him.

"Hang on a min," she called out. She climbed off the bed, pulling her gown together, and looked through the peephole. It was Peter.

"Hello, you. Had enough of the youthful exuberance then?" she asked smiling.

He came in and closed the door. In seconds, they were in each other's arms as if they hadn't seen each other for weeks. "My God, I've missed you," he said, nuzzling her neck. "It's been bloody awful trying to keep my hands off you."

"You can say that again," she said, giggling.

The talked until the early hours about the event earlier in the week and concluded there was nothing to do but put it away until the weekend. There was Falmouth to think of, and that would be a great distraction.

Spring had come early; it had been beautifully sunny for the past week or so. She was looking forward to the drive to Cornwall as it wasn't an area she knew at all. Pictures of the hotel looked fabulous; it was right on the beach at Gyllyngvase and offered a gym, spa, and balconies.

The team breakfasted together and started off almost in a convoy about 9:30. Georgina looked over to Peter and said mysteriously, "As planned then."

He smiled and nodded.

"Oh do behave you two," moaned Jude.

"That's enough from you, madam," Georgina said with a laugh.

She left about half an hour later and headed down the A38. She passed the turnoff to Teignmouth and smiled. She would have a talk with her father but thought that could wait. She passed through Ashburton and approached the site of her accident several months earlier. She noticed the fence was still broken. Seeing it gave her a sick feeling and raised the hairs on the back of her neck.

It took her close to an hour to get to the Little Chef off the Carkeel roundabout west of Plymouth. She saw Peter sitting in a window seat sipping coffee. They chatted over coffee and set off in their respective cars toward Truro and Falmouth. En route, he called her and said he would stop at a supermarket so they wouldn't arrive together.

There wasn't too much traffic on the road, so they made good time and arrived at the hotel just after 2:00 and 2:30 respectively. The rest of the team were there waiting for her to allocate the rooms.

"What kept you, boss? As if we didn't know," Roz said with mock frustration in her tone.

"What's your problem? We haven't got the office until three, and you can't book in until four," Georgina said with a laugh.

"No, but we could have charged drinks to your room," said the lad of the team, Nathan, pretending to hide behind Simon. "That's what Simon suggested."

"Nathan, at times, you have good ideas, but trust me, that ain't one."

She always enjoyed the banter between the members of her team. They had gelled over the previous audit, and the result had been a profitable, successful project finished on time. With that and the partial result from Redruth, she was happy to let them have a bit of fun for a day or so. They would see it as a perk and would be grateful, but they hadn't yet seen the workload for the next four weeks, which would require long hours.

In the snazzy bar, she ordered a round of drinks for everyone and suggested they sit on the patio as it was a beautiful afternoon. There would be plenty of time for them to be shut up in the office. The guys chatted for the next hour or so while Georgina went to reception and made friends with the girls behind the desk. She wanted to make sure her staff could get at least soup and sandwiches late at night if the restaurant was closed. She also wanted to get some sort of discount on the team's usually big bar bills. Pete, the manager, was obliging on that score.

"How about I make it easier for you? Ten percent off all drinks? As long as they don't try it with the wine. That's all charged to the restaurant."

"Peter, you're a gem. How do we work it?"

"I'll give each of you one of our club cards. The bar staff will recognize them and take it off each round they buy. That'll be easier than them running tabs and such."

Georgina thought Pete was a godsend. She got the impression he was gay, and she made a mental note to make sure the team didn't act inappropriately.

She made her way to the patio. "Hey chaps, how's it going? Here are the keys. We're getting ten percent off the bar bills."

"Good work, boss. Takes the sting out of hotel charges I suppose. They've just charged me four pounds ninety for a beer!"

"The price you pay for good digs I'm afraid, Simon. Listen, guys. The manager's name is Pete, and he's with us. Don't take the piss, though, please! Oh, and he's gay, so no daft antics."

She left them and headed toward the office. She needed it set up the way she wanted it, and so after half an hour or so, having moved some of the desks and file racks to make it easier for the guys to work together, she headed to her room. A whole wall of it was floor-to-ceiling, wall-to-wall glass overlooking the beach, and she had a sun-drenched balcony as well, a piece of heaven. The room faced west, so she knew she would struggle with the temptation to go there during the day. It was idyllic. Never one to miss an opportunity to grab some sun, she shed her business suit and donned a T-shirt and skirt. *All I need now is a glass of wine.*

# CHAPTER 46

# A Hint of Things to Come

THE SETTING SUN CAST A reddish hue on the sea. It was approaching 5:30 and beginning to cool. A knock brought Georgina out of her reverie. She rose from the patio lounger and shivered a little, realizing she'd become cold. Looking at her watch, she saw she had been asleep for the best part of an hour.

She opened the door. A smiling Peter entered the room, kissed her lightly on the cheek, and set down a bottle of Chardonnay and glasses. "I thought I'd leave you for a while. You looked as if you needed a bit of downtime."

"Hi love, and thanks. I sat on the balcony and fell asleep in the sun."

"I can tell. Your nose has caught the sun."

He took out the corkscrew he seemed to always carry.

"I do hope that's chilled," Georgina said with a laugh.

"Would I dare? Of course. It's from the bar."

Georgina took the glass he offered and sank into the soft sofa. "So what are the others up to? Behaving themselves?" She was concerned that as they'd been there since around midday, they had consumed a fair amount of alcohol, and it was only their first night there.

"They were talking about dinner around seven-thirty. Roz is hammered, and Simon's being daft, but I don't think they've had too much," he said, seeming to anticipate her concerns. "I think they slowed down by going out on the patio. They were all on beer, I think."

She showered and changed clothes. They joined the team in the restaurant. Peter had been right about their levels of intoxication. Roz, still on beer, was unsteady on her feet. Georgina whispered to her, "I reckon that's enough, don't you? Are you up for the meal, or do you want to give it a miss? You have a heavy day tomorrow."

She knew from experience that the power of suggestion worked well with Roz in these situations and that she'd take the hint. A couple of minutes later, Roz stood unsteadily and announced in a slurred voice, "That's me done. I'm going to bed." No one was surprised.

After that, the meal went off without a hitch and the evening ended quite early after Georgina belabored the point about the following day being a bitch.

But as she had hoped, the project went off without a hitch. Everyone did a good job, and the hotel was more than considerate, driven, Georgina believed, by Pete the manager.

She and Peter were able to spend a lot of quiet time together. They enjoyed a couple of evenings a week exploring restaurants in the area. One evening, they decided to explore Newquay, a town with two lives. In the winter, the locals just went about their business but weren't very profitable because so many of the shops and bars were geared toward tourists. But from Easter on, the population quadrupled; it was a surfers' paradise and offered a huge amount of hen and stag weekends. Almost every house seemed to have a B&B sign in the window.

That evening, the two arrived in Newquay for a quiet meal with some good music. As they parked, they heard a soulful sax. They smiled at each other and headed toward the sound, which seemed to be coming from a restaurant/jazz bar, Soul to Sole.

"Is that live?" asked Peter.

"Surely not this time of the year."

They were greeted by a middle-aged man who looked like a sixties throwback in flared jeans, colorful cotton shirt, and sandals.

"Hi there, folks. Table for two is it? Got one by the window. That okay?"

They followed him to the table. They discovering the music was a CD.

"You guys don't look like you're on holiday. What brings you to our little piece of heaven?"

"We're working here for a few weeks," volunteered Peter. "We heard the music. It's fabulous! What is it?"

"Isn't it brilliant? A saxophonist and pianist from the United States. Bob James and David Sanborn. The CD's called 'Double Vision.' Hold up. I'll start it from the beginning."

Peter and Georgina were enthralled. The waiter left them alone for about ten minutes, sensing they were happy just to listen. After all, they were the only punters he'd had all evening.

"So guys, what can I get you? A bottle of white, maybe? Got some lovely Chardonnay in."

"Why not?" Georgina said. "Where's it from … er … What's your name?"

"Sorry, love. I'm Sean. It's my place. The Chardonnay is eastern Australian and is beautifully crisp."

"Hi, Sean. Yeah, that'll be great. What's on special tonight? I fancy some fish."

Peter pulled a face. He feared fish bones. "Bring us the wine, and we'll have a look at the menu," he said, smiling at Georgina, who knew what was going through his mind.

The wine lived up to Sean's recommendation. Georgina ordered Dover sole and Peter settled for a filet. The evening was perfect. They looked out across the bay while soaking up the wonderful music and enjoying what they both said was one of the best meals they'd had in years.

They both agreed that evening was a turning point in their relationship. Maybe it was relief that it was out in the open. Maybe it was a coming together of two like-minded people who fit each other like gloves. They engaged in soul searching and asking the what ifs, things they'd never done before.

As each weekend arrived, the team members would usually head home by midafternoon Friday. Once she'd collated the figures,

Georgina would leave around 5:00. She regularly head up the A38, get to Plymouth around 6:30, and head for the Barbican, where she and Peter would have a quiet meal before going their separate ways.

His situation at home was becoming more untenable; his wife was playing the emotional blackmail card constantly and stirring up additional drama. His and Georgina's partings on Friday evening were always bittersweet. Each of them was hoping for the end of the audit, when Georgina would move out. They would leave each other, promising to keep their chins up.

Georgina was torn. She wanted to spend as much time with the girls as possible, but she knew Alan would have planned the weekend around his choice of activities and she would have little or no input. But anything was better than nothing, she told herself. She would tag along and try to give the girls as much of her time as possible.

Sunday afternoons saw her back on the road, saddened and sobbing. *This has got to end. It's not doing anyone any good, least of all my two little darlings.*

She arrived at the hotel about six and was pleasantly surprised to see Peter's car. She checked into her room and called him. Unusually, he answered only after several rings. "Yes?" he asked in a subdued voice.

"Hi, love. It's me. You okay? You sound odd."

"Not really. I'll be okay in a bit. Give me a while, will you? See you downstairs later?"

Georgina had never heard him like that before; he was always positive, in control. "Yes, sure, if that's what you want. You sure I can't help?"

"No, just leave it. I'll be down later."

Not having experienced that side of Peter, she didn't know how to react. It was her nature that if something needed confronting, you did it there and then; to just "leave it" was alien to her.

She went to the office and started going through the figures. It was the penultimate week; only nine working days left. There were always concerns that the last-minute accounting wouldn't come in on time. She decided to leave him to his own devices that evening. She ordered a sandwich.

She got stuck in her work, and before she knew it, it was 9:30. She stretched. She called his room. No answer. She left the office and went to his room with trepidation. She had no idea what mood he was in or how she would react to whatever it was.

She put her ear to the door. No sound. She knocked. She heard sounds of movement. The door slowly opened. Peter looked disheveled, grey. His eyes were bloodshot and downcast.

"Darling, what is it? Why didn't you call me?"

"Look, love, I'm sorry, but I'm not up to company tonight. Let's talk tomorrow, can we? Please, just leave me alone for now."

Georgina silently walked down the hallway without looking back. In her room, she sat on the bed almost in a state of shock. That wasn't how she'd expected the evening to go, and she had no idea how the next day would go. However, she knew the most important thing was to get the audit in on time and successfully.

# CHAPTER 47

## Signs of Dependency

DURING THE FOLLOWING DAYS, GEORGINA had little time to herself. She got to the office early, usually having breakfast there. At the end of the day, she would take all the files from the team and write up client reports long into the evening. She and Peter spent very little time together except for when she had to chase him for his files. His head obviously wasn't on the job, but she realized he wasn't about to come to her for help.

The days came and went until the end of the week. They said their farewell on Friday. He made some excuses ... needed to get back ... had stuff to sort out. In a way, Georgina was quite pleased because she had never had to handle anyone who was suffering such depression.

After the final weekend of the audit, she got back to the hotel about six and was surprised to see Peter's car. She walked up to the reception. The manager greeted her. "Hello there, you. Last week then? Got it all done?"

"Yes, last week, and just about done. Should be able to wind it up Wednesday night, relax on Thursday, and debrief on Friday." An idea came to her. "Listen, Pete. We usually do something special on the last night. How about you take the night off and join us?"

"I'd love to, but I've got two girls off this week, and the main one, Kathy, is the only one I can leave to take over. But it's a great idea.

Listen. Why don't we do something special for you guys? How about a garden party? We could lay up a large table in the garden and serve your meal out there."

Georgina smiled, thinking the guys would love it. "Brilliant. Let's chat later. Hey! What time did Peter arrive today?"

Pete checked the book. "Actually, he checked in late last night. Had a bit of a problem at home apparently and came back early. Either that or he's keen."

They both laughed. Pete had been so supportive, and even when the lads had gotten a bit rowdy, he managed to move them out of the main bar and into a smaller adjoining room almost without them noticing.

She went to her room and changed clothes. It was a beautiful evening; the sun was pouring in through the patio doors. She pulled out the bottle of wine she'd brought in a cool box, grabbed some glasses, and headed to Peter's room not really knowing what to expect but thinking no one could be in a bad mood for more than a week.

She tapped on the door. "Wine waiter, sir. Just what the doctor ordered."

The door opened after a couple of seconds. Peter looked terrible. He stepped to one side as she entered the room.

"Darling, what is it? Why are you like this? Why did you come down yesterday?"

"Sit down, love. I have to talk to you." He walked to the sofa.

She made her way to the dresser and opened the wine. She poured two glasses and handed him one. "Okay, love, talk to me."

"Oh Lord, where do I start? Well, last weekend, she went nuts. Threatened to kill herself, and in front of the boys. They ended up screaming at me. That it was all my fault … I didn't know what to do … Anyway, I went back on Friday, and she told the boys she was moving in with her boyfriend. Yeah, great, eh? Apparently, she's rented a flat, and she's going to live with that plonker she's been seeing." He took a large swig of wine. "I can't do this anymore, love. I've spoken to Jane, and she said we can use her place 'cuz she and Mick stay at his when they go home. Let's just pack up and go. I just need to get away."

Georgina was slowly realizing what he was suggesting. He wanted her to leave the hotel, the audit—her job—and go to Oxford with him.

"But darling, you know I can't do that. It'll be done on Thursday, so we can get off on Friday. You must know I can't leave, darling. Everyone's bonus depends on this last lot of figures, including yours, love."

"But I can't work … I just can't go out … You must see that."

Georgina thought for a minute. "Look. I tell you what. You stay up here, I'll sign you off sick, and get your last clients covered. That means you'll get your bonus. Once the books closed, which should be Thursday, we can head off then. How's that sound?"

He was crying. His head was in his hands. He looked completely broken. "Okay, but you'll come with me on Thursday, won't you? I can't do this on my own."

Assuring him she would and that she wouldn't tell the team, she finished her wine, took his face in her hands, and kissed him gently.

"Look darling, I'll have a word with Pete and get your meals sent up to your room. I'll make some excuse to the guys so they'll keep away. I'll come up after work if that's okay."

He agreed to what was a solution of sorts. When she suggested she go back to her room, he readily agreed.

She kissed him again and said a quiet "Night night."

She made her way to reception and was glad to see Pete was in the back office. "Pete, can I have a word?"

"Yeah. Come on in." He smiled and put his paperwork aside.

"Pete, I could do with a bit help, please. Peter's in a mess … terrible troubles at home. He needed to get away. But the thing is he can't work. He needs peace and quiet until the end of the project. I can sign him off sick, so as far as the bank's concerned, he was taken ill once he'd gotten here, but could you get him his meals up in his room? No special treatment, just what he'd normally have but taken up to him? If you'd like, I could take it up. Doable?"

Pete wasn't fazed at all. "Absolutely no problem, love. I'll put him on the service list. No one needs to know. Tell him it's fine. If he doesn't want housekeeping to come in, that's fine as well."

*Easier than I thought. This guy's a star.* "Thanks, Pete. I owe you big-time."

And so she pulled the final days of the audit together successfully; the other team members accepted what she had told them about Peter and left him alone.

On Wednesday evening, the hotel laid on a trestle table in the garden and served them a beautiful meal in the setting sun. Georgina was saddened that Peter wasn't able to join in the fun, but she would usually pop up to his room after dinner and sit with him for a while, enjoying some wine.

She stood the team down after breakfast on Thursday, and they drifted off during the day, promising to be on time for the debriefing the following Monday. She had cleared most of the office out on the Wednesday evening after leaving Peter, so there wasn't too much for her to do on Thursday once she'd paid the hotel account and loaded up the car with the office and her bags.

She headed to Peter's room, and as she rounded the corner of the hallway, she noticed his room door was on the latch. She approached it quietly. She pushed it open slightly. "Hey, love. You there? Peter, love, are you in here?"

He appeared in the hallway behind her. "Sorry, darling. I've been loading up the car. Are you ready to go? I know I am. I'll be so glad to get out of this bloody room."

She smiled as he passed his hand over her hair just as he'd done so many times before. She was relieved to see that he seemed to be almost back to his old self.

"Yes, I'm done. So what's the plan? You've had plenty of time to think about it, haven't you?" She laughed.

"Too bloody right I have. Yeah, let's get outta here. I had a voicemail from Jane earlier saying she was cool with us using her place as long as we wanted. She left the key for me down at reception." He smiled at Georgina. "What are you doing? You're coming with me, right?"

Georgina had worked out in her mind how this could play out. She would follow him up to Oxford, stay over until Monday morning, and head to Bristol for the debrief. She would make excuses for Peter, saying he'd gone home. Then she could ask for some time off saying she had stuff she needed to sort out at home.

The next project was in Gloucester; it was only a short one, so they could put Roz in as acting team leader for a couple of weeks. This would give her and Peter time to make a plan.

"Yes, love, of course. Let's get on the road. I'll follow you. Let's stop, say, at Taunton for coffee. We can chill over the weekend and talk this through."

They headed to reception; Pete was behind the desk. "Hey guys, you off?"

"Pete, you've been a pal. I hope we haven't been too much of a nightmare for you. Let's keep in touch!" Georgina gave him a huge hug. "Thank you," she whispered.

"You, my dear, are more than welcome. And you pal, take it easy, all right?"

Peter smiled. "You betcha. Thanks."

They headed to the car park. "See you up the road, darling," Georgina said.

# CHAPTER 48

❧

## On or Off? Who Knows?

AFTER AN INTENSE WEEKEND WITH Peter, Georgina left for the debriefing. After the formalities were over and the pats on the backs handed out, she headed back to Oxford for a couple of weeks' vacation.

She and Peter had discussed at length what the next few months would bring. One of the biggest decisions was that Peter would leave the job. It was too intense for him especially at the moment. She would stay at her father's because as arranged, she'd moved out of house, leaving Alan and the girls. She asked her father if she could stay until she could get something else more permanent, and he had agreed. She and Peter would meet up when they could.

He had wanted them to rent a place together, but there was a huge flaw in this as she saw it. She didn't want to just flip from one relationship to another. That was and never had been her plan. *What would the girls think? That I'd dumped their dad for someone else? That absolutely wasn't the case.* It was terribly important to her that they understood why she and their dad had separated.

There was also the more sensitive issue of finance. Peter wasn't going to be working for a while, and so any outgoings would have to come from her, and she wasn't sure she wanted to be the breadwinner in this relationship.

So it was agreed; she would go down to her father's house at the weekend and spend time with the family while she and Peter stayed at Jane's during the week. It wasn't the best arrangement because the atmosphere in the house was always somewhat tense.

Georgina worked the Gloucester audit after her break and did some house hunting. She'd have liked to be in or around Bristol, but after talking with some estate agents, she realized she couldn't afford that, so she eventually settled for a one-bedroom flat in Weston super Mare. It wasn't ideal, but at least it would be hers.

The girls came to see her on weekends, but it was far from ideal—one slept with her and the other on the recliner in the lounge. After about nine months, she realized she had to offer the girls a more comfortable reason to see her. She sold the flat and bought a larger, two-bedroom house a few roads away. It was more suitable, and she was able to make it a cozy, welcoming haven for her and the girls.

During this time, Alan had changed his situation as well. Instead of staying in Plymouth as they'd agreed, he was again headhunted and took a job way up country in Cambridgeshire. Without any consultation, he took the girls out of the school, got rid of Trisha the nanny, and started afresh. He'd also apparently been seeing one of the staff in Plymouth, and within a year of the divorce being finalized, he'd remarried.

This made it so much more difficult for Georgina to get the girls down to her at the weekends, but she and Alan would meet halfway as often as possible, and the girls would get in the car and chatter endlessly about Pauline, their new stepmum. They, especially Jackie, didn't get on very well with her. The first hour of the journey would be taken up by "She said …" and "Then she …" Georgina had to put a thirty-minute time limit on Pauline, and then they'd spend the rest of the time enjoying the closeness that mums and daughters ought to have.

For the next couple of years, Peter became a sort of on-again off-again partner. He'd turn up and say he'd left Sandra and would stay for a couple of months. Then the guilt would take over and he would run back to her. This reduced Georgina to the role of mistress—part-time mistress at that.

She struggled explaining to the girls why sometimes he was there and other times nowhere to be seen. They seemed to accept it, but she knew they were confused. There was time when it got too much for Georgina too. She couldn't concentrate on anything, and her work was suffering. She knew she was depressed, but because she had always been so positive, it was hard for her to admit it to herself.

She even got to the stage of believing that if it would never get any better, what was the point? Her state of mind allowed every negative thing in her life to rush to the forefront of her mind—her childhood, being dumped by her biological parents, being hated by her adopted parents, the boys, the girls ... All she seemed to do was make others unhappy. So maybe ... Somehow, she came out of that black period mainly because she couldn't handle how the girls and she supposed the boys would be affected by such a drastic, selfish action.

The problem was that most of the time when Peter was with her, they had a brilliant relationship, and he and the girls got on very well; he thought the world of them, and they appeared to reciprocate.

At the beginning of 1990, he got his divorce; she hoped things would settle down. They were both working, though Georgina had by that time left the bank; they had decided that weeks away on audits weren't conducive to a new relationship. Her new job was as a financial consultant for an estate agency, and while she enjoyed the work and the fact that it was a typical nine-to-five job, it didn't stimulate her at all.

They talked at length about their future and so started planning a wedding for December. The girls were excited to be bridesmaids, but only if they didn't have to wear "silly" dresses. That amused Georgina to no end; they settled on pencil-black skirts with lilac jackets. They looked so grown up, but of course they were growing up—Jackie was thirteen and Leslie was eleven.

Then financial disaster struck. Within weeks of each other, Peter and Georgina were laid off. Luckily, Georgina had already paid for most of the wedding costs, so that wasn't too much of an issue, but the main problem was the loss of company cars. This of course made going for interviews difficult, but they somehow managed and eventually landed jobs—not necessarily what they'd have chosen, but at least they had incomes.

The wedding took place on a very cold but sunny December morning with the girls looking lovely if not frozen. The guest list was made up of Georgina's friends, the team from the bank, who turned up mob handed, and Pete from the hotel. A surprise attendee was Peter's youngest son. He'd decided to support his dad. Peter was over the moon; he saw it as a start of getting his boys back.

The next four or five years were a mix of good and bad. Peter was still riddled with guilt because his boys had turned from him totally and had gone completely off the rails. They had gotten mixed up with an unsavory crowd and had started experimenting with drugs, including eventually heroin. They were living on the streets in Bristol, and on occasions when Georgina would go shopping, she would see the boys begging in shop doorways. She would hide behind doors and move around the stores to avoid their spotting her; she didn't want to give them any money and enable their habits. This situation affected her relationship with Peter, who would respond when they'd call at perhaps 3:00 a.m. "He's in trouble … needs money … got to find him."

Peter struggled to keep his jobs because he'd be out for hours searching Bristol for the boys. And they would constantly tap him for money, as much as £300 a month. Georgina couldn't make any plans because if the boys phoned, he would leave wherever they were at the time and disappear for hours, days, even weeks.

In the end, Georgina couldn't take any longer. While she loved him dearly, she realized he couldn't continue like that and survive. After one terrible weekend, she confronted him; she said he needed a place of his own so he wouldn't be torn between his responsibility to the boys and her. He left. They met up occasionally for coffee, but she realized that marriage number three was ending.

Over the next few months it became apparent he was seeing someone else. In fact, he told her in one of his darker moments that the woman actually understood what he was going through.

However, several months later, he suggested getting together with her over coffee. After a while, he declared undying love for her. He said he'd made a terrible mistake and couldn't live without her. He'd ended his affair and wanted to come home.

Georgina was stunned. Regardless of what had gone before, she still loved him. So once again, she gave in. That evening, he arrived at the house with his worldly goods in a couple of black plastic sacks. They talked long into the night. Georgina believed that he had missed her and was recommitting to their marriage.

Something that became apparent to Georgina was that Peter had never really felt he belonged in her little house; he said he often felt like a lodger there. Georgina realized the necessity of compromise; she reluctantly agreed to put the house on the market and buy another together. But her financial head told her this was a stupid thing to do considering the current state of the property market. Her house had at one time dropped 30 percent in value over the eight years she'd owned it. It had improved slightly to 10 percent below the purchase price. Nonetheless, she had about £9,000 in equity, a substantial deposit on another place. But Peter also wanted all new furniture, a complete new start. Again, Georgina capitulated, wanting to make him happy.

Over the next couple of months, her house was sold, and they took on the tedious job of viewing properties looking for just the right one. They eventually agreed on a suitable property a mile or so from where they lived. Ignoring the voices in her head saying *Don't do this!* she went ahead with the purchase though after buying the furniture, they could make only a much smaller down payment. The market was fragile, and she had a 95 percent mortgage.

In the end, they moved to a three-bedroom house with new beds, three-piece suite, new dining set, and much more. While she agreed it looked very nice, she thought it was all a ridiculous waste of money.

Unfortunately, even then, Peter wasn't happy. She was aware of phone calls coming in on the second line they'd installed for his work; he'd close his door and talk for a long time at most peculiar times of the day and night.

In March, only six weeks after they'd moved in, it all came to a head. She confronted him about his behavior. The last straw had been the charade of a day they'd just spent with some friends of Georgina. Playing the happy husband with Georgina's friends Luigi and Heather, they drove back from Nailsworth in silence. She knew it was the end. She spent the journey in the passenger seat looking out the window, tears rolling down her face.

At home, she couldn't contain herself. "What the hell was all that about? Why the hell are you still here? You obviously don't want to be here, do you?"

"No, you're right. I can't do this anymore. You just don't understand—"

"I tell you what I understand. I understand you're still seeing Sharon. I know she's phoning here constantly. And I understand that all that I've done for you, the house, the furniture, just isn't enough. Peter, I love you enough to let you go if you don't want to be here. But there's one thing I don't understand. Why if you felt like this did you commit me to this house, which I don't need, and all the new stuff if you had no intention of staying?"

He sat on the sofa in silence.

She continued. "You might be surprised at this, but I just knew this was going to happen. So believe it or not, I actually went to a solicitor last week to establish were I would stand. I'll go back to them next week and file the divorce papers. Let's just put it down to experience, shall we?"

He was in panic. He'd assumed it would be him making the decisions. "Christ, you don't hang about, do you? Fine. I'll go. But I'll have to stay until I can get a place."

They lived a horribly uncomfortable existence until May. Georgina would bypass the lounge, where he stayed, make a meal, and eat it in her room, an exile in her own house. They spoke very little as they saw each other rarely. When returning from work, she would pray his car was not there. When he finally moved out, it was a huge relief.

# CHAPTER 49

## *Let's Be Honest*

ONE THING, HOWEVER, THAT SEEMED to have change for the better was her relationship with her father. How it happened was almost an accident.

A week or so after they had decided to divorce, her father and Margaret were on a trip around Wales and had suggested they would call in on the way home to Devon. She had told Peter he wasn't to come anywhere near the house that day because she didn't want to have to explain matters to her father. "I don't care what you do or where you go, but I don't want you anywhere near here, understand?"

He grunted, "Yeah, whatever."

The afternoon of the visit arrived; she greeted them at the door.

"Hello, my love, and how are you today? How lovely to see you," oozed her dad. She was determined not to let the past weeks interfere with the visit, so she smiled sweetly and ushered them in.

"Hello there, Dad. Isn't it a lovely day? You've had a lovely drive I would think."

They exchanged hugs. She offered to make tea. While she was in the kitchen, they exchanged small talk about the weather and their trip around Wales.

"So this is your new home then," said Margaret. "It's lovely and airy, isn't it?"

"Where's your young man today?" asked her father.

That was it. She tried to hold it together but burst into a flood of tears.

"My love, what on earth is it? Can we help?"

It all came out—the original split-up, the reconciliation, the new house, the affair.

"Oh my love, I'm so sorry. But why didn't you tell us? You shouldn't have had to cope with all this on your own."

For some reason, that was the switch. With no thought of what they would think, out it all poured—how she was always desperate for his approval. How she would never tell him anything was wrong in case he thought less of her. She even told him about how she felt when he had accused her and Alan of "scrounging" that Christmas, which had caused her to not communicate with him for nearly eight years. *Had he not realized that was why? Obviously not!*

He looked from her to Margaret, mortified. "Oh my goodness, my love. I just didn't know you felt that way." He turned to Margaret and said in a whisper, "Mummy, I wasn't really that bad, was I?"

Margaret patted Georgina's hand and told her husband, "Actually, you were."

He was devastated. They continued to talk frankly for a while after that, and for the first time, Georgina felt she had gotten through to him.

An hour or so later, he and Margaret took their leave. For the first time, he took Georgina in his arms, hugged her, and gave her a kiss. That was the start of what would become a far more honest relationship between father and daughter.

There was another unexpected chink in the misery. Alan's marriage had fallen apart, and he wanted to get away from Cambridgeshire. She was more than happy when he spoke to her one day while doing the exchange trip for the girls. He wanted to get away and decided to move to Weston.

"You don't mind, do you? I just need a fresh start," he said.

"What about work? Is there anything going with any of the stores?"

"I'm not sure, love, but I'll find something. It can't be that hard. Jackie's happy to come as well. She's spoken to her work, and they'll give her a transfer."

Since leaving college, she'd been working for a large international insurance company and enjoyed the work, so it made sense to her to move with her Dad. Leslie, on the other hand, didn't want to leave. She had a good network of friends and enjoyed her job. They decided she and some friends would rent the house from her dad.

Alan and Jackie moved down and actually stayed with Georgina for a while. There was a thought that maybe she and Alan could rekindle their affection for each other, but after a few weeks, it became obvious that wouldn't work; they'd grown into very different people, or maybe it was only Georgina. He rented a place of his own.

Free to make her own decisions for the first time in many years, Georgina decided to return to her financial roots; she took a job as an advisor for a company that had recently won a national contract to provide the three UK emergency services with mortgage and investment advice. She loved traveling the southwest of England from the tip of Cornwall to Gloucestershire. But the company and its ethics left a lot to be desired, and so after about eighteen months, she decided to leave.

Her clients in the southwest were saddened when she told them of her intention to leave; they were so supportive that they encouraged her to set up a similar company. She thus became at age forty-nine self-employed for the first time; she was independent financially and emotionally.

Her company grew in stature over the next few years from a one-man band to an efficient, well-run, and well-respected company with nine on staff. The region she started with grew to beyond the Midlands. She worked the hardest she'd ever worked in her life and enjoyed every minute of it. She would sometimes drive four hundred miles a day, and while it was exhausting, she had the satisfaction of offering a superb service and being exceptionally well paid for it. She had never been so financially secure in her life. She determined not to throw it away on relationships that if history was any record would only get in her way.

In 2003, knowing that there were aspects of the company she wasn't giving enough attention to, one of the staff members she took on was Christine, the wife of someone she'd known in her previous employment. She was exceptionally well qualified at handling statistics and computer programs and identifying business opportunities, areas Georgina admitted she wasn't particularly good in herself.

But on a personal front, Christine and Georgina were poles apart. Christina's main aim in life was to brag to friends about how much money she and her husband had; by default, her friends were judged by how much their houses were worth and how much they spent on cars, holidays, and so on.

Georgina wasn't looking for a new best friend. She just wanted help taking the company to the next level. There was friction between them; Christine thought that as they were working so closely with each other that they should automatically become best buddies. The problem was that Georgina didn't really like her or her husband, one of the coarsest, most-vulgar men she'd ever met.

The two women had many heated arguments, something Georgina wasn't used to. She'd always avoided conflict as much as possible, but Christine appeared to revel in screaming matches, and it didn't matter whom it was with. On many occasions, the staff would be forced to be party to her childish temper tantrums, cursing, and swearing at them like an angry fishwife.

After a couple of years, while accepting that the company had grown because of Christine's abilities, Georgina wanted to end the relationship. But her old insecurities raised their ugly heads; she worried about finding someone with the same skill set and prepared to work the hours Christine did. It wasn't unusual for her to come up with an idea on a particular avenue of growth and spend the whole weekend researching it.

So Georgina pushed her dislike to one side for the benefit of the company. In hindsight, she realized that she could have found someone with comparable skills considering the salary she was paying Christine.

The company grew from strength to strength, and on a personal front, in 1997, she had joined an international service charity organization because she realized that though her work took up so much of her time, there ought to be something else in her life, more than a distraction—another dimension.

She was an active member for a couple of years, and in 2002, she was elected president of her local club, which comprised like-minded people who wanted to put something back into their communities.

Being the person she was, Georgina didn't stop there. Over the next eight years, she became a zone chair, served as club president four more times, and became a district officer, initially joining the leadership team and then becoming the public relations officer for the organization in the southwest.

# CHAPTER 50

## *Independent Success*

HER COMPANY THRIVED EVEN THROUGH the property market crash of 2007. Georgina's company found a new avenue to follow. While property prices plummeted month after month down as much as 40 percent, there was a government initiative set in place to encourage first-time buyers by helping with down payments. Georgina and Christine made visits to the housing associations around the country and offered the company's services to provide advice on the new programs. They were invariably well received; this became the main stream of income for the company through those hard times. It also meant that there was a need for specially trained staff, and so they were able to offer work to three unemployed advisors to work specifically of this project. They quickly became the go-to company for what was called the first-time buyer assisted scheme, and they profited greatly by it.

While more than happy with her success, Georgina still struggled with Christine's personality. She decided to think about retiring. She would be sixty in 2010 and wanted to go out on a high note. She asked Christine to discuss the options available. Christine, true to form, made it all about her. What were her options? What would be the rewards?

Georgina laid it out as simply as she could. She suggested she would reduce her hours gradually over the next couple of years with a possible end date of 2012. Her idea was to work two months and then take two months off.

Christine immediately jumped to the assumption that she would be doing more work for the same pay, something Georgina had expected. To counter this argument, Georgina offered her 50 percent of the company. She felt it was only fair; Christine would have responsibility for day-to-day operations while she was away.

Christine felt this was a reasonable offer but wondered what would happen when Georgina retired completely. She was assured that she would be given the opportunity to purchase the remaining 50 percent at a price to be determined by an independent valuation at that time.

The plan began to take shape. Georgina would work two months and then go to her second home in Canada or her property on the Mediterranean coast of Turkey throughout the year. Christine of course had her concerns about handling Georgina's work for the two months as well as her own. She knew they had their individual strengths; she was no good at doing what Georgina was so good at—putting people at their ease, gaining their confidence, and coaxing business out of on many occasions very skeptical and suspicious clients. Her attitude was simply, "This is what it is—take it or leave it."

Georgina's response to that was to decide what aspects of her work she could delegate. There was of course more money to play with for possible additional staff as Georgina would of course take only a 50 percent income over the twelve months.

In 2011, she was nominated for and elected as vice district governor for the charity she worked with. She knew she couldn't take two months off at a time and handle the charity work, so she reverted to working two and a half days a week still with the aim of completely retiring in 2012.

This pleased Christine; Georgina would be available Thursday, Friday, Saturday, Sunday, Monday and Tuesday, and of course, because Georgina had made a commitment to the charity not to travel for three years, she was also available on the phone the rest of the week, which of course Christine took advantage of.

In quiet times, Georgina would sometimes find herself wondering what would have happened if she had stayed married to Peter. But then, common sense would prevail; she realized she'd never have started her company. He would have drained the finances, and she certainly wouldn't have been as secure as she was; her standard of living was high. She also wouldn't have advanced to the position of governor with her charity; he would have considered that a personal affront to his alpha male status in the relationship.

And yet there it was again—the sense of failure. The boys—three marriages—the girls. But so what? She was good at something! She could earn lots of money. But if she asked herself would she rather have had her children around her, she would have said of course. But in a way, her constant striving to do better, to earn more, and to buy more property was her way of convincing herself she was good at something.

Over the years since she'd started her company, she'd spread her wings and had gone to Portugal a couple of times on holiday. She enjoyed it so much that she bought an apartment there and remodeled and redecorated it. It was close to the airport, so once a month, she would finish work on Wednesday evening, catch a plane to Faro, and enjoy a relaxing few days in the sun. She'd fly back on Sunday refreshed and ready to get back on the treadmill on Monday.

It was as if she needed projects as distractions. She bought a property in Turkey that she rented out, and then another in the same country. She would occasionally travel there ostensibly to check on her properties but also enjoy the beautiful country. She'd also bought several small flats in and around Weston that she rented out and would hopefully provide her with a pension in years to come.

Over the years, she had built up the facade of a confident, capable person who would let nothing stand in her way. In fact, at times, she would believe it herself.

One constant joy was the relationships she had with her girls. They were living nearby, and she wanted to make up in some small way for their early years. Jackie had married in 1999 and over the next five years had had two children. Georgina enjoyed being involved in their lives though she felt she wasn't the best grandma because she was always so busy. Nonetheless, she tried as best she could to be a part of their lives.

Back when Jackie had been preparing for her wedding, out of the blue one evening, she told Georgina, "Mum, I want to find my brothers. Wouldn't it be great if they could come to the wedding?"

"Good God, love! Where did that come from?"

"I've always wanted to meet up with them again, and I can't think of a better reason than the wedding!"

Georgina didn't know how to handle that. The boys hadn't made any attempt to contact her; she believed and hoped their lives were complete enough that they didn't want or need her in their lives.

"Darling, it's not that simple, is it? We don't know what their lives are, and we've got no right to go barging into their lives just because it's a 'great' reason. I believe if they'd have wanted to know me or us, they would have gotten in touch through that adoption register. I've updated it every time I've moved."

Jackie didn't agree; she was very family oriented. All she could think of was that they were her brothers so of course wanted to know her. "Grandpa found you!"

"Yes love, and look how that turned out. He did that to appease his guilt, and let's face it, it hasn't always been a smooth ride, has it? I sometime wish he'd just left it alone. You know that."

"But at least he tried!"

That conversation played repeatedly in Georgina's mind for the next few weeks, but she always came to the same conclusion—she felt she had no right to interfere in their lives without being invited to do so.

Jackie didn't mention it again, but Georgina knew it was important to her. She wondered if Leslie felt the same way. She didn't think she did. She'd never seemed concerned about them and hadn't asked about them. Georgina wondered if the two girls had ever talked it through. She had no idea what she'd do if the boys did come looking for her. The guilt had never left her, and there were many occasions sometimes in the dark of night that she would think, *I wonder ...*

The last she had heard, they were still in Hereford. Coincidentally, her work regularly took her there. As she drove the streets, she'd scan the crowded streets and wonder if she would recognize them if she saw them.

She continued with her reduced hours while successfully completing the year as second vice district governor and the next year as first vice. Because of the workload, she knew she couldn't be a successful district governor unless she gave it her all, so after the elections in March, she told Christine of her decision to finish with the company that Christmas a year earlier than planned.

That caused Christine to blow a gasket. "You've let us all down! You're thinking only about yourself. What about me? How the hell can I get everything in place?"

"But I don't understand," Georgina said. "You must have been expecting this. We've discussed it often enough. You've been all but running it for the past eighteen months. And you'll have additional income to take on another admin girl to free yourself up to see the clients."

"Yeah, well, I don't want to see more bloody clients, do I? Oh forget it! Just do what you want. You'll do that anyway! You're just a selfish cow."

The next six months were to say the least uncomfortable. Georgina didn't want to be confronted by the vitriolic sniping and the sarcastic comments, so she no longer regularly went to the office, preferring to work from home, which meant she had as little as possible to do with Christine.

In September, they had their meeting with the accountant and eventually settled on the amount Christine would pay for the remaining 50 percent of the company. Of course, the meeting was not without the "That's not fair!" and "What about me?" complaints and questions, but it was settled. Georgina would hand over her shares of the company around Christmas of 2012, Christine would pay a monthly sum for three years, and then full ownership of the company would be transferred into her name.

But even that didn't go smoothly; Christine started a huge argument mid-November because of something that had been totally taken out of context and didn't actually confirm the facts. It ended in a terrible screaming match in the office.

Georgina hated the confrontation. No one had ever provoked Georgina's anger to such a degree. Georgina easily came to the conclusion that enough was enough. She told Christine she would finish working there and then. The retirement document was rewritten again and again as Christine always wanted the last say. She insisted on certain phrases relating to contact with clients, and she demanded Georgina returned all laptops, phones, and so on—ridiculous demands according to Georgina's lawyer.

"I know you've spoken to some clients! You're in breach of the agreement, so I'm not signing it" was Christina's favorite cry. In fact, Georgina had received several calls from clients, but each time, she had explained the circumstances to them and advised that they call Christine. "But I don't want to deal with her. She doesn't do it like you" was the reply she received on several occasions. Still, she tried to put their minds at rest, assuring them that while Christine had a different style, she was as knowledgeable and as competent as Georgina was.

This went on from November through Christmas and into the new year. It took a terrible toll on Georgina, who became so depressed that she began to wonder if it was all worth fighting for. Luckily, she pulled herself out of her depression without the family being any the wiser.

Eventually, the document was acceptable to both parties. Christine was a hard-working, capable owner who would take the company Georgina has brought from nothing in a different direction, but Georgina knew she had to let go. Her health had suffered due to Christina's anger and aggression.

She eventually kicked herself into action; she was approaching the end of her year as first vice governor and threw herself into planning for her year as governor. She had her cabinet in place, a team of forty-nine other volunteers who had agreed to work with her for the year. And of course she was excited about the international convention in Milan and all the training she had to do prior to leaving for it on July 1.

So Georgina was retired but committing a huge amount of time to her charity work. She saw the girls usually at least once a week. What with her schedule, Jackie's work, the fact that Jackie's husband had odd hours as a first responder, and Leslie's long hours in Bristol, that was about the best they could hope for.

So when one Monday evening, when Jackie called to ask, "Hey Mum, do you fancy coming to dinner on Thursday?" Georgina was surprised.

"Why, what a lovely thought. What's brought it on? It's a school night after all."

"I know, but Leslie's coming, and I thought you might like a night out."

"Don't see why not then. What sort of time?"

"The kids go to bed about half past seven, so I like to get them fed early, but then, Les won't get here until about six, so shall we say six?"

"Sounds like a plan, darling. See you then."

Georgina pondered the unusual invitation but got back to her work.

Thursday came, and Georgina set off from home about half past five. She hadn't seen the little ones for about ten days, so it would be lovely to catch up with them albeit briefly before their bedtime.

She rang the doorbell and heard screams of "Grandma! Grandma!" from Victoria, who threw the huge red door open. "Hello, Grandma!" She threw her arms around Georgina.

"What a welcome! Hello, darling. What are you up to? Where's your brother?"

"Watching the telly of course! Where else would he be?"

Georgina chuckled. They walked into the lounge and saw Joshua engrossed in an action film on the huge, flat-screen TV that took up half the wall.

"Hi, Josh! Any chance of a cuddle then?"

"Er ... Yeah ... Okay." He tore himself away from the TV just long enough to run to Georgina and give her a hug and kiss before racing back to his show.

She laughed and followed Vicki to the kitchen.

"Howdy, Mummy. You okay?" asked Jackie. "Cup of tea?"

"Hi, love. That would be lovely," Georgina said as she kissed her daughter.

"This is nice then. Don't usually do weekdays, do we?"

"Yes, but I don't usually get to see both of you at once."

Leslie turned up a few minutes later, and after general chitchat about kids and work, Jackie served a lovely dinner of roast pork and loads of veg. They ate and conversed in between occasional interruption from the little ones. It was a pleasant hour or so. Georgina said, "Well it's just about eight, so I'd better be going. I've got a report to get together."

"Right you two!" said Jackie in her best mum's voice but noticeably not acknowledging Georgina's comment. "It's bedtime. Upstairs now please. Teeth, PJs, and I'll be up in a while. Say night night to Auntie Les and Grandma."

The two dutifully did the rounds of hugs and kisses and disappeared. Georgina stood.

"Er … Mum, sit a minute, will you?" Jackie said, looking at Leslie for support. "We've got something to talk to you about."

Georgina frowned. "What is it? Anything wrong?"

"Well no, there's nothing wrong, but we have something to tell you," Leslie said.     Jackie stepped in. "So Mum, do you remember getting an email from a bloke called Phillip saying something about Anthony?"

Georgina panicked. She *had* seen an email about a week ago and had thought about it ever since. She had been in a quandary, but now …

"Les got it first. He obviously picked up on the name Carter. But then I got it, so I suppose he'd linked her and me."

"Where's this going, girls?" Georgina asked, not wanting to know the answer.

"We've both had an email from Anthony. He wants to meet us. I know you're going away, but it's on the eleventh of December, 'cuz it's close to their wedding anniversary, and they're at Centre Parks, and we're going down there."

"You've done what? Without talking to me first? You're kidding! How could you?" Tears were running down her face. She didn't know if it was due to anger or frustration or what. *How could they have done all this without asking me if I minded?*

"Mum, we're sorry ... We—"

"How could you? Can't you see that after all this time if anyone's to see him, the first person to see him, speak to him ... should be me?"

"Mum, we didn't mean to upset you. It was just so ... spur of the moment."

"Bloody right it was spur of the moment! Can't you see this is far too important to just act on a whim? You have no idea how I feel, do you? Did it ever cross your mind how I'd feel? For fuck's sake!" She fought back tears. "For thirty-five years I've missed my boys! For thirty-five years I've resisted the temptation to contact them in case it buggered up their lives. For thirty-five years I've dreamed of them contacting me. And now you're going to meet Anthony without me and I'm not even in the country. Christ! How could you!"

Georgina struggled into her jacket and headed to the door. "Sorry. I'm going. I need to let this lot sink in. Bye." She got to the front door. She looked back and saw her daughters crying.

Something crossed her mind. "Just out of interest, who else knows about this?"

Jackie spoke. "Paul of course."

Leslie chipped in, "Sorry, Mum. I mentioned it to Dad."

"What? I don't believe this! Just great! Your husband and my ex, whom you may have forgotten by the way, was the guy who actually stopped me from having the boys back! That makes it even bloody worse!" She stepped out. "I need some time. Just leave me alone. I'll be in touch."

The girls followed her to the car. "Mum, we're sorry. We didn't mean to upset you!"

Georgina laughed through her angry tears "You sure as hell got that wrong, didn't you?"

# CHAPTER 51

## Dreams into Reality

OVER THE NEXT FEW DAYS, Georgina tried to come to terms with the fact that something she'd dreamed of for so long was about to happen. But instead of it being her and her boys somewhere quiet, talking about what had happened and why and hoping against hope they forgave her … Instead of that, her two daughters, who had no idea of the full story, were going to meet him and chat about Lord knows what without her there!

She quickly concluded that she must speak to him even if just over the phone. How would he feel if she didn't contact him? That wasn't even a consideration, but she was being backed into a corner, having to do this without any preparation. What would she say? What would he say? Did he hate her for deserting them? There surely had to be some resentment. Was this just an opportunity to get his own back? And what would he say to the girls? Could he turn them against her?

She drove home considering all the what ifs. The other issue was that she was leaving for Canada in five days. No time to plan. She didn't know what she would say.

Arriving back home, she ignored the message light flashing on the phone. She couldn't speak to anyone. She dumped her clothes and climbed into bed sobbing. *This is not how it was meant to be!* She had dreamed of the day … running into each other's arms … sitting in a restaurant. And then not knowing what to say … them screaming at her that she'd ruined their lives. So many different scenarios. *Why oh why have they done this without my knowing?* The question kept playing in her mind until she dozed off into fitful sleep.

The next morning, she didn't feel at all rested. She had a blinding headache. The anxiety returned. She had to act. *Today!* The girls had given her his number. She determined to phone him that evening, so she had all day to plan it.

Both girls rang during the day, but she couldn't speak to them. She couldn't remember ever being as angry with them as she had been the previous night. Or as hurt that they couldn't understand she should be the first to meet him. Her! She wasn't ready to pretend everything was okay. Not just then.

Throughout the day, she mentally rehearsed the call. But without knowing what his reaction would be, how could she know how to approach it? The girls called again. Again she ignored them. *This is ridiculous. If he's angry and aggressive, I'll hang up. And what will that achieve, you silly cow? Think positive! What's the worst that can happen?*

Around 6:30, she dialed the number. "Hello?"

She froze. She couldn't speak.

"Hello? Umm, is that you, Mum?"

*Christ! He's calling me mum! Maybe this will be okay after all. But isn't Julie Townsend his mum?* "Umm, yes, love, it's me. How are you?" *What a bloody stupid thing to say!* It was her long-lost son who she'd dreamed about talking to for years and all she could come up with was, "How are you?"

"Mum, don't cry. You'll make me start!" Her younger son's voice was soft.

"Oh Anthony, it shouldn't be like this! This isn't how I wanted it to be! I don't know what to say … what to expect! Oh my dearest boy. I'm so sorry! Can you ever forgive me?"

The words tumbled out not as she'd planned. She could hear in his voice he was either in tears or close to it.

"Mum, please, don't be upset. Please don't cry. You don't have anything to be sorry about. There's nothing to forgive. I mean it."

Georgina struggled to comprehend what he was saying. It was as if there were no past to forgive, no recrimination.

"Anthony darling, I've prayed for this for more than thirty years, but I didn't imagine for one moment it would be like this. You know I go away in a few days, don't you?"

"Yes Mum, I know, and it's okay."

"But it's not okay, love. You're going to meet up with your sisters in a few days. And speak to them before we've even met. I wanted to talk to you first. It's all the wrong way round."

"I know, but that's my fault, honest. Don't be mad at the girls. Once I'd found them, I just wanted to meet them. I didn't really think about how it ought to be."

Georgina was finally speaking to her baby boy. She hated the fact that the girls would meet him before her, but that couldn't be helped.

"We can meet up as soon as you get back, can't we?" Anthony asked. "But we can talk on the phone if you like. And then in January, Chris and I will come down and we can meet then."

*Oh Lord!* She hadn't banked on him having a wife or that she'd be there. "That would be lovely, but I'd really like … if you don't mind of course … that it's just the two of us. I'm sure she'd understand, wouldn't she?"

There was silence for a few seconds. "Yeah, I expect so. But she's been there for me all this time. And if it wasn't for her, I'd be a sniveling wreck by now. She's my rock. And she wants to meet you too."

"I see. Of course, but maybe when you come down in January, maybe she'd like to spend half an hour or so with the girls so that we can, well, just say hello on our own? There's so much we have to talk about, isn't there?"

"Yeah, I expect that'll be fine. But please, don't be mad at the girls. I pushed them to meet us."

She realized that maybe she had been a bit hard on the girls, but without all the facts, what else was she supposed to have done? They should have realized she had to come first in the process. But she would try to make amends with the girls.

The next few days went by in a haze. She kept replaying in her mind her conversation with Anthony. Because of her commitment not to travel during her term of district governor, it would be her last opportunity to visit Canada for two and a half years. She needed to winterize the house and close it down. She left a few days later to Canada. She had made the girls promise to let her know how they had all gotten on.

This they did, full of enthusiasm and joy at having met their big brother. They had talked for hours, and he had given them each a gift of a silver necklace with three hearts entwined. They loved them and the sentiment behind them.

It had been arranged that a week after she returned from Canada, he and his wife, Chris, would drive down from London. Jackie was to come up to her mum's and take Chris to Weston for a while, and then, with Leslie and the children, they would all meet up at the Windmill, a restaurant on the estuary for a family lunch.

# CHAPTER 52

*Forgiveness*

SEVEN WEEKS LATER, SHE FLEW into Heathrow and headed down the M4 motorway to her apartment. It was a two-hour journey, and her thoughts on the drive down, weaving in and out of the heavy traffic, were divided into two parts. The first was *I'm home*, and the second and most dominant in her mind was, *Not long before I meet Anthony. How will it go? Will he accept my reasons for doing what I did? Will he like me?*

Arriving home, things settled back into a sort of routine, and then very soon, the day arrived that Anthony was to drive down. She was an absolute bag of nerves. She hadn't slept, and she had stomach cramps.

Around noon, she got a call from him saying they were just coming past the services on the motorway and would be there in about ten minutes.

She paced the floor, moving from one room to another, straightening the curtains, smoothing the bed, flushing the toilet—anything to take her mind off the road outside.

True to form, Jackie arrived a few minutes prior to the arranged time just as an unfamiliar blue VW Polo pulled in. She watched Jackie and Anthony climb out of their respective cars and hug in the middle of the road. As they separated, she saw that his wife, Chris, had gotten out as well and was getting into Jackie's car. *Thank God! I have him to myself.*

The two girls drove off, leaving Georgina wondering what she should do. Should she open the patio doors? Wave through the glass? Go out to greet him? Wait at the door? It all seemed so like a play with actors not knowing their positions on stage.

She eventually made her way to the door. As she opened it, there was Anthony just turning into the path. He was almost hiding behind a huge bouquet of red roses. As they approached each other, he lowered the flowers. They embraced with an energy and a spilling of emotion that cut through the previous thirty-five years.

They were in tears and laughing. "Oh darling, it's so wonderful to see you. Please come on in."

He followed her into the apartment and closed the door. They entered the lounge and turned to each other. Still clutching the roses, they embraced again. They parted after a few seconds. He presented her with the flowers. "For you, Mum. Hope you like them."

They talked for an hour or so, conscious of the fact they were to soon meet the others. The conversation was very lighthearted and didn't get into any depth about the past. She didn't want this opportunity to end. There was so much they needed to talk about, but maybe, she thought, only she needed that. Her son seemed to be completely accepting of her actions and feeling no malice toward her at all.

It was she, she realized, that wanted or rather needed the opportunity to tell him why she'd done what she'd done. The reasons for her actions and how she felt about it. She was looking for forgiveness and acceptance but couldn't believe she already had them.

One of the things they did discuss at length was David. Apparently, he was almost an outcast to the family, not being in contact with the Townsends, his brother, his ex-wife or his children, two girls aged thirteen and eleven.

A big issue that obviously concerned Anthony more was what might happen if she met him. He told her of an episode when he had been successful in finding their father. He had phoned Mike, and they'd had an interesting albeit brief conversation. Anthony had felt duty bound to phone his brother. He'd left a message saying he had tracked down their father, and he gave his number. David didn't call him back or make any contact, so Anthony didn't know whether he'd spoken to Mike, but later that week, when Anthony phoned his father again, he was greeted with a very hostile response.

"Look, don't ever phone here again! We don't want anything to do with you." That was from Mike's second wife; apparently, Mike didn't want to speak to him.

He was devastated and immediately phoned his brother. "Did you speak to our dad?" he asked David accusingly.

"I sure did! I told him what a loser he was and how he'd fucked up our lives. I enjoyed it. I don't think he'll want to hear from us again."

"Thanks, you bastard! You might not have wanted to know him, but I did!"

Anthony had told her this because he admitted that he had been afraid that if she wanted to speak with David, he'd do the same to her, and if that happened, maybe she wouldn't want to know him either. He was terrified! Now that he'd found them all, he didn't want anything to spoil his newfound family.

She did her best to assure him that as far as she was concerned that would never be the case. But silently, she wasn't sure how she'd cope if David did come looking for her. But hey, one son at a time was fine.

They drew the chatting to a close and drove to the Windmill, a local restaurant overlooking the estuary, to find the rest of the family there. They sat around a big table in the window and had a very pleasant meal with the conversation flowing very naturally. She should have been pleased, she knew, but there was still an uncomfortable niggle playing in the back of her mind that it was all too much too soon. Here they all were playing happy family as if they'd known each other for years when Anthony and Chris were strangers. It all seemed too easy. There had to be a period of getting to know each other surely.

Soon after, Anthony and Chris said their farewells with promises to keep in touch and headed back to London. Georgina was ready to make her way back to the apartment for some alone time to assess how it had all gone. After assuring the girls she was fine and giving the little ones hugs and kisses, she went home.

It became a familiar ritual each morning and evening that she and the girls would receive a "Good morning ladies" and then a "Night night," and while it was a novelty, it gave her a feeling of completeness that maybe she was forgiven. At least by him.

The next few weeks passed without event, and then one evening, she received a call from Anthony inviting her to London. Apparently, Chris's mum and dad were holding a family barbecue and had suggested to Anthony that maybe he'd like to invite Georgina. She thought it was extremely odd that they would want to meet her, but apparently, Chris had told them all about the long-lost mum and they were more than happy to welcome her into the family. But again, Georgina felt it was as all too easy and too soon. She needed to get to know her son before being included in his wife's family.

"But what about Julie and Simon? Are they invited too?" she asked.

"Well Mum, Julie has never really got on with Chris, and so the two families have never mixed. But another thing. I was talking to Mum and Dad, you know, Julie and Simon—"

"Darling, they've been your mum and dad for an awfully long time. Don't be silly, you should call them that."

"Oh, okay then." He started again. "Mum and Dad really want to see you again. So if you come up here for the weekend, we can do the barbecue on Saturday and then see ... er ... Mum and Dad on Sunday. What do you think?"

It seemed he wanted to show her off like a new possession. She wasn't sure she wanted to be enveloped in this extended family; she was barely getting used to having a son and daughter-in-law for God's sake!

She parked it for a while until a couple of days later, he called again. "Mum, you will come up next weekend, won't you? We thought you could book into the local Premier Lodge. We haven't got a lot of room." He sounded apologetic. "Please, I'd really love for you to come."

It obviously meant a lot to him. She agreed. She wasn't sure what she was letting herself in for, but maybe this was his way of getting some answers if someone else asked them. She accepted the invitation and would take whatever was coming her way.

She told the girls of her plans, and they too thought it was odd that Chris's family would want to meet her so soon, but they did see why Julie and Simon would want to see her again. They seem to think it was a gesture of something like, "We looked after him well, didn't we?"

So the following Saturday, she drove up to the outskirts of London to meet up with her son and daughter-in-law. She went to their flat and had a cup of tea in their tiny lounge before they headed to the hotel to get her checked in.

Anthony drove them to the family gathering at a modern house off a quiet residential road. Georgina entered with trepidation, but she soon realized it was a normal family barbecue. No one asked any questions, and they all treated her as if they'd known her for years. *Here we go again. Constant small talk. Did no one ever talk about meaningful things?*

They left around seven. Georgina suggested that they just take her back to the hotel as she was tired. Actually, she was emotionally drained. So much anticipation. All for nothing. Again!

They arranged to join her for breakfast about nine the following morning.

As soon as they'd left, she undressed, climbed into bed, and pretended to watch some rubbishy game show on TV before dropping off into a fitful sleep.

In the morning, she showered and made her way downstairs. Anthony and Chris were there, and they headed into the dining room. They chatted as they tucked into the huge buffet breakfast on offer.

After a while, Anthony dropped the bombshell that Julie and Simon were expecting them around 11:00 so they ought to get off. "Actually, Mum, I mean Julie, isn't very well. She's got a liver problem, and sometimes, she just takes to her bed. She was okay about an hour ago when I rang, but that's nothing to go by. So if she's not about, don't take it personally, will you?"

They arrived at the house a short time later, and she was greeted by Simon and Julie as if she were a long-lost friend. Again the familiar story. No recriminations, no serious conversation other than confirmation that David was unfortunately not in communication with any of them and that he'd become a bit of a problem.

After a while, Anthony made a move that suggested it was time to leave. He had seen the signs of Julie fading fast and thought it better to leave.

Saying her good-byes, thank yous, and promises to keep in touch, they left and headed to a pub for lunch.

Anthony explained that Julie hadn't been well for some time and was waiting for a liver transplant. She certainly seemed frail. Georgina wondered what she really thought of her. There she was again, assuming the Townsends had an axe to grind.

She just found it completely bemusing that everyone was just treating it as business as usual. It seemed she was the only one who understood the enormity of the situation. *Doesn't anyone understand how important this is to me?* She just wanted to get to know her son, not his wife or her parents or these other people who had nothing to do with her.

She said her farewells a while later after lunch and headed back to Bristol. It had been only the second time she'd seen her son in thirty-five years, and they'd spent a weekend as if they'd know each other all their lives. Not a single mention of the past. Not a single memory. Not one recollection of any sort. But she was beginning to think she was asking for something she wasn't going to get.

# CHAPTER 53

## Welcome to the Family

OVER THE NEXT FEW MONTHS, Anthony would drive down every couple of months. One weekend, she took Vicki and Josh to see them, again staying in the hotel, but it turned out well because the kids had a whale of a time mucking out and generally making themselves useful at the stables where Chris kept her horse.

It gave Anthony and Georgina a rare opportunity to spend some valuable time together as they strolled arm in arm along the towpath by the River Thames at Marlow. At last, they had an opportunity to touch on a very small part of his childhood and his memories. It was a fleeting moment but one Georgina truly relished. It was such a brief interlude, but Georgina felt she had had the chance to peer through a very small window into his life as a child with the Townsends.

Around this time, Georgina went down to Devon to see her father, who was not at all well but nevertheless enjoyed company occasionally. She mentioned having been in touch with Anthony. He expressed a wish to meet him as well. "He is my grandson after all," he'd said the day Georgina had broached the subject.

"Well, if you're sure, Dad. I'll mention it to him."

This she did the next time she spoke to Anthony. "The thing is, love, he's not too well, and I'd hate for you not to have known him."

There was a moment's silence. "Well, yes, I suppose. Maybe next time we come down?"

Again, he was suggesting that his wife join them.

"Well, to be honest, love, I think it would be better if it was just you and me, please. That would be okay, wouldn't it?"

Eventually, it was arranged he would take a day off in a couple of weeks and the two of them would drive down to see his grandfather. Georgina wondered if this would be the opportunity to speak openly.

The day arrived, and they set off for the eighty-mile drive to Devon. But no matter how much she tried, Georgina was unable to get him to open up about his childhood or his feelings about what had happened to the two of them.

It was a pleasant meeting; the three had lunch at the village pub. Her father asked several searching questions of Anthony but got little insight into Anthony's feelings.

They left midafternoon. Georgina gave up trying to get him to open up, and they resorted to the ridiculous small talk of people who didn't know each other and had nothing in common. Georgina was upset, but her son was oblivious to it all, or so it seemed.

At the end of January came the sad news that Julie had only weeks to live. Anthony assumed the responsibility of preparing things for his dad, and one of those was trying to get David up to see his mother before she passed away. Texts were sent, phone calls were made, but to no avail. And then the news that everyone was dreading. She had passed away.

Anthony phoned Georgina to tell her the news and surprisingly said he wanted her to come to the funeral, as did Simon apparently. She could see that this was fraught with problems; she would remain an outsider especially as Anthony and David were to everyone else burying their mother.

And then there was David. How could she not speak to him? But Anthony was adamant. "Please, Mum. I just want to know you're there. Please?"

How could she refuse his first request to her in his life? She would go and support him. But from afar.

"That's fine, Mum. Thank you. It means so much."

It seemed that Anthony had to convince his brother to attend the funeral, and finally, it was agreed he would come from Southampton the night before the funeral. It was terribly sad, but Simon had told Anthony he didn't want David in his house. Anthony booked a bed and breakfast for the night.

Georgina had traveled up the day before, having booked a hotel near the crematorium. Anthony called her and said that he, Simon, and Chris were going out for a meal that evening and would like her to join them. She thought it odd but was learning not to question things.

"But what about David? Isn't he going too?"

"Absolutely not. Dad doesn't want him there, but he does want you. So you'll come, won't you?"

She reluctantly agreed, and they had had a pleasant evening, Anthony and Simon exchanging "Do you remember …?" episodes.

They left her at the hotel. She turned in with fear and trepidation of what the next day would bring. She would be in the presence of both her sons but allowed to speak to only one.

A miserable, grey day dawned, the right mood for a funeral. She showered trying to fend off the looming headache threatening to take over her head. She dressed and went down to breakfast. She didn't have much of an appetite, so she made do with a couple of cups of coffee and some fruit.

The funeral was at 10:00, so around 9:45, Georgina drove to the crematorium Anthony had shown her the previous day. She was dreading the whole thing because she knew she didn't belong there. She drove into the car park and walked toward a group of people standing by the doors, none of whom she knew. She stood slightly apart from them. She felt a slight touch on her arm. Chris's mother. "Don't worry, love. You can stand with us. It'll be okay."

*What a generous thing to do*, thought Georgina. It made her feel less like the outsider she was. "Thank you, Jill. I really don't belong here."

"Maybe not, but Anthony wanted you here, didn't he? So it's for him."

Georgina saw the funeral cars pull in. The first one was the hearse. The second contained the family. She was mesmerized as she saw Simon followed by Pam and Anthony. The door on the other side of the car opened and out stepped what could only be her firstborn, David. She lost sight of them all as they entered the chapel.

Everyone started to move forward, and again, Jill gently took her arm. The three walked slowly into the chapel and took their seat two rows behind the family. Georgina started to cry quietly as she realized that her two sons were within reach of her for the first time in so long. The sadness that overwhelmed her was that she could have so easily reached out and touched David. She was so close to him, but he didn't know. He wouldn't know her even if she were standing next to him.

The service was lovely and understated, and all too soon, everyone started to move toward the doors. She could see Jill and Mick were anxious to get to Chris, who looked upset, so touching Jill's arm, Georgina said through her tears, "Please, Jill. I'm fine. You go to Chris. She needs you."

"Are you sure you're okay?" asked Jill, looking relieved. Georgina took a deep breath. "Yes of course. Go."

Georgina made her way into the cool, hazy sunlight and stood apart from the crowd, which was drifting toward Simon and the boys. She watched Anthony help his dad. *What a support he is, poor love.* She sobbed quietly and realized that most of the people had made their way to the family. She knew she couldn't go there. She glanced to Anthony. He was making his way toward her. *What is he doing? What if David sees him?*

He didn't seem to care. He made his way through the crowd and reached her in seconds. "Mum, I'm sorry. Are you okay? Do you want to see David?"

She sobbed into his shoulder as he held her. "Darling, of course I do, but I understand it's not possible, so no, darling. I'm going to go. You must go back to your dad. I'll be fine. Maybe we can speak tomorrow." She sounded brave, but she was racked with tears.

"Oh Mum, I'm so sorry. I shouldn't have asked you to come."

"Don't worry, love. I'll be fine. You go now."

He dutifully turned away and with tears in his eyes made his way back to his brother and dad.

Georgina wove her way back to the car. She entered it and broke down in floods of tears. There was her boy, but she couldn't touch him. She was in a terrible place. She had never imagined that the first time she would see her son again she wouldn't be able to touch him let alone speak to him. All she could do was mourn the missed opportunity.

Just then, she was startled by a knock on the window. It was Mick, Chris's dad. "Look love, you can't drive like this. Take my key and go back to the house. We'll be back maybe in an hour. Go on. Take a bit of time."

Georgina was flabbergasted at the kindly thought from this guy who hardly knew her. But she couldn't. Trying to control herself, she said, "No, that's fine, Mick. Thank you. I'll be okay. Thank you. You're so kind."

"Well, only if you're sure. But take it steady, won't you?"

Georgina did as she said. She sat behind the tinted glass and sadly watched as the boys got back in the funeral car with Simon. It slowly drove away. After a few minutes, she gathered herself together as best she could and began her long, lonely journey home.

She just couldn't stop crying, but she hated herself for making it about her. It was poor Julie's funeral, and all she was thinking about was herself. She despised herself but couldn't stop the feelings. She just had to get away.

She'd been on the road for about twenty minutes and suddenly her mobile phone rang. She took a deep breath and answered.

It was Anthony. "Hey, Mum. You okay? Mick said you were so upset."

"I'm fine, love. You get back to Simon. He needs you more than me." She tried to hold back her tears to no avail.

"Mum, I'm so sorry. I should never have asked you to come. Look, pull over at the next pull in, and I'll bring David to you."

"No, I can't! I'm all right, honest. I'll text you when I get home. Now go!"

"Well, okay, if you're sure. I love you, Mum. Be safe."

She drove back in a deep depression. She desperately needed to hear a friendly voice. She thought of calling Jackie to find out if she'd come by, but she was reminded it was Josh's birthday party. Jackie was up to her eyes in the party and the dozen or so kids at the house, and so trying to make light of her heavy mood, she told her daughter she'd call her the next day.

The next call she made was to Lesley. "Hi, darling! Where are you?" She tried to sound normal but knew it wasn't a very convincing performance.

"On the train home. Be there in about ten minutes. Why? You okay? You sound weird."

No point in trying to hide it. "It was awful. I was about five feet from David but couldn't touch him." The tears started again. "I'm sorry, love. Any chance you could come up for an hour?"

"Yeah, okay. Can't stop too long though."

Georgina arrived home absolutely drained. She went straight to her bedroom. She just wanted to snuggle up in her duvet and hide from everyone. She removed her clothes. After cleaning her teeth, she climbed into her bed and tried to get the pictures out of her mind.

She must have dozed for a while. She was awakened by the front door opening and the usual "Ola, Mother" coming from Leslie.

Georgina looked at the clock and saw that it was nearly seven. She had slept for at least half an hour but didn't feel any better for it.

"Do you fancy a cuppa, Mum? I'll put the kettle on. You can tell me all about it."

She soon returned with a cup of Georgina's favorite, lemon and ginger tea. Perching on the bed, she said, "Come on then. What happened?"

Georgina told her some of the events of the day but focused on the nearness of David and the fact she couldn't even touch him. She continued to sob just at the thought of it. "Poor old Ma. I said all along you shouldn't go. I always said it was bloody stupid! And I told Anthony the same. He had no right to ask you to go! Pillock!"

After a while, Georgina composed herself. They were able to chat normally about some less-traumatic matters until they heard a loud knock on the door.

"Oh Lord, if that's Jean, tell her I'm asleep. I can't be doing with her tonight."

She slid down the bed in case the neighbor got past Leslie.

She didn't hear the voice. She let Leslie take care of whomever it was.

"Er, Mum, someone to see you," Leslie said.

Georgina looked up and froze. Standing in the doorway was Anthony still in the suit he'd worn at the funeral.

"Darling? What on earth? How did you get here? Why?"

"Mum, I was so worried that you'd driven home so upset that I wanted to make sure you were okay. I really am so sorry I got you to come up today. It never crossed my mind that you'd be so upset. I should have thought about it more. Are you okay?"

More tears fell. She wiped her eyes. "Yes, I'm fine, love, just so tired. Darling, I came to support you. You wanted me to come, so I did. I couldn't have not come, but I had no idea how bad it would be. Don't know what I was expecting. I was surprised at the strength of my feelings. Don't know why, though. I should have thought ..."

"Told you it was a daft idea," piped in Leslie. "I don't know what you thought would happen, but it's done now, and you don't have to worry about it anymore. Listen, Ma, I've got to get off. Got an early start in the morning."

She kissed her, Anthony, and Chris, who had remained in the hallway all that time.

"We need to get off too, Mum. I promised Dad I'd call before bedtime. Will you be okay?"

"Yes, I'll be fine. I can't believe you drove all that way just to check up on me. A phone call would have done." Georgina took his hand and kissed it. "You're very dear to me. You know that, don't you?"

After an exchange of hugs and kisses, they left, promising to call her when they reached home.

She was on her own. She pulled the duvet over her and prayed for sleep.

The next months were more settled. Anthony and Chris drove down to see Georgina and the girls every second month. Georgina was settling in to her life, which was more relaxed as she no longer had any major responsibilities other than the family. There was obviously no work, and the commitment to the charity had reduced almost to zero. She would very soon return to being a grass-roots member who attended a monthly meeting and took part in local volunteer projects. She was able to look forward to the future, which would be split between Canada and England each year.

She had of course discussed what she hoped would be her plans with the family. The last thing she wanted was for them to feel she was deserting them. They were all very receptive to her plans, saying they were happy as long as they would be able to speak to her by phone regularly. Knowing she had their blessing, Georgina made plans to fly to Canada in the August once she'd finished her governorship at the end of June.

But before that could happen, she was scheduled to have knee replacement surgery, which had been on the cards for a few years. It was getting to the stage that she was unable to walk very far without it giving out. The operation had been scheduled at the end of April, which actually encroached on her charity work because she wasn't able to drive for six weeks. But true to form, she missed only one event because she had so many offers of help with transport. And within two weeks of the operation, she was to be seen in full-length ball gown and four-inch heels and crutches at a charter anniversary dinner in Devon.

Her recovery all went according to plan, and she flew out to her beloved Canada as planned. It was to be the first time she would spend such a long time there—five months. Her life in Canada was very different from anything she'd experienced, which was why she wanted to keep coming back. She decided to sell her European properties. That was not the best financial decision she'd ever made because the euro zone was suffering terribly and property prices were plummeting. However, she accepted the loss and concentrated on traveling between the UK and Canada.

The Canadians were not worldly; they accepted their lot and saw no reason to change their life style. Originally, there was a thriving fishing industry that employed the majority of adult men, but for many years, the cod had been so depleted that there was hardly any work for those of any age. Many were forced to look for work elsewhere—Toronto, Fort McMurry, Yellow Knife, and even barren Labrador. The lifestyle was simple, and that to Georgina's way of thinking was not a criticism—quite the opposite. Community spirit was all encompassing; if anyone was struggling, sick, or just not doing well, the whole community would rally round.

Georgina had bought a lovely typically eastern Canadian wooden house in 2004, and it was a haven. The house was in a little hamlet of 186 people but no shops, pubs, restaurants, or public transport. The nearest shops were in a small town ten miles away, and the main center was sixty miles away. And even that was smaller than most villages in the UK.

She had been accepted by the community though no one knew anything of her life; regardless, they liked her. She had never known such acceptance. Who she was, what she'd been through, what she'd done—none of this mattered to them. For the first time in her life, she could be completely herself. She had nothing to prove, no image to maintain, no one to approve of her.

From early on, she had needed to be accepted, liked. She had to be the best at whatever role she took on. But in Canada, none of that mattered. No fancy clothes, no expensive jewelry, no fancy car. It had been what she had been subconsciously looking for her whole life. And here it was, her little piece of heaven.

She had told Anthony, Jackie, and Leslie how at peace she felt there and that she would like to split her time between her home in the UK and her home in Canada if they were okay with that. She didn't want them and of course the grandchildren to think she was deserting them again. They were happy about it as long as they could speak to her regularly and get her emails with photos and news.

Jackie, Paul, and their two children visited her in 2009 and had had a whale of a time skating on the frozen sea, going to the local ice hockey stadium twelve miles away, and joining in with the impromptu get-togethers that were always happening. She was so pleased that they'd come. They could see firsthand how happy and contented she was.

And so it became the norm. She would make the most of the family from February through to August, spending as much time as she could with them, and then mid-August, she would fly to her second home and become an honorary Canadian.

She joined a branch of the same charity and very quickly became a club member; she became an integral member of a church and sang in two choirs. About once a month, she and friends would sing to the seniors in the long-term care unit at a hospital.

She had found true peace within herself, with her surroundings, and with the people she surrounded herself with. Of course she looked forward to returning to the UK to see the family, hug them, and catch up with their news.

One day in April, while she was at her apartment in the UK with not much of anything to do, the phone rang. She rose from the chair, and a newly replaced knee gave a bit of a twinge. *Ouch!* "Hello?"

"Oh, hi there. Are you the Georgina who had two sons back in the seventies and walked out on them?"

Georgina swayed and grabbed for the table. "Who's this? Who are you?" Her voice trembled.

"I'm the other one!"

Printed in the United States
By Bookmasters